CHRIST AND HUMA

There is no one who writes with such incision
irony. This is a book which will speak to readers across both the disciplines and the
professions, from academic theologian to Lieutenant-General.

Iain Torrance, President, Princeton Theological Seminary, New Jersey

In this engaging and lively study, George Newlands seeks to connect distinctive
Christological claims with the more universal moral discourse of human rights.
In doing so, he outlines important ways in which Christian theological ethics may
appropriate secular claims while remaining faithful to its central theme.

David Fergusson, Professor of Divinity, University of Edinburgh

Human rights is one of the most important geopolitical issues in the modern world. Jesus Christ is the centre of Christianity. Yet there exists almost no analysis of the significance of Christology for human rights. This book focuses on the connections. Examination of rights reveals tensions, ambiguities and conflicts.

This book constructs a Christology which centres on a Christ of the vulnerable and the margins. It explores the interface between religion, law, politics and violence, East and West, North and South. The history of the use of sacred texts as 'texts of terror' is examined, and theological links to legal and political dimensions explored. Criteria are developed for action to make an effective difference to human rights enforcement and resolution between cultures and religions on rights.

THEOLOGY AND RELIGION IN INTERDISCIPLINARY PERSPECTIVE SERIES

Series Editors

Professor Douglas Davies, University of Durham, UK
Professor Richard Fenn, Princeton Theological Seminary, New Jersey, USA

Creativity through shared perspectives lies at the heart of Ashgate's series *Theology and Religion in Interdisciplinary Perspective*. Central religious and theological topics can be raised to a higher order of expression and clarity when approached through interdisciplinary perspectives; this new series aims to provide a pool of potential theories and worked out examples as a resource for ongoing debate, fostering intellectual curiosity rather than guarding traditional academic boundaries and extending, rather than acting as a simple guide to, an already well-defined field. Major theological issues of contemporary society and thought, as well as some long established ideas, are explored in terms of current research across appropriate disciplines and with an international compass. The books in the series will prove of particular value to students, academics, and others who see the benefit to be derived from bringing together ideas and information that often exist in relative isolation.

Also in the series

The Return of the Primitive
A New Sociological Theory of Religion
Richard K. Fenn
ISBN-10: 0 7546 0419 5 (HBK)
ISBN-10: 0 7546 0420 9 (PBK)

Christian Language and its Mutations
Essays in Sociological Understanding
David Martin
ISBN-10: 0 7546 0739 9 (HBK)
ISBN-10: 0 7546 0740 2 (PBK)

Christ and Human Rights

The Transformative Engagement

GEORGE NEWLANDS
University of Glasgow, UK

ASHGATE

Published by
Ashgate Publishing Limited
Gower House
Croft Road
Aldershot
Hampshire GU11 3HR
England

Ashgate Publishing Company
Suite 420
101 Cherry Street
Burlington, VT 05401-4405
USA

Ashgate website: http://www.ashgate.com

British Library Cataloguing in Publication Data
Newlands, G.M., 1941–
    Christ and human rights : the transformative engagement. –
    (Theology and religion in interdisciplinary perspective)
    1. Jesus Christ – Person and offices 2. Human rights –
    Religious aspects – Christianity
    I. Title
    261.7

Library of Congress Cataloging-in-Publication Data
Newlands, G.M., 1941–
    Christ and human rights : the transformative engagement / George
Newlands.—1st ed.
        p. cm.
    ISBN 0-7546-5201-7 (hardcover : alk. paper)—ISBN 0-7546-5210-6 (pbk. :
    alk. paper)
    1. Human rights—Religious aspects—Christianity. I. Title.

    BT738.15.N49 2006
    261.7—dc22

                                                                2005026467

ISBN-13: 978-0-7546-5201-4 (HBK)
ISBN-10: 0-7546-5201-7 (HBK)
ISBN-13: 978-0-7546-5210-6 (PBK)
ISBN-10: 0-7546-5210-6 (PBK)

Printed and bound in Great Britain by MPG Books Ltd., Bodmin, Cornwall.

Igneous, sedimentary,
conglomerate, metamorphic rock-
strata, in which particular grace,
individual love, decency, endurance,
are traced across the faults.
(Geoffrey Hill, *The Triumph of Love*, 1994LI)

Contents

Preface

Human rights provide no panacea to the world crisis, but they are a critical part of any solution. Religions are not easy allies to engage, but the struggle for human rights cannot be won without them. Witte, 1996, xviii

Perhaps we should stand, from the start, with the crucified Jesus and the vulnerable God he makes known to us. Placher, 1994,128

And yet the impressive thing about human rights, it seems to me, is how effectively they have functioned despite all their manifest limitations and obscurities. Yes, the promulgation of human rights, by international institutions, hardly guarantees assent- and even assent hardly guarantees anything in particular. The miracle is how well we have done even without such guarantees. The substance of these rights will indeed always be contested and interpreted; but it doesn't mean that they aren't useful instruments for drawing attention to the many ways in which people are brutal to one another. Appiah, 2005, 264

This book is about Christ and human rights. There is already a huge volume of literature around this area, and it may be useful to say, at the beginning, what this study is about, and what it is not, and why it has been written now. Human beings have been engaged in different forms of charity work since the earliest times, but thinking and action on human rights have only come to prominence in their modern forms. Although the nature of human rights has been, and remains, controversial, there was a widespread recognition in 1945 that basic human norms of conduct had been flagrantly violated by the Nazis and that efforts should be made to prevent a recurrence. Human rights action has been encouraged by both religious and by secular visions. For Christians, human rights notions have been developed in relation to understandings of the relationship between God and humanity. Christian faith understands God centrally through Jesus Christ, as the focus and incarnation of the divine nature as unconditional love. Reflections on the transcendent mystery of Christ are formalized in the discipline of Christology. Christologies are discussed here as ways of engaging with the relationship between faith and human rights issues.

I shall argue that the central Christian doctrine of Christology has much to contribute to a 'thick culture' in which global human rights may be positively advanced. I will address the considerable gap in our knowledge of why Christology has not been able to play a more decisive historical role in this area, and consider how a hermeneutical retrieval of the tradition in the service of the future may be achieved.

Can the understanding of Christ make a significant contribution to the theory and practice of human rights? Are fundamental shifts in Christology needed to maximize the contribution of Christianity to human rights issues? Would the cause of human rights be better served by detaching it from all religion and ideology? This study examines in depth the historical tensions between the Christian gospel and rights, and the scope and limitations of the language of rights. It seeks to provide concrete proposals for confronting rights issues in contemporary contexts.

The direction of this research tradition follows on from my earlier studies in theology and culture, *Generosity and the Christian Future* (SPCK, 1997), *John and Donald Baillie – Transatlantic Theology,* (Peter Lang, 2002) and *The Transformative Imagination – Rethinking Intercultural Theology* (Ashgate, 2004). I am grateful to numerous friends and colleagues for their support in the writing of this study – perhaps I can mention Richard Amesbury, David Beckett, Brian Blount, Susan Brown, Camille Cook, Chip Dobbs-Allsopp, Bob Dykstra, Keith Ewing, Richard Fenn, David Fergusson, Tim Hughes, Stacy Johnson, Joe Kramp, Bruce McCormack, Bob MacLennan, Ian Markham, Paul Middleton, Pat Miller, David Smith, Mark Taylor, Iain Torrance, Wentzel and Hester Van Huyssteen, David Wall and Nick Wyatt for their friendship and many conversations about human rights issues. My warm thanks are also due to the University of Glasgow for granting me study leave, to the faculty and students of Princeton Theological Seminary for their generous hospitality, and to Elizabeth for checking the typescript and for much else besides.

George Newlands
University of Glasgow
August 2005

CHAPTER 1

Introduction:
The Centrality of Rights

Human rights are perhaps the most important geopolitical concept of the present era. Jesus Christ is the centre of Christian faith. Can the understanding of Christ make a significant contribution to the theory and practice of human rights? Why has Christianity so often been associated with domination rather than justice? Are fundamental shifts in Christology needed to maximize the contribution of Christianity to human rights issues? Would the cause of human rights be better served by detaching it from all religion and ideology? This book examines in depth the historical tensions between the Christian gospel and rights, and the scope and limitations of the language of rights. It seeks to provide concrete proposals for facing rights issues in contemporary contexts.

Christ and Human Rights is a study in theology. It involves issues in ethics, worship, politics and culture. The central strand is the exploration of theological issues. It seems likely that basic theological issues, as well as political and cultural issues, lie at the root of much practice in this field. Negotiating these issues where they continue to divide, respecting difference while maintaining dialogue, remains central to movement on rights issues. This study seeks, in the first instance, neither to condemn nor to defend the churches' record on human rights issues, but to understand the context in which decisions and actions that may seem incomprehensible today occurred. On that basis, it should then be possible to suggest specific contributions for the present. Nevertheless, whatever progress we can make today, future generations will no doubt conclude that we still had much to learn about human rights in the twenty-first century.[1]

---

1   John Langan has produced an excellent summary of the relationships of human rights to Christian Ethics (in Biggar *et al.*, 1986, 119ff.) in his article 'Human Rights Theory: A Basis for Pluralism Open to Christian Ethics'. He highlights ways in which Christian ethics can complement or challenge human rights theory:

    1.   It can stress the limited and instrumental character of many human rights
       'The point of exercising HR is to enable us to act rightly and to achieve our human (and Christian) destiny in a humane way.'
    2.   It can stress the full range of human rights as against partial and reductive conceptions of humanity.
    3.   It can provide links between symbols and histories of a particular religious tradition and the universal values and claims of human rights theory.
    4   It can deepen the sense of history and the sense of community, both of which are often left in obscurity or taken for granted in liberal forms of human rights theory.
    5.   The Christian ethical tradition, through its emotionally powerful symbols and the reality of the common life from which it grows, can contribute motivation and commitment to the long, uneven struggle for the realization of human rights in our world. This struggle by

Many, perhaps most, Christians have no experience of discrimination or even friends who have been discriminated against – churches have long abandoned the practice of burning witches. There are also vivid examples of counterdiscrimination, when people adopt an aggressive victim status in order to dominate others and distort reality. But, still, there are huge numbers of victims of human rights abuses in the world – even, sadly, within the churches themselves.[2]

It must be said at the outset that there is nothing self-evident about the role of Christ in the advocacy of human rights. On the one hand, it may be said that Christ has nothing to do with rights; on the other, it can so be argued that, historically, Christ has been a figure used to counter human rights – notably racism, slavery and the emancipation of women – and that this is a perfectly legitimate theological interpretation. I shall suggest that this is a misunderstanding of the centre of the faith and will further argue that Jesus Christ is the basis for an urgent Christian support of human rights. Against the more bleak record may be placed the impressive work undertaken by many different sorts of Christian NGOs in alleviating poverty and suffering in the contemporary world.

Christianity is embedded in community. Churches, like other bodies, have, and have had, a complex relationship with human rights. Christian churches and Christian thinkers have made contributions to human rights issues and human rights actions. There was, for example, a decisive Christian input to the United Nations Declaration on Human Rights in 1945, and, especially between 1975 and 1985, churches were active in promoting human rights, abandoning their earlier stance of suspicion and joining in a widespread, and to a large extent American-led, drive for universal human rights. During this period there was frequent dialogue with non-church bodies, and it became common to speak of first-, second- and third-generation rights issues, moving from individual freedoms to economic and social and then to global and environmental rights.

There have also been several new and different waves of anti-rights sentiments. Within and outside the churches – in legal studies, in politics, in theology and elsewhere – objections to rights issues and rights culture have arisen, some with traditional and some with more recent roots. The Marxist critique of liberal Western rights talk made churches cautious about endorsing what might be seen as bourgeois values. The word 'liberal' became deeply suspect in many areas of discourse.[3] Churches were inevitably concerned to distance themselves from a politicisation of rights which served some interests but not others. The linking of humanitarian, political and global strategic aims by nation-states could be positively damaging to human rights work on the ground by NGOs, including churches. Equally, churches

---

Christians is to be sustained through sharing in the mystery of life and death of the Christ who came that we might have life and have it more abundantly.

2   A new resource is *The Journal of Hate Studies*, produced by Gonzaga University, Spokane, WA: see www.gonzaga.edu/against hate. The Christian Identity federation is a good example of what is often a deadly combination of hate and reactionary religion.

3   'I'm telling you, it's a sick, sick nation that turned the word ' "liberal" into an expletive' (Iain Banks, 2002, 204).

might be deeply reluctant to expose their own internal structures, social arrangements and lines of authority to human rights scrutiny. Here, traditional assumptions about the independence and autonomy of churches from human scrutiny – old and outdated privileges – are conveniently recalled. On a worldwide frame theology and church have moved further away from patterns of liberal dialogue towards patterns of communitarian affirmation and evangelical affirmation yet the more serious question always remained: do Christians have rights and should they talk of, and exercise rights in discipleship to a God who, in Christ, is an utterly self-giving, self-dispossessing God?

In brief, all these movements were to lead – with due exceptions as always – in the present day (2005) to a marked decline in the momentum of Christian reflection on human rights. In some respects, this may be welcomed. The point has been made; there is no longer an issue. Christian communities do in fact work effectively everywhere for humanitarian causes and for the prevention of injustice – through the Catholic Agency for Overseas Development CAFOD (Catholic Agency for Overseas Development), Christian Aid, the Tear Fund and so on. After a scholarly contest to triumph in being the most non-triumphalist, it becomes clear that many church traditions have contributed to human rights talk, although most have, at the same time, inhibited human rights action. Rights talk can never be seen as a trump card in complex conversations. Rhetoric and advocacy have both positive and negative effects. Some discussions benefit from moratorium.

And yet it is always unwise to assume that, because points have been made, there is no more to be done. The history of black people in North America shows how apparent victories easily dissolve into the former unacceptable status quo. The history of Jewish people in Europe shows how apparent assimilation and general acceptance can be followed by swift and brutal annihilation. The world of post-9/11 is marked by growing religious fundamentalisms of different colours, and these are unlikely to disappear soon. Marginalized communities can rarely afford to be entirely complacent, discrimination against individuals is a fact of everyday life, and positive benefits such as adequate food are denied to a large portion of the world's population. The continuing energetic encouragement of a critical, carefully constructed human rights culture may be an inadequate strategy, *sub specie aeternitatis*. It is one which, I shall argue, all societies should be encouraged to continue to pursue vigilantly. It is a goal on which Christians, as disciples of a loving God, should be consistently and determinedly focused at all times.

Christian faith does not come to the meeting place of dialogue and engagement on human rights as a white knight with a spotless record. It comes as flawed and often disgraced. Yet innumerable individuals and communities have made tremendous concrete contributions to rights issues, very often through anonymous self-sacrifice in forgotten places, and church voices played a central role in the genesis of the 1945 UN Charter. Rights are an issue where persistence in taking small steps remains imperative, whatever the setbacks and challenges.

Why Do Human Rights Matter?

Put simply, human rights matter because they can inspire action to diminish man's inhumanity to man, to discourage the torture, genocide and other manifest evils which remain a continuing and endemic feature of human society. From a Christian standpoint, human rights issues are related intimately to central concepts of the gospel, to the understanding of humanity before God, to righteousness and justice. They embrace considerations of mercy, reconciliation and hospitality, and they focus on the treatment of the marginalized and of strangers. For Christians, they stem from the understanding of Christ as the centre of forgiveness, reconciliation and generosity.

What *are* human rights and do they exist? These questions are the subject of continuing debate. When I use the term 'human rights', I shall be trying to speak about a human ability to enjoy certain basic capacities which are constitutive of human living – the ability to survive and to enjoy reasonable health and freedom of action, to express one's views without hindrance, to associate with other people without arbitrary constraints and without fear of torture or detention. All highly debateable issues, you might say. They are. And shouldn't we also be talking about human responsibilities, or human wrongs rather than human rights? Well, perhaps. But as it has been appositely said:

> Outside the cocooned world of the academy, people are still victims of torture, still subjected to genocide, still deprived of basic freedoms and still dying through starvation. We should remember these people before we decide to forget about rights. (Jones, 1994, 227)

What are the relations between ethics, Christian ethics and Christology? In a nutshell, ethics is concerned with the development of critical theories of conduct, right and wrong, desirable and undesirable, and the comparative analysis of these different theories. Morality is the negotiation and implementation of codes of behaviour in practice. Christian ethics seeks to make a contribution to ethical theory and its practical consequences for morality, in the light of the Christian faith. Christology as the exploration of the nature of God's action in Jesus Christ is at the centre of faith, encouraging a Christomorphic view of the world. As such, it is pivotal to Christian views of the ethical dilemmas flagged up in the language and practice of human rights. Although Christian ethics has wider sources than Christology, in that it draws on the whole biblical tradition, the tradition of the Christian community and contemporary social and philosophical reflection, this study will centre on the Christological matrix, because it is paradoxically at once absolutely central and often thought to be at the root of Christian blindness to human rights issues through the centuries.

Although there is endless debate over their grounds and justification, human rights, as embodied in law, are not mysterious or difficult to grasp. For example, the British Human Rights Act of 1998, enacting European legislation into Scottish and English law, has 14 articles. The first article declares that the state must respect the rights set out in the articles. The second states that everyone's right to life shall be protected by law. The third prohibits torture or degrading treatment. The fourth prohibits slavery or forced labour. The fifth guarantees the right to personal liberty and security. The sixth ensures the right to a fair trial. The seventh ensures no punishment without a relevant law. The eighth concerns respect for privacy and family life. The remainder cover: freedom of thought, conscience and religion (Art. 9); freedom of expression (Art.10); freedom of assembly and association (Art.11); the right to marry and to found a family (Art. 12); the right to an effective remedy (Art. 13); and freedom from discrimination in any of the issues mentioned in the other articles (Art.14). Additional protocols cover the right to the peaceful enjoyment of possessions, to education and to free elections, and reiterate the abolition of the death penalty. The interpretation of these rights, however, is a matter of continuing legal debate and development.

It seems clear that human rights will continue to be of central importance to our human future. Prohibitions against genocide, murder, slavery, torture, prolonged arbitrary imprisonment and systematic racial discrimination will always be important for human flourishing. Human rights theory will remain subject to healthy debate and constructive disagreement in all its dimensions.[4] If it is to be implemented effectively, it will have to be related to wider cultural frameworks. For some people, this means being embedded in a secular culture, without all the traditional divisiveness of religious commitment. For others in many parts of the world, it will mean engagement with religion as an integral part of culture.

Christian theology is unable to take a purist stance on this debate. The Christian gospel implies commitment to dialogue both with the secular and the religious. Both perspectives have important insights into the human condition, and both are open to distortion and abuse. We can use neither our human rights theory nor our religious commitment as a trump card. Rather, we must seek to draw benefit for humanity from a web of connections and a number of different theories in order to work together with others to deliver practical outcomes in human rights – freedom from coercion and conditions for the reality of human flourishing.

---

4   There are good reasons for this constructive disagreement, which we shall explore throughout this study. Cf. especially Appiah (2005, ch 6, 'Rooted Cosmopolitanism', 212ff).

> Practically speaking, we do not resolve disagreements in principle about why we want to save this child from drowning if, in fact, we agree that this child must be saved. But what if you believe that the child is meant to die because an ancestor has called her, and I do not?
>
> I want to suggest that there was something wrong with the original picture of how dialogue should be grounded. It was based on the idea that we must find points of agreement at the level of principle: here is human nature; here is what human nature dictates. What we learn from efforts at actual intercultural dialogue – what we learn from travel, but also from poems or novels, or films from other places – is that we can identify points of agreement that are much more local and contingent than this. (Appiah, 2005, 253)

Appiah advocates a 'metaphysical ecumenism, responsive to the moral vocabularies we find on the ground' (2005, 267).

We needn't be unduly troubled by the fact that metaphysical debate is unlikely to produce consensus, because human rights can, and therefore should, be sustained without metaphysical consensus. (Ibid.)

Whilst human rights are one of the most important geopolitical issues in the modern world, systematic theological attention to the subject, though significant, has been very limited. Moreover, given the history of persecution in the name of Christ, Christology may seem an unlikely catalyst for such dialogue. Yet Jesus Christ has always been the centre of Christianity, and I believe that it should be possible to put reflection on Christ at the centre of a research project on human rights. Christian ethics shares in all human ethical concerns. But the character of Jesus Christ in his life, death and resurrection colours all Christian thinking about rights, duties, justice and the whole spectrum of overlapping concerns., Paradoxically, it may be that the very ambiguity of the Christian response to Christ in the area of human rights over the centuries can help us better understand the choices which we are called to make. That would, of course, correspond to a central feature of Donald Baillie's famous *God was in Christ* (1948), the paradox of grace.

It is precisely in the particularity of Christ that we are invited to share in the universality of the concerns of other world religions and of humanist ethical endeavour. The paradox extends further. Christians believe that Jesus Christ is centrally relevant to all aspects of human life. Yet the more we are inclined to use Christology to produce instant solutions to human rights issues, the less success we are likely to have. It is likely to be more profitable to see the Christian framework as a perspective of eschatological hope, a vision of the peace of God, and to work towards this with as much patience and modesty as we can find. Henri Nouwen's notion of *The Wounded Healer* (1972), though of limited application, may be relevant to the role of Christian community in reinforcing rights culture in society.

Why are human rights so important? The reasons are, at a basic level, quite simple. In the twenty-first century, large numbers of people continue to be abused, tortured and murdered. Large numbers continue to die of hunger and disease when the resources are there to prevent this. Large numbers suffer from all kinds of discrimination to a degree that is serious enough to damage their lives in quite unnecessary ways. Despite giant strides in human social progress, descent into barbarism seems as easy in our current century as it has ever been. Action needs to be taken constantly to reduce and prevent these evils. This, at least, is agreed by most people today, even if they may not always avoid aspects of discrimination, large or small, themselves. It seems, too, that human rights are likely to remain central to any work on global ethics.[5]

---

5   There is a very useful overview of recent human rights writing in Little (1999, 151f). In addition, David Little's definitions on human rights, in his essay 'The Nature and Basis of Human Rights' (1993, 73ff) are especially useful:

> Since a human right is a complex idea with moral, legal and other aspects, we must make some preliminary clarifications. Given that a 'right' *simpliciter* is an entitlement to demand a certain performance or forbearance on pain of sanction for non-compliance; that a 'moral right' is a right regarded as authoritative in that it takes precedence over other action, and is legitimate in part for considering the welfare of others, and that a 'legal right' is warranted and enforced within a legal system, a 'human right' then, is understood as having the following five characteristics, according to the prevailing 'human rights vocabulary'.

Much else remains controversial and highly contested. The nature of human rights, their scope and how to achieve them, how to negotiate conflicts of rights, how to create the political climate in which rights may be best achieved, how to deal with diverse combinations of rights talk with other ideals, often of a conflicting nature – all of this is the subject of continuing debate. Often, difficult practical decisions have to be made, and are decided on an ad hoc basis. It is important that Christian perspectives should be fed into reflection at an early stage, as a contribution to the framework in which decisions are taken.

Human rights talk may be distinguished, but not entirely separated, from other social and political considerations. We have seen nations use human rights as a weapon of propaganda against other nations with which they are in dispute on other grounds. States may stop talking about rights when this could embarrass allies, invite the publicity of countercharges or politically liberate people whose views could be uncongenial. The experience of Amnesty International has been a history of dealing with such complexity and seeking to avoid being used for extraneous political reasons. Talk of human rights does not take away the need for politics and diplomacy, or that for wider reflection on citizenship: it is only one avenue, albeit an important one, to social communicative action. As communication changes – most recently through the Internet – rights issues develop new and unexpected dimensions.[6]

If human rights are so very important to human well-being, then it is clearly incumbent on all traditions of thought and action, religious or non-religious, which believe they have a distinctive contribution to make to the human future, to engage seriously with rights issues. For Christianity this involves theology and practice. Since Christology is at the centre of Christianity, it should be engaged in this process.

---

1. It is a moral right advanced as a legal right. It should, as we pointed out earlier, 'be protected by the rule of law' thus constituting a standard for the conduct of government and the administration of force.
2. It is regarded as protecting something of indispensable human importance.
3. It is ascribed 'naturally', which is to say that it is not earned or achieved, nor is it disallowed by virtue of race, creed, ethnic origin or gender.
4. Some human rights can be forfeited or suspended under prescribed conditions (for example,. a public emergency), but several 'primary' or basic rights are considered indefeasible under any circumstances.
5. It is universally claimable by (or on behalf of) all people against all (appropriately situated) others, or by (or on behalf of) certain generic categories of people, such as 'women' or 'children'. Those who are appropriately subject to such claims are said to have 'correlative human duties'.

6   The Internet provides new resources of Human Rights action. In *Human Rights and the Internet* (Hick *et al.*, 2000) there are excellent discussions of the advantages and disadvantages of the Internet in the fight against human rights violations. These include the possibilities of wider communication, the dangers of hate sites (ibid., 141), the battle between human rights groups and oppressive governments attempting to hack into their websites (illustrated in relation to East Timor (ibid.,133ff)), the problems of protecting children and the need, on occasion, for encryption software such as PGP (Pretty Good Privacy). There are useful lists of human rights resources on the Internet (ibid.,100ff, 117ff), including Oneworld.org, OCMT (the World Organization Against Torture) and so on.

Currently there is remarkably little extant literature on Christology and human rights. There may be good reasons for the gap. Although the connections are inescapable in theory, making the appropriate ones may not be easy. But it must at least be both possible and desirable to take steps towards an ongoing task.

There are, however, important areas of reflection and practice which overlap with both Christology and human rights. These include humanity before God, righteousness and justice, mercy, reconciliation, and hospitality. Christ is often seen in the Christian tradition as the centre of forgiveness and generosity, of commitment to marginality, to specific sorts of strangers. It will be part of this project to draw together these webs of connection.[7]

Here, I need to sound a note of caution. It would be unwise to imagine that even a widespread agreement on the main characteristics of human rights will in itself solve the many human rights problems in contemporary society. We have noted that societies, groups and individuals are often notoriously selective in the ways in which they espouse human rights issues. This selectivity is seen in the disagreements on rights between Eastern and Western states during the Cold War, and between North and South. Churches and other religious organizations enthusiastically and piously support human rights causes in faraway countries while continuing to discriminate systematically against members of their own communities at home. In reaction

---

7   An excellent deployment of webs of connections is made in Ian Markham's *A Theology of Engagement* (2003), a study devoted to the dialogue between Christian thought and action and other traditions, religious and secular, in contemporary society. Inclusion is a keyword in the engagement process. Engagement is to be understood as 'an encounter that subsequently shapes the theology itself' (Markham. 2003, 10). It is described more closely, as: assimilation – the constructive use of categories from non-Christian sources; resistance – the ability to reject sources as incompatible with the heart of the Christian tradition; and overhearing – the process of illumination from discussion within another religious tradition. Assimilation as a process has been valuable even when the content remains subject to critique. Resistance leads to precision in expression and has characterized the development of doctrines of the incarnation.

Assimilation is deployed by Markham in engagement with human rights, enabling theology to negotiate – an issue on which the church has a very chequered record. Resistance may also enable the defence of human rights, illustrated through resistance to the concept of the sovereign state, with reference to Austria, Kosovo and Chile. God is more basic to humanity than the state. Resistance points to a human rights construction of theological engagement with black and feminist issues. Markham is characteristically trenchant: 'I take the oppression of women by men as given. Christian theology has at its most benign treated women as invisible; and at its most wicked, it has provided a justification for this cruelty' (ibid., 87–8). Repentance and modification of the tradition are urgently needed. Similar conditions apply in the development of black theology.

Markham returns to overhearing, examining the clash of discourses concerning the secular, in the West and in India. He considers the ramifications of Hindu nationalism through the eyes of Chandhoke and Chatterjee. Here, religious sensibilities and group rights have to be respected. This leads to further reflection on Hinduism, inclusivity and toleration. Beyond this there is need of an inclusive cultural vision in which the economic consensus around capitalism may be humanely articulated. This is focused on the response to globalization. Complexity and ambiguity may be revelatory (ibid., 187).

We turn to the shape of an engaged theology: 'So the theologian needs to be both in the middle and on the edge' – centred in the believing community but 'forcing the community to listen to the truth of God as it is in non-Christian traditions' (ibid., 209).

we may be tempted to despair over the whole process. But the weaknesses only underline the need to move forward with consistency. The reality of hypocrisy has to be weighed against the reality of the symbolic importance of human rights language. When human rights theory becomes embedded in human rights culture the chances of effective outcomes increase. Where Christianity in particular is concerned, it may be that awareness of our ambiguous record can lead to action in repentance, which may incorporate an effective element of humanity and provisionality into the process.

The human rights debate takes place on several levels. There are academic arguments for and against rights concepts. Rights arguments may get in the way of practical action on justice issues. Rights language may be manipulated to facilitate oppression. These levels are reflected in theological debate. There are academic arguments for and against the theological use of rights language. Rights language may not always be the best for dealing with issues which are more suited to a notion like forgiveness. Here, too, rights language is manipulated for the sake of oppression. Christian and Christological arguments have been, are being, and will continue to be, used in ways which will oppress minorities who deviate from traditional norms. The argument of this book is that they can be liberating, provided that the roots of oppression are laid bare and addressed.

On the other hand, there are a huge number of coercive and manipulative people who do not believe in God. Abandoning faith does not always make people more sensitive to the needs of others! They may become obsessed with other, penultimate values and these may become a new form of idolatry.

But some people who have a vision of Jesus as the instantiation of the vulnerable God *do* have a sense of the need for mutuality and reciprocity, this is something worth advocating. It should be the mark of an open and progressive theology that it constructs a robust case for its preferred perspective, but that it is not afraid to embrace insights – sometimes critical insights – from different perspectives, where these are available.[8]

---

8   It is important in this process to take a charitable, rather than a pejorative, view of these alternative perspectives if they are to be maximally useful, and to avoid caricature. As Glasgow's Archbishop Robert Leighton famously said in a slightly different context – and he knew all about theological controversy:

Nobody, I believe, will deny, that we are to form our judgement of the true nature of the human mind, not from sloth and stupidity of the most degenerate and vilest of men, but from the sentiments and fervent desires of the best and wisest of the species.(Theological Lectures, 5, *Of the Immortality of the Soul.*)

CHAPTER 2

Jesus Christ and the Hope of Rights

For Christian faith, Jesus Christ in his life, death and resurrection shows us the character of God as a God of unconditional love, peace and justice. Christ is the crucified God, the executed God, always in solidarity with the marginalized. As such, Christ is, and will remain, a vital source of hope of justice, compassion and rights for all humanity. But today Christianity is often perceived as oppressive, in the past and the present. Despite the work already done, there is still a need for more precise accounting for this contradiction, and for strategies to produce more constructive outcomes in the future.

Embodying the Love of God

Jesus Christ is at the centre of Christian faith. Christian faith holds that Jesus in his life, his ministry, his death and his resurrection embodies the generous love of God for all humanity. In his incarnation he manifests the character of God in the created world. In Christ, God was reconciling the world to himself. Christ is ground of hope for a future of justice, peace, and human flourishing. Christian faith and life is Christocentric, as the great twentieth-century theologian Karl Barth tirelessly insisted.

Reflection upon Christ comes to the churches through a tradition including scripture, community and interpretation. The scriptures importantly include the Old Testament as well as the New. For Jews and Christians the Hebrew scriptures have been a constant source of understanding of the faithful love of God. Judaism has produced important reflections and valuable impetus for human rights as an expression of that love. But none of this stream of human consciousness has been free from the contradictions and tensions inherent in any culturally embedded tradition. Christocentric faith can become Christomonist, using Christ as a kind of trump card, to echo language used in rights talk, to override all other considerations. Passages from the scriptures can, and often continue to, serve to override the teaching and significance of Christ as the icon of God's love. This creates situations where stereotyping of one side of an argument does not solve the problems. Faithful and generous Christians continued to keep slaves for centuries.[1] Some Christians continue to practise what others regard as moral slavery in relation to groups such as women and gays.[2] It will be a central part of my argument to suggest that it is precisely this conflict concerning the significance of Christ in the light of the roles

---

1   For example, famously, Thomas Jefferson. Cf. Genovese (1998).

2   Catharine MacKinnon in Haydon (2001) and Richards (1999).

of scripture and tradition in interpretation that accounts for the extremely ambiguous record of Christianity in relation to human rights through the centuries.

Of course, everything that we know of Christ comes to us through scripture and tradition, past and present. There is a very great deal that we do not know about Jesus Christ. We have become aware, in recent decades, of the cultural relativity of our own research traditions and of the need for constant critical reappraisal of what we take to be assured results. We may be certain that perspectives will change and develop in the future. This does not mean, however, that we can have no confidence that the state of research to date is much superior to the position 100 years ago. There is a dialectic between the hermeneutics of suspicion and suspicion of that suspicion.

There are grounds for asserting against relativizing criticism that Jesus of Nazareth, in his life and death, was concerned for individual human dignity and for social justice. He was committed to unconditional love for all human beings, both in his teaching and in his actions. Christian faith trusts that this concern was the instantiation of the love of God the creator of the universe, and that, through the events which are collectively understood as the resurrection, this love was universalized and made effective as a decisive contribution to the well-being of all humanity. All of Christian doctrine becomes relevant to human rights concerns.

God is love. Response to this love has been articulated in countless ways in Christian community, often in relation to justice. The language of rights has been a newcomer to this practice. But of course there are connections between love and justice and the new discourse of rights. It may be thought that attention to rights has always been included in concern for love and justice. Yet one discovery of recent decades may be that there may be aspects of rights language which need to be made explicit in order for love and justice to be fully served. There may be much more to human well-being than rights – apprehension of the effective love of God and of our fellow human beings, for example. But there may also be reasons to believe that modern alertness to human rights can be a powerful catalyst for human flourishing, to which the religious and the non-religious can contribute equally, and in which Christian faith can suggest important initiatives.

> Perhaps we should stand, from the start, with the crucified Jesus and the vulnerable God he makes known to us. (Placher,1994,128)

William Placher's *Jesus The Savior – The Meaning of Jesus Christ for Christian Faith* (Placher, 2001a) expands the discussion of the vulnerable God in Christology. Both this book and *Narratives of a Vulnerable God*, from which the above quotation is taken, are brilliant reminders of the intimate connection between doctrine and ethics, and between Christology and human rights. Placher reiterates the equal importance of the life of Jesus, the crucifixion and the resurrection for faith, and, in a highly instructive analysis, relates these dimensions from a classical Reformed perspective to three classical human rights issues of Christian ethical concern, namely homosexuality, prisons and war. His work is an illuminating example of the power of the combination of classical and emancipatory theology.

The ministry of Jesus is prophetic and points to the coming reign of God. Through Jesus' actions God is encountered by those around him – an encounter which often challenges order and respectability. Jesus' bodiliness reminds us that having a body is part of being human. He modelled the compassion and care that we ought to show to others. Discussion of biblical passages is framed through the ministry of Jesus:

> Jesus clearly did not deliver his most forceful condemnations about the sins that generated the most social antagonism in his culture, as homosexuality often does in ours, but rather reserved them for the flaws in those his society viewed as most respectable... Here as elsewhere, Jesus stood with the outsiders, the disreputable, and the fearful, rather than the self-confident and self-righteous. (Placher, 2001a, 101)

Crucifixion: 'The whole course of Christ's obedience led him to crucifixion'

The gospels are passion narratives. The memory of the cross and the presence of Christ are at the centre of the central act of Christian worship, the Eucharist. The cross is a cross of solidarity, sacrifice, reconciliation and redemption as the victory of love. This should make us think, as we rarely do, about the penal system: 'We live in a country gone mad on sending people to prison.' (Placher, 2001a, 150). But the Bible talks of release to the captives, and Jesus speaks of visiting prisoners. If Christ has taken upon himself the sins of the world, punishment becomes problematic. Yet thousands of prisoners receive no visitors at all.

Resurrection

Resurrection was an important part of the hope of Israel. It indicates that the cross was not the end of the Christian story, and affirms the eternal value to God of every human life. From resurrection comes faith, as in the breaking of bread on the road to Emmaus, and the reign of God. In the framework of the peace of God, violence and war are exposed for the evils they are:

> We take it for granted that we should kill and be killed in the name of our nations. Christians should at least dream of a time when that too will seem part of the horrible past. Christ invites us to follow him in love, and offers us eternal life....But it isn't easy. Resurrection lies on the other side of the cross, and hope follows only on the risks of love. (Placher, 2001a,197–8)

There is much more to human life than human rights – neither life nor theology can be reduced to human rights alone. Undue concentration on a particular issue can often diminish the enjoyment of full lives. The Christian gospel is concerned with salvation, reconciliation, the fullness of human flourishing in all its aspects, in life and beyond life. Human life is built up through the development of satisfying personal and social relationships, through appropriate economic and political arrangements, through the development of the humanities and the sciences. Through Jesus Christ, Christians believe, God's love as a transformative force of grace is effective throughout[3] the cosmos. Yet when human rights are abused, rather like when a vital organ of the human body fails, the results have a pervasive detrimental effect on the whole of society. That is why theology may welcome, without qualification, the recent prominence of human rights issues in global affairs and will seek to make its own contribution to human rights advocacy through critical appraisal of its own traditions and resources.

Violence, coercion and torture are the enemies of human rights. They perfectly exemplify the actuality of sin.[4] There is a thread of violence and coercion which runs through the sources of Christianity, and which will be the subject of our close attention in succeeding chapters. But there is also a thread of non-violence, of self-giving, self-affirming love which, as the Fourth Gospel has it, shines in the darkness as a beacon of hope. This light is the incarnation of God in Jesus Christ, an icon of the divine love. It is this positive side of Christian faith which provides an antidote to despair. While there is everything to be said for realism, obstacles are only overcome when we have the courage to trust to the beacons of light rather than to giving in the face of the darkness. I shall suggest later that there are other distinctive and effective lights, both in the world religions and in secular thought. Here, I concentrate on Christ.[5]

There are countless varieties of Christologies, but all point, in their diverse ways, to the particular and lasting significance of Jesus Christ for human welfare. More absolutist Christologies are concerned not to understate the vital role of Jesus Christ in the understanding of God, and of the entire created order, in Christian understanding. More modest Christologies are concerned to safeguard the connections between Jesus and all human beings, while not alienating those who do not share their views

---

3   Human dignity, the realization of which is the aim of human rights, cannot be reduced to dimensions that can be encompassed by a short or narrow list of 'basic' human rights. All human rights are basic rights in the fundamental sense that systematic violations of any human right preclude realizing a life of full human dignity – that is, prevent one from enjoying the minimum conditions necessary for a life worthy of a human being. (Donnelly, 1989, 37–9)

4   Roger Haight neatly articulated the connection between oppression and sin in his early book *An Alternative Vision*:

> One sees social institutions that not only structure human freedoms of people, but also crush them, oppress their very being, cause suffering and push many towards untimely and unnecessary death. These structures are more than the effect of sin: such social structures may be called rightfully sin, and not merely the effects of sin, since they are not merely evil and products of nature. (Haight, 1985, 148)

With this he contrasted the essence of a liberation spirituality:

> This spirituality has a faith that sees the Kingdom of God in the little bits and pieces of history where people are being served and cared for by other people. This faith sees God's hand working through human agency in this; these little victories in the struggle for the emancipation and liberation of other human beings are the ultimate experiential ground of faith that justifies hope. And finally, the faith and hope of this spirituality is informed by love, because only through participating in this movement in history can faith and hope continue to survive. (Ibid., 256)

5   This chapter seeks to provide an overall sketch of the issues involved, each of which will be addressed in later chapters.

by making totalizing claims. Both these dynamics are present in changing patterns in all Christian theology and practice.

Jesus Christ is central to Christian reflection on rights. This centrality may be expressed traditionally, in what is often described as foundationalist categories, or it may be expressed more cautiously in terms of a web of connections concerning the nature of the divine love and relationality. But the web and the foundations share a distinctive hermeneutical envelope, which prioritizes the life, death and resurrection of Jesus as the continuing source of unconditional regard and support.

The divine love seeks, creates, welcomes and relates in reciprocity with all other loves. This has been a classical theme of faith through the ages. But its instrument in human agency has often been able only very imperfectly to apprehend and to transmit that love. In our local cultures, whether in small circles or in huge tracts which we have culturally colonized, we have failed to recognize different responses of love as love. Love has become hate or indifference. This is a commonplace, but has to be acknowledged as part of the way things are.

The task of liberating, in each cultural situation, the communication of unconditional love from the limitations which hinder it remains incomplete. Although this problem is not, of course, unique to Christian perspectives, it is a primary objective of this study to consider how the Christian tradition in its continuities and irruptions may provide hints that may be utilized in other strategies for action. I hope to show that the language of rights may be particularly effective in this task.

The Way of Jesus

Christians have almost universally held that Jesus of Nazareth, in his life, teaching and actions, manifests the purpose of God for the created order, and in particular for human beings. They continue to argue about important areas of this life. How far was he committed to engaging in, and encouraging his followers to take, social and political action? To what degree did his teaching rest entirely within an apocalyptic framework?

Much about the culture in which he was embedded remains the subject of scholarly controversy. But it is always possible, and indeed it is necessary, to attempt an interim report on these issues, assuming that biblical scholarship is at least as capable of modest progress as all other scholarship in the humanities. It seems clear that Jesus was a teacher in the tradition of teaching in Israel, intensively devoted to Israel's God, and conscious of a need to live, teach and act as a messenger of salvific change, which was to come from God himself. His humanity was moulded by his devotion to God.

It also seems clear that he was in some ways faithful to rabbinic tradition and in other ways radical – socially, religiously and, just possibly, politically. As a result, he gathered a group of followers and had a remarkable influence on them and on others in the community in which he lived. He preached in word and action a message of what was perceived to be something approaching unconditional love. Attracting attention in a highly charged political maelstrom he came into conflict with the religious and political authorities and was executed by crucifixion.

After his death, some of his followers came to believe that he continued to be alive in some decisive and mysterious way, which they came to understand in terms of bringing individual salvation and the corporate expected reign of God. They came to affirm that, as St Paul phrased it, God was in Christ, reconciling the world to himself. For many centuries they tended on the whole (for there were always many different understandings of faith) to see this salvation in individual and otherworldly terms, as an escape from the consequences of moral sinfulness and a place in heaven. In time, some would reflect on God incarnate, the crucified God, the executed God, in a mysterious but effective solidarity with all the liminal, with all the marginalized and all the discriminated against. It is on the genesis and the fate of this latter strand that we shall now reflect.[6]

There are sources for theoretical reflection on human rights at many levels. There is also a powerful demonstration of the embedding of theory in the lives and cultural world of individuals and communities. Although, of course, not everyone has heard of Jesus Christ, this life is perhaps the most familiar life image in human history. For this reason it is worth reflecting that it has the potential to become a kind of condition of the possibility of helping to translate human rights theory into the establishment of a human rights culture. For Christian faith, this iconicity is based on the belief that, here, the creator of the universe participates definitively in human life.

Emphasizing the relation of Jesus Christ to the marginalized and to human rights is, of course, a characteristically modern preoccupation. Future generations will doubtless stress other dimensions. But I would claim that the link to human rights is an important positive development in Christology, which is likely to remain, and ought to remain, central to Christologies to come. It may be that Christianity will develop into an increasingly spiritualized and socially conservative religion, as Islam has tended to do in recent decades. But I regard it as vital that a witness to a socially and politically radical Christology should also continue as a witness to a tradition stemming from the centre of the gospel. If this dimension should become less widespread in world Christianity, persistence with it will become all the more important.

Turning to the biblical narratives, we find concern for the whole range of questions concerning God, creation and salvation, the future of humanity under God, the development of the relationship between God and human beings, relationships between men and women and social development. It would be unhelpful to view this

---

6   Richard Kearney puts it well:

How ironic it is to observe so many monotheistic followers still failing to recognise the message: that God speaks not through monuments of power and pomp but in stories and acts of love and justice, the giving to the least of creatures, the caring for orphans, widows and strangers; stories and acts which bear testimony – as transfiguring gestures do – to that God of little things that comes and goes, like the thin small voice, like the burning bush, like the voice crying in the wilderness, like the word made flesh, like the wind that blows where it wills. (Kearney, 2001, 51)

immense range always from the narrow focus of rights. Yet it is also important to explore this area, not least because its significance has so often been underrated by Christian tradition.

Liberating Narrative

Here, the emancipatory theologies offer a particular insight. An excellent example is Brian Blount's *Then the Whisper put on Flesh – New Testament Ethics in an African-American Context* (2001). Blount argues for the model of liberation as a lens for reconfiguring ethics. This enables him to read the synoptic gospels as an ethics of the kingdom, John as the Christology of a community of active resistance, Paul as theology enabling liberating ethics – at least on occasion – and Revelation as the witness of active resistance. More precisely, the synoptic gospels set up new paradigms of behaviour: 'For Mark, discipleship as a narrative theme follows from the realization of God's own boundary breaking behavior around and in Jesus'(Blount, 2001, 57). In Matthew we see the liberating ethics of a 'visible institution', the kingdom of heaven. In Luke there is a bias towards the poor and the oppressed in Jesus' teaching and action, in a reversal of common attitudes. In John love for God and humanity becomes a strategy of active resistance. In Paul there is also a basic liberating ethic of boundary-breaking, although Paul's choices might be different in some areas today, notably in slavery and sexuality (ibid., 149ff). In Revelation there is a pattern of active resistance in the face of massive evil.

Blount struggles with the question of what exactly the New Testament has to do with ethics, and here he follows Leander Keck:

> New Testament ethics may not look like what we have come to expect from a 'critical reflection on morality' because it is its own brand of ethics. It is not ethics formed round a philosophical construct. It is, instead, 'event ethics.' It is ethics orientated and structured around the event of Jesus' life, death and resurrection. (Blount, 2001, 17)

This, it seems to me, is precisely why any Christian reflection on human rights needs to deal centrally with Christology.

Why should people who have suffered at the hands of Christians even consider listening to Christian sources for human rights reflection? This basic question is illuminatingly tackled in Blount's discussion of slavery as an interpretive lens. Those who first learned of Christian faith, often in very distorted form, at the hands of their oppressors have nevertheless been able, in the past, to own Christian faith as a humanizing force, through a reconfigured ethics of liberation. 'Jesus can understand the pain, the tragedy, the hopelessness, the sorrow, and, most important, the hope'(Blount, 2001, 33). In the lens of liberation the Bible is read contextually, 'reading, respecting, sometimes rejecting' (ibid., 31). African-American slaves reconfigured the biblical message in order to retrieve it for their own situation.

Blount's narrative respects equally the value of the narratives of individual and community suffering. Are human rights concerned with individuals or communities?

The answer from the slave communities would seem to be emphatically that it is both, although neither romantic individualism nor romantic communitarianism will do. Critiques of neoliberal economic policies have alerted us today to the dangers of individualism. Sebastian Haffner's *Defying Hitler* (2002) provides a devastating critique of the romanticization of community:

> The general promiscuous comradeship to which the Nazis have seduced the Germans has debased this nation as nothing else could...Comradeship completely destroys the sense of responsibility for oneself, be it in the civilian, or worse still, the religious sense... The Nazis knew what they were doing when they made it the normal way of life for an entire nation (Haffner, 2002, 235f)

Of course, the abuse does not take away the proper use, but the dilemma of appropriate community is worth noting.

Brian Blount, in conclusion, faces up to the need for dialogue between black and white American communities who remain separate and distrustful of each other.

> In this dialogue the primary focus would not be on the establishment of universally normative ways of dealing with particular issues. It would instead encourage a cross-fertilisation of different cultural perspectives which would spark in turn new encounters with the text's meaning potential. Then and only then would the real goal be within reach. Then we would approach an interpretive reality where ethics enables the crossing of those boundaries that separate humans from God and disable productive and transformative human contact with one another. (Blount, 2001, 191)

I have quoted this study at length because the issues with which it deals seem to me to be applicable to other contemporary human rights issues. The love of God in Jesus Christ, as a boundary-breaking narrative and a signal of the hope for a different future, is of the essence of a Christian contribution to human rights.

Christ Against Human Rights

Brian Blount's interpretation highlighted, in an acute form, the danger of assuming that Christ will always be seen as an advocate of rights. Christianity was brought to the Americas by slavers and was fostered through the piety of plantation owners. They too, it might be argued in a postmodern framework, had their own legitimately contextual theology, in which they read the biblical texts in interaction with their own culture. Within their Christian community they had the right to the peaceful possession of their lawful property, and that included slaves. They exercised Christian charity and often lived blameless and pious lives, as did many who later practised apartheid. They, too, had legitimate interests and human rights. Above all, they had religious human rights, because their practices were integral to their religious beliefs, which were based on scripture. The same defence could be made of those who tortured heretics and witches. Were these also not religious human rights, ultimately part of obedience to Christ?

Rights conflict. Where they conflict, the more basic and fundamental rights prevail. Who decides? In a secular setting the courts decide. In a theological setting it comes down to debate and decision between different interpretations. I shall suggest that a Christ who blocks access to specific rights, which we shall examine, is a Christ misinterpreted. I shall propose that the character of God's love always privileges justice, equality and kindness. It is always on the side of the marginalized, but not if the marginalized have marginalized themselves through oppression and coercion. It is always the character of unconditional compassion. Discipleship leads unconditionally to human rights advocacy. As Bonhoeffer famously and tellingly put it, 'Only he who speaks up for the Jews should sing hymns in church'. For Jews, read any other persecuted group. But what about my human right to sing hymns regardless? That is indeed a human right, but it is overtaken by the greater need and injustice.

There is a Christ of unconditional love. But the tradition also contains a Christ of terror, a severe judge who will cast into hellfire all who break any of the detailed commands in the scriptural corpus. The judgement of God on unbelief, false belief or moral deviation has been a powerful driving force for the persecution of countless individuals throughout history. In medieval Christendom the vision of Christ the judge could be sufficient justification for torture and repression. In numerous small communities today, and even at family level, there remain various micro-tyrannies in which lives are wrecked by such imagery and the imagined threat that it implies (for current examples see the many websites on Christ and hellfire). Terrorism is never justified, and human rights are perhaps the best remedy.

Christians and Rights Talk

We shall come shortly to debates in philosophical and political literature about the value of rights talk, but already we should note that Christian theologians are themselves quite divided on the role of rights language in relation to the gospel.

In his sympathetic, but searching, critique of Christian notions of justice, especially in liberation theology, Daniel Bell writes of the 'terror' of justice, as it involves judgement and reparation. He is especially critical of the liberal discourse of rights, which he sees as arising from an Enlightenment perspective. Against this he places the therapy of forgiveness, as a gift of God in Christ. He recognizes the dangers of disempowerment for the already powerless, as well as the lack of empirical confirmation of an effective strategy of forgiveness. But he sees the Christian way as a 'refusal to cease suffering, a Christian therapy of desire over against a capitalist therapy of desire'. He concludes as follows:

> When history's losers, the crucified people, follow in the steps of Jesus and forgive their enemies, they are wagering on God. They are wagering that God is

who the Gospel proclaims God to be, the one who defeats sin and wipes away
every tear, not with the sword of a justice that upholds rights but with the gift of
forgiveness in Christ. (Bell, 2001, 195)

Daniel Bell's advocacy tends to stress the less satisfactory sides of an argument from
justice and rights, building on Aquinas and echoing traditional Catholic suspicion of
liberal values. It might also be thought to be in danger of a kind of triumphalism of
forgiveness, of the sort finely discussed by James Alison (Alison, 1993, 2001). For
Bell, the church and its penitential system become the keystone of the arch of human
well-being, in a kind of vulnerability which is itself imposed from above, reminding
us once again of the value of a more open, progressive approach to theology as a
contribution. But Bell's study, in its reflection on justice from a Christian perspective,
is a deeply thoughtful and well-constructed exploration of the other side of rights
language.

A more constructive engagement with rights language can be found in Nicholas
Wolterstorff's *Until Justice and Peace Embrace* (1983), a fine study which cannot
be faulted for neglecting attention to the deep underlying theological questions.
Wolterstorff combines justice with the theological sphere of *shalom*, and he
balances rights with duties. But he can still find an important Christian role for rights
language:

> Seeing that rights are claims to guarantees against threats makes clear that rights
> are God's charter for the weak and defenseless ones in society. A right is the
> legitimate claim for protection of those too weak to help themselves. It is the
> legitimate claim of the defenseless against the more devastating and common of
> life's threats which, at that time and place, are remediable. It is the claim of the
> little ones in society to restraint upon economic and political and physical forces
> that would otherwise be too strong for them to resist. (Wolterstorff, 1983, 84)

An impressive account of church groups acting against torture is given in William
T. Cavanaugh's *Torture and Eucharist* (1998). Cavanaugh, writing from a radical
orthodox position, stresses the importance of the rights of Christian groups against
a pure individualism. He emphasizes that torture works by isolating individuals.
In his Catholic hesitation about the individualist roots of Protestant human rights
thinking he follows a long tradition, reflected, for example, in Jacques Maritain's
1943 work, *The Rights of Man and Natural Law*. It was indeed church suspicion of
the individualist and the potentially secularizing tone of much early modern human
rights reflection that made the churches wary of engaging with it. Cavanaugh offers
a rare Christological reflection on the body of Christ as an antidote to torture and
of the Eucharist as 'performing the body of Christ'. He expresses this eloquently as
follows:

> Jesus' suffering is redemptive for the entire world. His one unrepeatable sacrifice,
> His death by torture on the cross, serves to abolish other blood sacrifices once and
> for all. We do not find other bodies to torture and sacrifice, but only remember
> the eucharist and the one sacrifice which takes away the world's pain.

> The Christian economy of pain, therefore, overcomes the incommunicability
> of pain on which the torturer relies. Torture is so useful; for isolating individuals
> in society from one another in large part because of the inability of people to
> share pain... Pain is incommunicable beyond the body, and the sufferer must
> suffer alone. Christians, nevertheless, make the bizarre claim that pain *can*
> be shared, precisely because people can be knitted together into one body.
> (Cavanaugh, 1998, 280)

It may be that Christians ought not always to assert rights for themselves. But it is important to be able to support the rights of others who may be defenceless in the face of violence. It would seem that neither rights nor forgiveness nor justice as concepts in themselves will be sufficient to articulate the Christian vision of the realm of God. The Christian contribution to society may perhaps be more a combination of incommensurable fragments, deployed together with non-Christian contributions in different ways at different times but always shaped by the eschatological vision of a Christomorphic trace in history, without which all predictions of the end of history will be incomplete.

In looking for insights between the various theological schools of interpretation it is usually fatal to be too purist and to imagine that any one approach has all the answers. For example, between the Christian visions of Jon Sobrino, Stanley Hauerwas and figures such as Adam von Trott (cf. MacDonogh, 1989) and the Kreisau Circle there are huge gulfs. For the latter it was absolutely necessary to become involved in all kinds of dangerous political compromise in order to kill Hitler. There are many ways of embracing resistance and crucifixion.

A Christology for Human Rights?

We have been emphasizing the humanity of God in Jesus Christ. The Christian faith has also sought to find words to articulate its sense of the divinity of Jesus Christ, not in opposition to, but in and through, his humanity. This recognition of transcendence, of the humanity of Jesus as extending participation beyond humanity into a distinctive relationship with God, the source of all existence, has been framed in very different sorts of language, symbol and metaphor throughout the history of Christian community. The search for appropriate language to articulate the gift of faith will always be an ongoing task that cannot be resolved through any particular cultural expression. Even within the same time and culture the language of faith will take different forms in relation to different questions, and cannot accomplish everything that needs to be said in one range of expression. I suggest that the language and culture of human rights may be one highly significant field – though certainly not the only one – for the articulation of the central Christian affirmation of incarnation and reconciliation. I do not wish to suggest that Christology is, in essence, only a Christology of human rights, but I do wish to contemplate a Christology for human rights. I would like to imagine such a Christology with a dynamic which not only reflects a sense of Jesus' human solidarity with our fellow human beings – that is crucially important – but also seeks to bring to some level of effective concrete expression at least the underlying divine love which Christians understand to be the ultimate ground of the way things are. A modest Christology should not be a diminished Christology.

The suggestion that Jesus Christ is the central Christian icon (and not an idol) of human rights engagement entails that all dimensions of Christ, both human and divine, are understood to be fully involved in rights concerns. A Christology that is immersed in human rights culture cannot be the private property of any single theological movement. It may start from many places, and it requires the wisdom and cooperation of different Christian perspectives if it is to be fully effective.

CHAPTER 3

Rights, Cultures and Transcendence: Ambiguity and Tension

The last 50 years have seen enormous advances not only in the statutory provision of human rights legislation, but also in the political importance of human rights. The UN now has a high commissioner for human rights. Groups opposed to human rights have had to take cognisance of rights in their responses, and many such bodies have taken over human rights language to defend their own positions. Claims to rights inevitably come into conflict with one another. It has become clear that human rights concepts, like many theological concepts, are highly contested.[1]

---

1   Although most of the literature cited in this study is from the post-1945 period, surprising items can be found on rights much earlier. E.P. Hurlbut, a New York lawyer, published *Essays on Human Rights and their Political Guarantees* in Edinburgh in 1847. This forward-looking piece, much of which revolves round the constitution of the State of New York, even has a special chapter on 'The Rights of Woman' (52ff). Hurlbut begins, 'Man was not "born to command," nor woman "to obey."' The chapter is an enlightened plea for property rights for women.

There is a superb colloquium on human rights in the *Journal of Religious Ethics*, 26(2), Fall, 1998 which has as its focus the 50th anniversary of the UDHR. Cf. Shue (1998, 266ff):

> Rights can be understood as social guarantees: or better, as systems of social guarantees... Any given right in the system will in practice be much more valuable to some people than to others because the respective circumstances of the individuals vary.
>
> ...These guarantees can be expressed as duties not to deprive, duties to protect, and duties to assist. I believe that every right has these three kinds of correlative duties, which range from negative duties to positive duties.

There is a good account of convergence and divergence in human rights in the essay by Little, . Sachedina and Kelsay, 'Human Rights and the World's Religions' in Bloom, Martin and Proudfoot (1996,213ff). They speak of 'clear and surprising parallels between the Western and Islamic traditions... Both traditions share a common framework within which to think about freedom of conscience and religious liberty' (236.)

Jack Donnelly's *The Concept of Human Rights* (1985), provides what is perhaps still the most clear and succinct account of the nature of human rights:

> Human rights are not 'given' to man by God, nature or the physical facts of life; to think of them in such terms is to remain tied to a vision of human beings as things. Like other social practices, human rights arise from human action. Human rights represent the choice of a particular moral vision of human potentiality and the institutions for realising that vision...We can say that the 'human nature' underlying human rights is a combination of 'natural, social, historical and moral elements'. (Donnelly, 1985, 31)

Donnelly again, in his article 'In Defense of the Universal Declaration Model', in Lyons and Mayall (2003, 21ff) gives a good integrated account of the complementarity of individual and group rights.

Christ and Human Rights

The literature on human rights, and especially the reports of legal cases involving human rights law, is huge. There are many different sorts of rights. Robert Drinan's *The Mobilization of Shame* (2001) – a world-view of human rights – gives a useful overview of current legal positions in global human rights, especially US attitudes, and provides a survey of the main charters, documents and courts of human rights Drinan considers economic and social rights, economic and political rights, women's rights, children's rights, protection against torture and against hunger, the rights of prisoners and the death penalty, and the right to freedom of religion. He also examines the human rights policies of successive US administrations. Other topics covered include the need always for an independent judiciary, the role of amnesty and reconciliation in achieving justice, as in South Africa, and refugee problems.

In *The Transformative Imagination* (Newlands, 2004) I included politics and human rights among the important dialogue partners of a contemporary theology, and examined the work of Gewirth (1982), Forsythe (2000) and others on rights. Some concentrate on philosophical analysis, others on cultural context.

Collections of human rights texts are inevitably highly selective. Many writers have supported some rights, but not others. In Michelene Ishay's *The Human Rights Reader* (1997) St Paul appears, in his Areopagus speech in Acts, as a supporter of free speech for Christians and St Augustine appears in *The City of God* as an advocate of peace rather than war. But on other issues they might seem opposed to the rights of other groups. In his 'Five Fables of Human Rights', cited by Ishay, Steven Lukes examines rights from the perspectives of different imaginary places – Utilitaria, Communitaria, Proletaria, Libertaria and Egalitaria. Each perspective involves different consequences for rights issues; Lukes prefers the last, equality of opportunity, as indicating the relevance of an ideal which can never in fact be reached. The essay in this volume which comes closest to the perspective of this present study is 'Liberalism and Human Rights: A Necessary Connection', by Rhoda Howard and Jack Donnelly. I am inclined to view a liberal approach as necessary but not sufficient.

There is a powerful plea for attention to needs in the context of rights in Goldewijk and Fortman (1999). Cf. Ch. 5, 'Human Dignity and Humiliation':

> A renewed focus on human dignity in the context of human rights implies at least three elements. The first is a clear insistence that human dignity provides a *critical standard* or basic norm to judge any person, group, organization, institution or action that denies human equality and freedom and thus humiliates and dehumanizes people. Second, the concept of dignity points to that area of being human in which *vulnerable* and *fragile* dimensions of human existence are recognized to have priority. Third, dignity offers a decisive indicator of the *sustainability* of efforts towards the everyday realization of human rights. (55)

Needs are also considered by Henry Shue (1980) in his plea for a basic level of subsistence as central to human rights. I have discussed elsewhere Kymlicka's (1989) work on group and individual rights (Newlands, 1997). In his *Taking Suffering Seriously* William Felice makes a strong plea for collective rights, but recognizes some dangers: 'Rights alone are not necessarily progressive, and, in fact, can serve to disguise exploitation rather than help mend it. Genocide has been committed under the banner of group rights, and therefore the *context* of these rights must be made explicit' (Felice, 1996, 181).

In critiques of liberal perspectives there has been much talk of monolithic foundations of enlightenment – rightly. But sometimes this has reflected an earlier monolithic foundationalism – and perhaps indicated new ones to come. The need is to develop pluralistic notion of value, but not against other perspectives in a polemical way. Even pluralists can be dogmatic ideologues, as in some pluralist Christologies. Critical perspectives must be porous and open – except to coercion.

Michael Ignatieff

Rather than offering yet another general survey of a huge raft of writers I want to focus here on the recent work of Michael Ignatieff. The achievements and the ambiguities of human rights concerns from a non-religious perspective are well documented in Ignatieff's excellent lectures on *Human Rights as Politics and Idolatry*, and in the responses to this (Ignatieff, 2001).

The purpose of human rights, he argues, is to protect human agency and therefore to protect human agents against abuse and oppression. Beyond this, rights do not claim to be morally comprehensive. Without rights, people lack agency. To minimize controversy and allow for moral pluralism we should avoid foundational arguments such as religious arguments. But this does not mean relativism. Rights are universal because they define the interests of the powerless. They involve a commitment to dialogue with people with whom we disagree – although they do imply non-negotiable concepts, such as the rights of individuals. Human rights interventions will not always be successful, but must be done with consistency. We should not make a creed out of rights – that would be idolatry.

In order to avoid abstraction and concentrate on the actual dynamics of human rights issues it is well worth looking more closely at Ignatieff's case. Ignatieff may be an appropriate central dialogue partner for this present study, both because of his expertise and because his earlier work on Isaiah Berlin makes his approach very similar to my own in working on intercultural theology, of which human rights theology is a distinctive dimension. He begins his first lecture, 'Human Rights as Politics' from the premise that when human beings have defensible rights – when their agency as individuals is protected and enhanced – they are less likely to be abused or oppressed. He concedes at once that the rights revolution was not led by states that already practised what they preached (as we shall see later, Christian theology starts from a similar position) and contends that '[h]uman rights has gone global by going local, embedding itself in the soil of cultures and worldviews independent of the West, in order to sustain ordinary people's struggles against unjust states and oppressive social practices' (Ignatieff, 2001, 7).

Human rights activism is not neutral. It involves politics, taking sides. But it is constrained by moral standards. Ignatieff sees the anti-slavery campaigns as a source of modern human rights activism: 'The most essential message of human rights is that there are no excuses for the inhuman use of human beings (ibid., 16).' What are the limits of human rights? After 1945 the communist tradition stressed economic and social rights, whereas the capitalist tradition emphasized political and civil rights – traditions affirmed in Helsinki in 1975. Ignatieff stresses that '[w]e cannot speak of human rights as trumps... The larger illusion I want to criticize is that human rights is above politics, a set of moral trump cards whose function is to bring political disputes to closure and conclusion'(ibid., 21). To take a concrete example, 'the problem in Western human rights policy is that by promoting ethnic self-determination, we may actually endanger the stability that is a pre-condition for protecting human rights'(ibid., 29). Although liberal democracy tends to support human rights, it does not always do so (as evidenced by the death penalty in the United States, for example), and other state forms may still provide minority rights protection.

Neither intervention nor non-intervention can guarantee success; the process is always fallible. The criteria for intervention include pervasive abuses of rights, a threat to a wider area and a real chance of stopping the abuses (this comes close to the traditional criteria for a just war). There may be wider geopolitical reasons – for example, the threat of global conflict. There are many pitfalls – the human rights conscience of the West may be exploited and human rights intervention can itself become abusive.

The second Ignatieff lecture, 'Human Rights as Idolatry' (Ignatieff, 2001, p. 53ff) was particularly apposite to this study of rights in relation to transcendence: 'Human rights is misunderstood...if it is seen as a "secular" religion. It is not a creed; it is not a metaphysics. To make it so is to turn it into a species of idolatry: humanism worshipping itself.' He argues that '[h]uman rights can command universal assent only as a decidedly "thin" theory of what is right, a definition of the minimum conditions for any kind of life at all'(ibid., 56). Human rights protect people's agency – that is Isaiah Berlin's negative liberty, 'the capacity of each individual to achieve rational intentions without let or hindrance' (ibid., 57).

Ignatieff considers challenges to human rights, from Islam, from East Asia and from the West itself. The West should neither equate Islam with fundamentalism nor concede too much to the Islamic model and the Asian/Singaporean challenge in a spirit of postmodern relativism. Western defenders of human rights have traded too much away. Individuals matter: 'Rights are meaningful only if they confer entitlements and immunities on individuals; they are worth having only if they can be enforced against institutions like the family, the state and the church' (ibid., 67). The test of human rights legitimacy is from the powerless: 'Relativism is the invariable ally of tyranny' (ibid.,74).

Ignatieff reflects upon 'the spiritual crisis' of human rights: 'Whereas the cultural crisis of human rights has been about the intercultural validity of human rights norms, the spiritual crisis concerns the ultimate metaphysical grounds for these norms' (ibid., 77). He quotes Charles Taylor to the effect that the concept of human rights 'could travel better if separated from some of its underlying justifications'. He disagrees with religious grounds – as advocated by Perry and Stackhouse – and, indeed, with a form of humanist idolatry: despite the degree of secular and religious hubris it attracts, there is nothing sacred about human rights Ignatieff advocates a humble humanism without rights inflation; all human beings should be protected from cruelty. There is a need for constant dialogue 'We need to stop thinking of human rights as trumps and begin thinking of them as a language that creates the basis for deliberation' (ibid., 95).

After Ignatieff

It is interesting that Ignatieff quotes Taylor on the side of his 'thin universalism', but Taylor has himself expressed concern that transcendence may be too quickly ruled out by Enlightenment perspectives on ethical issues. (Taylor, 1999; Newlands, 2004). I would like to think that an intercultural theology may contribute to this 'thin universalism' by bringing its tradition to the table not as a trump card, but as an equal contribution to the conversation. In this way it may perhaps be possible to see that religion is compatible with what is a genuine, rather than a privileged, political liberalism, which is open to conversation while maintaining its intolerance of oppression.

Let me try to clarify my position in relation to Michael Ignatieff's comments on religion. It seems to me that, although there is no need or necessity for transcendence, faith or God, there is, as a matter of fact – accidental fact if you like – human experience which understands itself in terms of these perspectives. We don't have to have God in order to be good, or to have humanity or human rights. Christians can, and sometimes do, engage in human rights without any such explicit reference – as, indeed, Ignatieff recommends. It is true that much of our religious imagery comes, *inter alia*, from specific cultures of the third millennium BCE. We compose our religious identities, like the rest of our human identity, from all sorts of influences. Indeed, our metaphors are also shaped by the ideologies of the ancient Mediterranean world, by Greece and Rome, and therefore with all the issues about power, domination and control that these carry with them.

But parallel to, and embedded in, these traditions are traditions of what people have understood as experience of faith. This occurs on a spectrum from pure fideism to faith supported by a cumulative, though not compelling, rational case. Located within this human tradition are the Jewish and Christian faiths. If there is a God of the sort envisaged in classical Christian faith, then it would not perhaps be unreasonable for our knowledge of God to come 'in, with and under' these traditions which have both religious and secular overtones. Although there certainly does not have to be a God, faith hangs on to the persuasion that there is.

At this point I want to indicate some important and salient points made in response to Ignatieff in the collected (2001) volume. In her Introduction, Amy Gutmann suggests that 'minimal' is not necessarily synonymous with 'maximally consensual' or 'easiest to enforce.'(xii): 'My disagreement with Ignatieff is over whether a human rights regime rests on a single foundation – the one agreeable to all, or to most people – or on several foundations, no one of which is likely to be agreeable to most people'(xviii). These might include human dignity, agency, equality and freedom.

Anthony Appiah suggests that human rights are more than an expression of Western Enlightenment values, and that group rights may be important, provided that they do not endanger individual rights (Ignatieff, 2001, p. 101ff). David Hollinger wants to keep the door open for people with thick theories of human rights 'because we need all the help we can get.'(ibid., 125). Thomas Laqueur highlights the role of the moral imagination (ibid., 127ff). Diane Orentlicher makes the point, particularly germane to this study, that 'universal acceptance of the human rights idea depends on its legitimation *within* diverse religious traditions, and not just *alongside* them' (ibid., 141ff). Human rights not only challenges state power but 'often requires fundamental transformation of belief systems….For this reason I am inclined to share An-Na'im's belief that human rights advocates would do well "to seriously engage religion" rather than seek to exclude religious discourse from the intercultural process of constructing and construing human rights'(ibid., 156)

In response to his critics Ignatieff notes that 'modern international rights conceives of victims as rights –bearers.'(ibid., 163). He sees a way of reconciling group rights and national belonging: 'There is no reason in principle why citizens cannot enjoy two types of rights at once – those that they enjoy with all other citizens and those that they enjoy by virtue of their particular minority status'(ibid., 168). Although democracy does not guarantee rights, 'the advent of democracy improves the human rights of those who do not happen to belong to the electoral majority' (ibid.,172). Ignatieff's recent Gifford lectures develop the human rights theme further, with particular reference to Terrorism and the temptation to resort to torture in counterterrorism. He explores the growth of nihilism and the appropriate response to it, stressing the need to avoid an unnecessary guilt complex and to defend robustly the values of justice, human dignity and liberal democracy for which we stand.[2]

Christ and Consensus

In this study of Christology and human rights we shall be concerned precisely 'to seriously engage religion'; through analysis of the strengths and weaknesses of the Christian tradition. I have myself expressed the Christian position like this:

> Christians believe, as characterised in the incarnation of Jesus Christ. They bring
> the way of Jesus Christ, as an icon of humanity as God intends it, to the table
> for consideration. They believe that all human beings are created to be fulfilled
> in the image of God, and to be fulfilled with dignity and well being. They do

---

2   In his Scribner Lectures (Princeton University, April 2005) Ronald Dworkin underlined the important distinction between liberty and freedom. A theory of liberty will explain why freedom should be protected. A government does not compromise liberty by limiting freedom – for example, by creating taxes – provided that this is done with an appropriate distributive justification. Despite popular rhetoric, freedom is not a political value, but liberty is.

not wish to impose this vision on others. But they offer it in the belief that it has infinite value for the human future. Schleiermacher held that all human beings have a sense, in their self-consciousness, of absolute dependence on a higher transcendent source, but this is often inhibited by a corruption of this sense through cultural and personal factors. As a matter of empirical observation this is clearly not the case, and experience is notably deceptive. There is however an awareness in most societies that our humanity is largely shaped by our relationships with others, by the recognition of difference. This means that the formal possibility of relationship to a transcendent other is not unintelligible in human conversation. The concrete condition of this possibility is specified in particular religious traditions, and in Christianity through faith in God through Jesus Christ. (Newlands, 2004, 102)

The problem obviously remains, however – underlined again in the Ignatieff colloquium – of how to engage transcendence with human rights in such a way that religion does not colonize rights, and that rights language does not rule out the religious dimension as being inevitably hegemonic and intolerant. We shall return to this issue again and again, but at this stage I want to introduce arguments which I believe may have value at least as a catalyst for continuing the dialogue.

In a 1996 essay (reprinted in Hayden, 2001) Charles Taylor reflected on the possibility of a world consensus on human rights. Such an 'overlapping consensus' on the condemnation of such activities as genocide, murder and slavery might be agreed on the basis of 'alternative, mutually incompatible justifications' (Hayden, 2001, 411). A distinction can be made between norms of conduct, based on a legal tradition, and views about human nature, society and the human good, which are their underlying justification. In the West, notions of subjective rights led to a rewriting of natural law theory in the seventeenth century. But the package can be untied. Buddhist conceptions of human rights might derive from a basic value of non-violence. The outcome might be the same, although the justification is different, leading to the possibility of a consensus on human rights and democracy, and to a Gadamerian 'fusion of horizons':

> To the extent that we can only acknowledge agreement with people who share the whole package, and are moved by the same heroes, the consensus will either never come or must be forced. (Taylor, 1999, 112)

It seems to me that this approach to a multiple justification of agreed aims is central to a viable Christian contribution to human rights, as well as to the effective articulation of the centrality of Jesus Christ for human welfare in the future. It would not be impossible to relate the kind of Islamic justification of human rights advocated by such scholars as An-Na'im to the Buddhist example cited by Taylor.

Martin Marty justifies the religious dimension in a slightly different way. Given the difficulties, why adduce religious approaches?

> At the very least, what is adduced here is an attempt to use one's own religion and religious outlook to help move beyond mere toleration to the defense and assurance of those in another religion who have other outlooks.. Not indifference to religion or the incomprehensibility of the other, but reflective difference, based

on the always ambiguous and problematic but resource-rich religious traditions, can become an instrument for enlarging and assuring human rights (cited in Witte, 1996,16)

It is particularly in areas such as Asia that the religious dimension of human rights becomes crucial. Chandra Muzaffar writes:

> The nature of the human being, his characteristics, his values, his strengths, his weaknesses, even his duties and his rights have been discussed through the ages by almost every strain within Hinduism, Buddhism, Taoism, Confucianism, Christianity, Islam and Sikhism. Contemplation on the human being is the very essence of religion. It is only logical therefore that in Asia (and perhaps in other parts of the world too) human rights thinkers and activists open their minds to ideas on the human being embodied in those great religious philosophies which ordinary women and men on our continent continue to cherish in the depths of their hearts. (Muzaffar, 2002, 99)

The consequences of this approach may mean seeking to learn from approaches which are, on the face of it, diametrically opposed, and trying to think them through in a constructive tension. Max Stackhouse's study of human rights is based on universal norms deriving from the created order (Stackhouse, 1984.) In an article cited in Witte (1996), Stackhouse strongly criticizes Rorty's and Lyotard's postmodern attack on foundationalism. Yet it may also be possible to learn from postmodern justification. Rorty notes that torturers are often simply unable to regard their victims as fellow human beings, often because of racial prejudice. He views such people as deprived not so much of moral knowledge as of security and sympathy and believes that trust and sentiment need to be developed. He proposes challenging such incapacity with narratives that create bonds of sympathy through a process of 'sentimental education' (Rorty, cited in Hayden 2001, 254).[3]

A cumulative approach also has the huge advantage of potentially including the vast raft of perspectives which have traditionally been on the margins of classical European debate: African perspectives on human rights, feminist (for example Catharine MacKinnon in Hayden (2001)) and gay perspectives (for example, Donnelly and Nussbaum in Hayden (2001); Nussbaum and Olyan, 1998), and perspectives on environmental rights. MacKinnon points out that rape in conflict situations, such as genocidal rape in the Balkan wars, is often misinterpreted by male commentators. Donnelly cites the 1998 crucifixion of Matthew Shepard in Wyoming

---

3   The history of the concept of sympathy has been traced from the Cambridge Platonists by Jennifer Herdt (1997). We may note its theological role in Abelard and McLeod Campbell. We shall return to Richard Rorty on this subject: 'We shouldn't claim that our reason sets us apart from other animals, but instead we are set apart by our ability to feel for each other much more than animals can' (from Rorty's 'Human Rights, Rationality and Sentimentality' in Shute and Rorty (1993).

Rorty's view of the role of religion in the public sphere is well illustrated in his dialogue with Wolterstorff, in the *Journal of Religious Ethics*, 31(3), Spring, 2003, pp 129ff. He is, unsurprisingly, critical of the triumphalist tone of much recent theology: 'When I am told by Stout that opponents of humility such as Hauerwas, Macintyre and Millbank are now favoured over Rauschenbusch and Niebuhr, I fear for the republic!'

and underlines the difficulty of achieving real protection against discrimination for sexual minorities under international law. We might expect the Christological reflections of emancipatory theologies to be helpful in acting as a catalyst for such cumulative justification – although we have to admit that such a Christian catalyst has to be purified in the fires of repentance, since Christian intervention in issues of racism, sex and gender has been particularly ambiguous.

The price of consensus?

Taking Taylor's analysis further, we might reflect, too, that, although it is vital to work out clearly the role of Christology in underpinning a Christian contribution to human rights, and to spell out this dimension publicly, the effective deployment of this dimension might not always lead to explicit Christian language in the praxis of rights issues. Although there was a huge Christian input into existing documentation, there is nowhere, so far as I am aware, any reference to Jesus Christ, or indeed to any other central figure in the major world religions, in the enabling legislation and related documentation. This may be entirely appropriate. We may perhaps learn from Ignatieff's discussion also not to use Christology as if it were automatically a trump card.

Christian perspectives on geopolitical issues are often concerned to highlight actual and potential shortcomings in alternative approaches, whether secular or religious. It seems to me that constructive dialogue is most likely to take place when Christian views are introduced as distinctive contributions that simply exist in their own right, rather than as solutions to gaps in other traditions.[4]

Consensus and legal critique

It may be salutary to end this chapter by considering writers who raise serious questions about human rights from a democratic perspective, through a concern for civil liberties. Mary Ann Glendon's *Rights Talk: The Impoverishment of Political Discourse* begins with America, the land of rights, where the language has suffered from hyperinflation: 'By needlessly indulging in excessively simplistic forms of rights talk in our pluralistic society, we needlessly multiply occasions for civil discord (Glendon, 1991, 15).

---

4   There is a comprehensive discussion of the relation of religion to political liberalism in Dombrowski (2001). Cf. also the collection edited by P.J. Weithman (1997) especially the essays by N. Wolterstorff, who criticizes the restrictions on religion often proposed by political liberalism, and T.P. Jackson, who brings a Christian 'civic agapism' to political discussion. In this debate it is important to be fair to both sides of the discussion. Wolterstorff is a good example of a conservative theologian who is committed to social issues and whose proposals could hardly be regarded as oppressive to non-Christians.

Theology will bring to the table the admission that it, too, has had, and still has, oppressive structures. The issue of a strategy to combat structures of oppression from within is tackled effectively in Mark Taylor (1990, esp. 111f, 157f). Taylor writes powerfully of the Christ of emancipatory reconciliation and of 'refiguring Christ for today's Christopraxis'.

There is an illusion of absoluteness about rights – this is illustrated from the treatment of property rights in American law. We see ourselves as isolated individuals, 'lone rights-bearers', and we may lose any sense of responsibility, social or legal, to help others. We need a sense of sociality and an awareness of the international character of rights reflection. Precisely because rights language is important, it needs to be used with caution and precision. Tolerance, dialogue and civility, rather than inflamed rhetoric, offers the best way forward (Glendon, 1991, 171f).

It is perhaps still significant that writers in a Catholic tradition, such as Glendon (who became the first head of a papal academy in 2004) and Elshtain, are more immediately conscious of the communal dimensions of rights, whereas thinkers with a Protestant background think more obviously of individual rights. Constructive conversation therefore requires paying attention to all avenues.[5]

Tolerance, patience, generosity and all the many dimensions of love will be as important for achieving human welfare as rights talk alone. This may be part of the necessary culture in which human rights can flourish – a culture to which the shape of Christ may make a valuable contribution as an open Christomorphic dimension and a safe space for dialogue and action.[6]

Equally crushing, at least in the first instance, is the collection edited by Campbell, Ewing and Tomkins, *Sceptical Essays on Human Rights* (2001). Tomkins marshals the issues deftly in his Introduction: 'The Human Rights Act 1998 was one of the most widely celebrated statutes to have been passed by parliament in many years. Nowhere were the celebrations more pronounced or more intense than among communities of lawyers' (Campbell *et al.*, 2001, 1). Much of his argument is directed against the danger of tasks proper to the democratically elected legislature being taken over by an unelected, and perhaps elitist, judiciary:

---

5   Stanley Hauerwas famously criticized human rights in a number of places:

   Indeed, we overlook too easily how the language of 'rights,' in spite of its potential for good, contains within its logic a powerful justification for violence. Our rights language 'absolutizes the relative' in the name of a universal that is profoundly limited and limiting just to the extent that it tempts us to substitute some moral ideal for our faithfulness to God. (Hauerwas, 1983, 61)

It is, of course, important not to absolutize the relative. But cruel and unnatural acts are also commonly done in an absolutized supposed faithfulness to God.

6   This will inevitably include the vexed issue of cultural relativism, to which we shall return. Wilson offers a robust critique, but the issues are not easily resolved:

   For their doctrine to be coherent, cultural relativists seem to hold a nineteenth-century notion of culture as discrete and homogeneous, as the product of isolation, and as the basis of all difference and similarity between human beings. Their relativism is predicated upon bounded conceptions of linguistic and cultural systems, but it falls apart in contexts of hybridity, creolisation, intermixture and the overlapping of political traditions. (Wilson, 1997, 9)

   We should not adopt a diffusionist view of globalisation since it does not just imply a process of homogenisation and integration, but involves a proliferation of diversity as well. (Ibid., 12)

Cf. 'The solution, or rather the "good" multiculturalism must arrive at a blend of sharing and difference' (T.H. Eriksen in Wilson, 1997, 63).

> In England judicial decisions tend to reflect the culture of the common law, in which there is a privileging of individual rights over collective rights, and a concentration on rights based on property as of absolute value. The interpretation of a bill of rights can enhance the judicial role and serve to weaken the importance and power of elected bodies. Legal examples point to various incongruities, rough edges, nonsense, or limitations imposed by the Human Rights Act in the fields of devolution, labour law, discrimination, tort law, criminal justice, and minority protection law. (Campbell *et al.*, 2001, 7)

Such problems arise equally in laws outside Britain.

In the essays there are various forms of scepticism – about rights as such in relationships between the individual and the state, about the wisdom of having rights enforced by judges, and about the content of specific rights enshrined in the ECHR and therefore in the Human Rights Act. Rights talk is inherently antagonistic: it imagines a paradigm in which there are two parties and therefore squeezes out room for a third 'public interest' voice; it reduces the relationship between citizen and state to a quasi-legal contract; and it is 'insufficiently sensitive to the hegemonic power of its own discourse'(ibid., 8).

The authors highlight the gaps in the British Human Rights Act:

> Property is protected for those who possess it, but the homeless have no right to be housed. Religious freedom is protected, but not an adequate standard of health care. And so on, and on. Social and economic rights are nowhere to be seen in the new liberal order: only a select few rights have been 'brought home' in the Not-Very-Many-Human Rights-Act of 1998. (Campbell *et al.*, 2001,10)

Particularly telling is Keith Ewing's essay on 'The Unbalanced Constitution' in which he shows how corporations have regularly used human rights legislation to foster their own commercial interests – to dilute attempts to control corruption, to attack restrictions on tobacco advertising or on election spending by rich political parties (Campbell *et al.*, 2001,103ff.). There is a danger of promoting liberty at the expense of equality. Ewing argues that '[p]aradoxically for those sceptical about Bills of Rights on the grounds of democratic principle, the Human Rights Act has thus created a democratic imperative for even more entrenched rights'(ibid.,116).

A reader sceptical about the scepticism might, of course, gently wonder whether there is some rivalry between a judicial and an academic oligarchy here. But the legal discussion perhaps helps to show that the very serious gains to be made and losses to be sustained in human rights issues would benefit from the input of a number of disciplines in dialogue. There is a case to be made for the intercultural and interdisciplinary use of the imagination to transform the intractable abuses which remain so often at the heart of our society.

However, as we shall see in a later chapter, the legal critique of rights is central to the consideration of practical outcomes. In 1986 Tom Campbell and his colleagues stressed that the rhetoric of human rights has to be grounded in laws if it is to be effective (Campbell *et al.*, 1986). Human rights rhetoric is often of little use in specific cases, and may sometimes be counterproductive:

> That effective human rights require to be particularized and realized in law is clear. What is in question is whether these essential steps to articulate and realize the social cash-value of such rights undermine or underline the persuasive force of generalized declarations of human rights. (Campbell, in Campbell *et al.*, 1986, 13)

A sharp postmodern account of the development of human rights has been given by Costas Douzinas in *The End of Human Rights: Critical Legal Thought at the Turn of the Century* (2000). Against traditional liberal individualism, Douzinas refers to Levinas on *the face*, to relate rights to the ethics of alterity:

> The other is incomparably unique; she is external to categories, norms and principles, in her face humanity is annulled to leave her the only one of her kind, bearer of all the dignity in the world, the most equal among equals... On this bedrock of total uniqueness which has nothing to do with the selfishness of individuality or the safety and certainty of community, both abstract individualism and particular universalism find their inescapable limit. (Douzinas, 2000, 350)

Alterity is focused by reflecting on the position of the refugee:

> We cannot escape the other and rid ourselves of the stranger. The refugee is the representative of total otherness and the symbol of our own exile, the sign that ego cannot find peace and security in a secluded and protected existence. (Douzinas, 2000, 358)

However, we should always perhaps bear in mind that philosophers and theologians are not always accurate prophets, and that we need not see the discussion as inevitably culminating in the postmodern. None of us is in a position to mortgage the future. The point could be made from one of the most recent studies, William Talbott's excellent book, *Which Rights should be Universal.* Talbott discusses the development of judgement rights, including security and subsistence rights. He notes Sen's striking discovery that serious famines and mass starvations have more political than natural origins, and invariably occur under totalitarian regimes, and also Sen's demonstration of how patriarchal institutions harm women (Talbott, 2005, 99). Talbott summarizes his argument as follows:

> The ground of basic human rights is the capacity of normal adult human beings to make reliable judgements about what is good for them. Basic human rights are the guarantees that enable people to develop and exercise their autonomy. (Talbott, 2005, 185)

He concludes:

> Following Mill, I have suggested that a rights-respecting democracy is an experimental society, where people engage in experiments in living to try to better understand what makes for a good life... The experiment began recently, less than 300 years ago. This is not the end of history. The experiment has hardly begun. (Talbott, 2005,188)

Talbott, like the rest of us, is not infallible, but he wisely does not pretend to be:

> Imagine what driving would be like if there were no traffic regulations at all, no speed limits, no stop lights, no stop or yield signs. Traffic would be much more congested and there would be many more accidents. All drivers would be much worse off. (Talbott, 2005, 144)

In general, this may be the case, but recent small-scale experiments in Holland have demonstrated that the removal of all lights and signs may increase safety by encouraging driver alertness!

Human rights are never completely achieved; they challenge us always to question the present through a utopian vision of the future. This perspective would overlap with my construal of Christology in terms of relationality. It is, however, by no means clear that there needs to be an absolute divide between modified liberal grammars of identity and postmodern alternatives – in this respect, we shall consider the work of Taylor, Appiah and Stout in later chapters. Drawing from both these traditions is the advantage of the postfoundational.

CHAPTER 4

Human Rights,
History and Christology

Exploring the Paradox

Human rights are not an obvious feature of the Christological traditions of the church. The New Testament struggles to make sense of the events concerning Jesus, his life, his teaching and the horrific and humiliating circumstances of his death. Different, and sometimes conflicting, interpretations swiftly arise. At least some of his followers are united in the belief that he has a central role in the continuing purposes of the God of Israel: faith in God begins to include faith that the salvific presence of God includes the presence of Jesus, in some continuing form. The early Christian communities began to understand Jesus as the resurrected one, or as a unique messianic prophet. No doubt some of the communities expected the breaking in of the kingdom of God with immediate political consequences. But what was to become the mainstream increasingly saw the future as the eschatological gift of eternal life, continuing beyond physical death, through the resurrected Christ. Here, somehow, the divine spirit was to be poured out bringing salvation to an increasingly widening community. Christians began to worship Jesus as God. Gradually, the various titles attributed to Jesus – especially as Lord, as Saviour, as Son of God, as Word – enabled Christians to achieve a deeper and more comprehensive understanding of the faith which they understood themselves to experience as a gift of grace.

The central concern of this community was to understand the relation of Jesus to God. Christologies developed. Doctrines of the incarnation arose. The relation of divine to human in Jesus, word to flesh, word to humanity, the role of the mind and will of God to the mind and will of a particular man – all these issues were high on the Christian agenda. For this there were theoretical, but also highly practical, reasons. Worship suggested that Christology and the urgent issue of how salvation from sin in the Hebrew tradition was to be achieved was no less important. On the positive side there was the apprehension that God was uniquely and transformatively present to the community. On the negative side there was a need to differentiate the community from other religious groups, both Jewish and gentile.

A community based on minor cultural groups that were facing hostility had no obvious motivation to consider social deprivation and human rights issues in the existing majority communities. More important was the need to plead for tolerance and protection for the small and vulnerable congregations. Notions of tolerance, and then of respect and claims to equality, took different shapes in different communities. The influential Pauline communities tended to refrain from asserting rights and instead to act in humility and kenosis. This could, of course, become a powerful catalyst for the need to care for and privilege the rights of others, especially when coupled with the concern for strangers which ran powerfully through Jesus' teaching and action. But this would come to fruition only when Christians became major players within the Roman empire.

The social consequences of the kingdom of God in the teaching of Jesus were love, peace and justice. This vision was entirely consonant with St Paul's understanding of the fruits of the spirit, patience, gentleness and love. But salvation was increasingly seen as an eschatological gift of faith, coming from, and leading to, the heavenly kingdom. The world of temporal affairs was held to be of only provisional significance, to be exchanged sooner or later for the kingdom of heaven. Christians are in the world, but not of it. Much more importantly they are in Christ, in mystical union. Communities which stress the sociopolitical aspects of Jesus' message are increasingly written out of the narrative – a signal example of the marginalization which takes place in the development of all religious traditions.

A Persecuting Church?

There can be little doubt that the huge emphasis on the development of classical Christological and Trinitarian doctrine with which theological students become familiar today accurately reflects the main emphasis of intellectual activity throughout much of the history of the church. It entailed the need for agreed doctrinal criteria and often led to the harsh treatment of those who produced minority reports.

The famous dictum that 'error has no rights' effectively hindered, and may still hinder, respect for basic human dignity within the churches. As the churches gained political significance, it became possible to mobilize the state against dissent. The assertion of theological certainty, which the cultural paradigms of the church increasingly seemed to require, led to religious intolerance and to persecution.

Christians were persecuted. Christians persecuted.

The early church

Brian Tierney has said that '[f]rom the beginning of the Christian era there were elements in the Christian tradition that could lead on either to a doctrine of religious liberty or to a practice of persecution' (Witte, 1996, 19). Luke Timothy Johnson puts it as follows: 'Christians have been, and continue to be, the least credible of witnesses to the blessings of tolerance and the human right to religious liberty' (ibid., 65). Paul Zagorin, begins his *How the Idea of Religious Toleration came to the West* with this comment:

> Of all the great world religions past and present, Christianity has been by far the most intolerant. This statement may come as a shock, but nevertheless it is true. In spite of the fact that Jesus Christ, the Jewish founder of the Christian religion, is shown in the New Testament as a prophet and savior who preached mutual love and non-violence to his followers, the Christian church was for a great part of its history an extremely intolerant institution. (Zagorin, 2003,1)

We may recall Michael Ignatieff's damning comment on Victorian prisons that as the penitentiary's technician of guilt, the chaplain provided the constant legitimation of institutional practice required for its functioning. (Ignatieff, 1979, 198)

Where is Christology in all of this? Here again there is a wide spectrum, and the most diverse approaches have their defenders. Biblical tradition seemed to point in opposite directions. On the one hand, love is the cardinal virtue; on the other hand, truth is paramount, and those who were in untruth or persuaded others of untrue doctrines were destroying souls and, for this, severe punishment was the divine command.

There were, of course, factors central to the Christological issue, which could affirm human dignity and commend unconditional empathy and compassion. Christians constantly heard sermons on texts exhorting compassion: on Matthew 5: 43, 'Love your enemies'; on John 15:12, 'Love one another, as I have loved you'; on Galatians 2: 20 and many other passages. Among the Apostolic Fathers, altruism characterizes the Letter to Diognetus, especially Chapter 7, and the tradition of altruism was well established in preaching and charitable action.

Liberty of religious conscience for Christians is praised, notably by Tertullian (*Apology*, 24.5–6 and 28.1) and Athenagoras (*Embassy*, 1–2). Lactantius, in a much quoted passage, goes further and defends all freedom of religion:

> Liberty has chosen to dwell in religion. For nothing is so much a matter of free will as religion, and no one can be required to worship what he does not will to worship. (*Divinarum Institutionum*, V.19, CSEL 19,463–5, PL6.1061 (Brian Tierney's translation))

Lactantius does appear to have held a consistent, though somewhat exceptional, theory of religious toleration. Beyond this there is evidence of a raft of concerns for what we would today regard as human rights issues – Gregory of Nyssa's (again rather isolated) clear condemnation of slavery, explicit concern for widows, the poor, and the sick, and the development of alms-giving arising out of biblical exposition. David Hart has shown how Gregory uses eschatology as a counter to the essentialism of Aristotelian natural theology, so that there is 'a continuous liberation of the creature' (Hart, 2001, 65).[1] Coercion divides the one body of humanity, while redemption comes through humanity in the form of a slave.

But the compulsions of the need for conformity combined in practice to drown out these motifs. It was to take the development of less authoritarian ways of thinking in society in general to lead the church to discover what it already had, but had largely buried. To do this it had to learn to restrain some of the exclusive tendencies of monotheism and the rhetoric of intolerance. There was a need to relativize – that

---

1 I am grateful to Iain Torrance for this reference and to other discussions of torture and slavery in the ancient world, and to Sarah Coakley for an illuminating lecture on Gregory as source of a theology of desire, as a guide to disentangling deadlock on sexuality. Hart's eschatological critique of essentialism could be applied to this issue also.

is, tone down – the rhetoric and the theological claims, legitimizing diversity. The claims of conscience continued to be debated throughout the Middle Ages – for example, in the comments of the *Glossa Ordinaria* on Romans 14:23.

As the quest to clarify the Christological mystery became ever more intense, it was not surprising that formulations which seemed to emphasize most effectively the supreme significance of Jesus Christ in the understanding of God came to be preferred. Politics entered the decision-making process at every stage. As it happened, the politically strongest formulation also coincided with the strongest theological options at the seminal councils of both Nicaea and Chalcedon, and these decisions contributed to the strength of Christianity in most parts of Christendom for the next 1,000 years. But there was a price to be paid in confirming precedents for monolithic theological structures and in excluding those who espoused alternative, but often equally faithful, perspectives. With regard to non-Christian perspectives of transcendence, an earlier appreciation of at least an element of complementarity between Christian and Graeco-Roman philosophical and theological values gave way to a consistent devaluing of anything that was not explicitly Christian. Paradigmatic for this tension between the explicitly Christian and underlying culture is the work of Augustine, whose astonishing knowledge and use of classical culture nevertheless led him to a decisive repudiation of many of its central values in favour of explicitly biblical and Christian perspectives.

Whilst it cannot be said that the mainstream of classical Christology was inimical to the development of human rights, it might be more accurately asserted that it could be, and was often, used to stifle diversity and dissent. Looking at the church from a modern perspective, William Frend concluded unsurprisingly that the early church was not a particularly liberal institution (Frend, 1969, 28ff).

Through Boethius, again a scholar steeped in classical culture and deeply moulded by Christian piety, the triumph of Christian over classical culture permeated the Middle Ages and shaped its theology. There are, of course, huge tracts of medieval thought which deviated from the mainstream. And certainly classical culture was not an inevitable friend of tolerance and respect for human dignity – slavery is the obvious example. Yet the tendency to assume that the one true doctrine could be found and then definitively formulated continued to militate against respect for diversity of perspective. This was paralleled by the centralization of bureaucracy in church and state. Augustine famously used, against the Donatists, the fateful interpretation of Luke 14:23 – *cogite intrare*. Persecution of error now had his prestigious support . A form of dualism of church and state came to be justified in what we term the Middle Ages, thus limiting Christian theological criticism of state practice in matters of justice.

Authoritative and comprehensive surveys of the role of concepts of humanity and *humanitas*, of cognate ideas such as *aequitas, misericordia, philanthropia, eleemosune,* and *xenodocheiea* indicate that the ancient world developed in a manner not too dissimilar to our own times. Churchmen preached on a huge spectrum of topics related to compassion and punishment with different emphases at different times. Politicians played politics with the concepts, honing them to the particular demands of *Realpolitik* of the particular period.

The Middle Ages

Church history is characterized by the well-known paradox of an amazing variety in faith and practice in many local areas, and of cultural pluralism and intercultural thinking shining through the work of a theologian such as Augustine, the great definer of orthodoxy, set against an enduring tendency to confuse unity with uniformity and to seek to force Christianity into a doctrinal and ethical straitjacket.

St Thomas Aquinas could link heresy and persecution easily: 'Unfaithfulness is an act of the intellect, but moved by the will.' Heretics were seen not only as traitors to the church, but as traitors to God. Heresy was inextricably linked with malice and mortal sin, and charges of moral turpitude in the form of sexual deviance were frequently cited in heresy proceedings.

Against this rather bleak narrative we may place the impressive charitable work carried out by monasteries, as an example of a positive Christological influence on society. Although the monasteries looked after the poor and disabled, biblical texts against the handicapped remained a powerful counterforce.

There were, however, other pointers towards rights. The idea that all persons possess natural rights appears to have arisen around the twelfth century. *Ius naturale*, for example, is discussed extensively by Ockham. An emphasis on the dignity of man and on humanity as created in the image of God created conditions conducive to the development of a human rights culture. The development of the doctrine of the just war, building on Roman law, illustrates the highly developed state of Christian moral theology during this period.

However, these factors were usually overridden by more potent theological and sociopolitical considerations. Even the reformist jurist and canonist Jean Gerson saw heretics not only as traitors to the church, but also as traitors to God. On the other hand, 'the Middle Ages' encompass a wide variety of culture, theory and practice and were very far from being the darkness before the Reformation dawn. Discussions in works by numerous medieval writers helped create the conditions for the possibility of a modern culture of rights, even though there is no direct evidence of this coming about. Not all of this material is purely 'Christian' – Ciceronian views of *humanitas* played a huge role in medieval thought, and rights issues were not as alien to the classical world as has often been imagined. Scholars have traced in Abelard and John of Salisbury, in Wyclif, in Christine de Pizan and Marsiglio of Padua, in Denck and Franck, in Vitoria and Las Casas, among others, theological reasons which could lead, in specific places and in particular circumstances, to convictions which could point to concordance with, and tolerance and respect for, human dignity and conscience, sometimes existing in contradiction, but all straws in the wind which could in time encourage different versions of human rights culture (see Nederman and Laursen, 1996; Laursen and Nederman 1998) .

Roger Ruston usefully examines the medieval background to human rights in his *Human Rights and the Image of God* (2004). His main focus is on St Thomas, Vitoria, Las Casas and Locke, but he also makes pertinent observations on the place of human rights in the churches, and especially in the Roman Catholic Church today.

Ruston's starting point is the Catholic Church's traditional suspicion towards rights discourse, based on its supposed Enlightenment origins and its stress on individualism, and the subsequent transition to a Catholic paradigm of rights, notably in Vatican II's *Dignitatis Humanae* of 1965. He sees a resistance to this openness in John Paul II's *Evangelium Vitae* of 1995, with its attack on a 'culture of death' 'This resistance is reflected in the fact that, of the 103 or so international conventions relating to human rights, the Holy See has subscribed to a mere 10' (Ruston, 2004, 43).

There are problems with an autocratic church government. Ruston notes that human rights within the church itself remain 'very much at the level of the theoretical' (51):

> The modern church has shown a distinct preference for passive rights over active rights in its internal life. This has caused it to give pre-eminence to welfare rights rather than to liberties both in its juridical structure and in its social teachings. (Ibid., 53)

St Thomas uses the *imago Dei* metaphor extensively to show that human beings, in distinction from all other animals, are made in the image of God and capable of knowing God. Nevertheless, slaves remain inferior, for slavery is a punishment for sin. Thus the treatment of slavery remains under the influence of Aristotle's notion that slaves are naturally in servitude. Ruston documents the opposition of Vitoria and Las Casas to the exploitation of the native peoples of America in the Spanish conquest. This protest began with a sermon by Fr. Antonio Montesino in 1510 which directly invokes Christ in the name of justice:

> I am the voice of Christ in the wilderness of this land … This voice says that you are all in mortal sin and that you will live and die in it for the cruelty with which you use these innocent people. Tell me, with what right, with what justice do you hold these Indians in such cruel and horrible slavery? (Ruston, 2004, 106)

Vitoria argued that the Indians had their own natural *dominium,* which should not be violated. Lack of Christian religious belief could be no excuse for war against them.

In this tradition Ruston sees a developing argument for objective rights based on equality and justice. He finds in Gerson an argument for individual liberties, without which a community cannot flourish. But the central figure in this tradition is Las Casas, who devoted his life to supporting the Indians against their oppressors. Here, too, there is a Christological strand combined with arguments from natural law.

> The evidence shows that Christ set a form for preaching the gospel that was one and the same…to win the mind with reasons, to win the will with motives, to

attract it, because the form is peaceful, gentle, kind, full of the taste of charity. (Ruston, 2004, 203)

But, as often, theory of rights was not followed by enforcement of rights: "For all the debates and the learned treatises the benefit to the Indians was apparently next to nothing' (ibid., 219).

Ruston sheds light on numerous aspects of the development of rights talk. Renaissance humanists were often more concerned for civil society than untutored nature and untutored barbarians, and therefore laid little stress on natural law.

Las Casas was generous towards the Indians but harsh towards heretics – then, as now, respect for difference was usually selective. On the other hand, he could invoke the legal maxim, '*Quod omnes tangit debet ab omnibus approbari*' ('What touches all should be approved by all') to call for government by consent, which could have potentially enormous consequences for church as well as society (ibid., 281).

The development of rights is traced further through Grotius, who compares the sovereign individual with the sovereign state, to Locke. There is no inexorable line from Locke to free-market neoliberalism (ibid., 324). Rights involve duties, coming, for Christians, from the commandment of Christ (ibid., 349) and concerning human beings as created in the image of God. There are important continuities, as well as discontinuities, between Locke and the tradition of natural law. Ruston concludes that neither individual rights nor social rights are enough by themselves – both are essential for a just society.

As more work is done on Bartolomé de Las Casas he begins to emerge as a prophetic figure in the history of rights discussion.[2] In his final letter to Pope Pius V, in 1566 he asks for anathemas against 'those who affirm that they are unable to receive the Gospel and eternal salvation, on the basis of their alleged lack of intelligence or acuity of mind, which they in fact do not lack, those Indians whose rights I have defended till my death, for the honor of God and the church'.

Ruston's work should be supplemented by Brian Tierney's meticulous examination of medieval distinctions in rights theory in his essay, 'Religion and Rights: A Medieval Perspective':

> In the twelfth century a concern for the moral integrity of human personality led to the first stirrings of natural rights theories. An autonomous church asserted its own rights and limited the power of the state so that it never became truly absolute. Individual civic rights grew up within a context of communal institutions that were shaped in part by the growing law of the church. These points have broader implications. They suggest that Western rights theories did not have their origin either in early modern capitalism or in late medieval nominalism; rather they are rooted more deeply in the tradition of Christian humanism that has shaped much of our political culture. (Tierney, 1997a, 174).

---

2   Rivera-Pagan (2003): *History of the Indies*. Cf. Pagan, 232,: ET in Rivera-Pagan (2002, 108–110 and appendix to art. 239).

He traces a line through Isidore of Seville, Gratian and Huguccio to Grotius and Christian Wolff, and on to the 1965 Vatican II *Declaration on Religious Liberty*. On the negative side, in 1215 the Fourth Lateran Council pronounced on the extermination of heretics, a fate reiterated in 1231 by the Emperor Frederick II. 'Committed to the judgement of the flames, they should be burned alive in the sight of the people' (Tierney, 1997b, 31)

Tierney notes that Aquinas discusses heresy in *Summa theologiae* 2.2ae. At 10.8 he considers arguments for tolerance, but accepts the Augustinian 'compel them to come in.'

Tierney also discusses Las Casas's view that 'liberty is a right implanted in men' in *De Regia Potestate* (Tierney 1997a, 302), and the significance of the Roman law *Quod omnes tangit (XII-648)*:

> All through the Middle Ages there were two attitudes – not just one – to the problem of equality and inequality. One could emphasize that hierarchical ranking was necessary in an ordered society; or one could emphasize that, because all men shared a common humanity, they were all by nature equal, and also by nature free (for no one had a right to dominate his equals). Both positions were ancient, one Platonic, the other Stoic. Both could be defended in terms of Christian doctrine. ... The distinctive feature of medieval thought was not that it preserved the old notion of hierarchy but that it introduced a radical innovation by using the egalitarian concept as a foundation for new legal and philosophical theories of government by consent. (Ibid.)

Finally, Tierney turns to John Peter Olivi and papal inerrancy. We do not yet have a full and adequate account of the development of the doctrine of papal infallibility. But we know enough already to be sure of one thing at least: if the whole story is ever written, Peter John Olivi will play a major part in it (Tierney, 1997a, 328).

Tierney's sober assessment contrasts with the more optimistic view of other commentators such as John Witte (2001, 93ff). In 'The Spirit of the Laws, the Laws of the Spirit', he reflects on religion and human rights in a new global era. 'We have seen the best of human rights protections inscribed on the books, but some of the worst of human rights violations inflicted on the ground' (Witte, 2001, 79). Witte identifies the need for a new human rights hermeneutic within religion. Medieval canon law was based, in part, on the concept of individual and corporate rights. It defined the rights of clergy, ecclesiastical organizations, church councils, the laity, the poor and the needy. The Protestant Reformation provided the basis for a further expansion of rights. Wittee concludes that '[r]eligion must be drawn into a constructive alliance with a regime of law, democracy and human rights, or they will be pitted against each other (Witte, 2001,106).

Reformation and rights?

What, then, of the Reformation? Anticipated in part by aspects of the Renaissance, the Reformation brought an appeal to individual judgement and individual conscience which was to stimulate a discussion of toleration a century later. But this was hampered by a tendency to equate the voice of conscience with the voice of God and therefore to breed a new authoritarianism. Calvin's Geneva, too, was built on the *consensus fidelium,* in which the individual in the Reformed polity was under divine obligation to obey the ruling presbyters, acting on behalf of the divinely elect community. Despite Luther's strongly Christological emphasis on Christian freedom and Calvin's proclamation of the absolute freedom of the sovereign God, freedom did not extend to freedom of life and opinion over and against the covenant community. The minute detail of surveillance exercised by seventeenth-century kirk sessions in Scotland is a classic example of these constraints. It was to take the Enlightenment to break the mould of authoritarian tradition and free up the many resources for affirming human dignity and individual rights which were frozen in the sediment of the classical Christological tradition. Of course, the Reformation also brought a new emphasis on the centrality of scripture. We shall explore further Reformation thinking on rights issues when we look at the tradition of interpretation of scripture in Chapter 5.

We shall not find anything like twentieth-century liberal culture in sixteenth-century Geneva. Freedom of conscience was balanced against a genuine fear of anarchy. Human dignity based on the image of God was related to the common good of the godly community as much as to the wishes of private individuals. And there were, of course, numerous factors in the history of Christian practice which did not apply in later centuries. For example, Luther explained evil in the world by a belief in demons who constantly had to be fought.

'It is the saints who burn the saints.' This striking phrase about the saints from Roland Bainton's *Studies in the Reformation* (Bainton, 1963, preface), pinpoints a problem at the heart of Christian reflection on human rights. It can be seen as pointing to the reality of the 'black hole' on rights issues for most of the history of Christianity, and at the same time perhaps indicates the complex tendency of Christians, ancient and modern, to court martyrdom in various guises like moths circling a flickering flame. On the other hand, it may be argued that such a comment merely demonstrates the folly of judging sixteenth-century issues by twenty-first-century standards. Despite a mountain of subsequent studies on rights and persecution – revisionist and anti-revisionist, postmodern and paleomodern – Bainton's classic studies are still worth reflecting upon.

Bainton argued that, to persecute, a man must believe that he is right, that the point in question is important and that coercion is effective. Catholics and Protestants had an absolute belief in the rightness of their positions. Conscience has no claims as such; a man must do what appears to him to be right. However, 'he must *be* right in order to have rights.'(Bainton, 1953, 215). Erasmus believed that scripture was not clear, and Castellio held that what we believe we must not pretend to know. However, Bainton also noted, these considerations might be necessary for tolerance but were certainly not sufficient: 'In the French Revolution reason and scepticism sent their victims to the guillotine'(ibid., 217).

Reliance on statistics on recorded executions among marginalized groups perhaps hardly reflects the mass of accumulated misery inflicted on people who did not conform to ecclesiastical norms. A notable example might be Argula von Grumbach, rescued from comparative oblivion by Peter Matheson after centuries of being silenced and then ignored.

Bainton was concerned primarily with religious liberty. Yet the basic issues which he studied in Reformation history are not peculiar to the sixteenth century, and he was also aware of the scapegoating of groups other than Christian heretics, notably the Jews. Although he notes that Luther could be scathing about the church as well as the Jews, he quotes the notorious lines from the later Luther: 'Burn their synagogues; take away their books, including the Bible. They should be compelled to work, denied food and shelter, preferably banished' (Bainton 1963, 43, citing WA LIII.536).

In Calvin he saw the springs of intolerance not in wickedness as such, but in theological conviction. Apparent injustice is part of the mystery of election: 'The most tender affections with which nature has endowed us and in which the best of men may otherwise indulge, these when they impede the vindication of God's glory he pronounces vicious' (ibid, 143, quoting *Calvini opera* XXIV.360). Castellio's classic response to these words, and to traditional pleas of defending community virtues against individual conscience, might seem as valid when applied to twenty-first century violations of human rights as it did in the sixteenth: 'To kill a man is not to defend a doctrine. It is to kill a man' (ibid, 177, citing *Contra Libellum Calvini*, Eb, Cal.77, 78).

Are there any links between these pointers to a human rights culture and the era in which rights was first to come of age? Bainton saw probable links between Castellio and Locke (ibid., 184). More recent scholarship has shown enormous complexity in the theory and practice of the cluster of overlapping issues surrounding tolerance, rights conscience and freedom of a kind that Bainton never imagined. Suspicion of liberal triumphalism leads to suspicion of suspicion in the research tradition of the history of political thought. Even Zagorin, in discussing theories of and defences of toleration in the second half of the sixteenth century, allows that Christians contributed to tolerance as well as to intolerance: 'The latter were the work of profoundly Christian if also unorthodox thinkers, not of minds inclined to religious indifference or unbelief; and the same is true of nearly all the major theorists of toleration in the seventeenth century'(Zagorin, 2003, 9).

The Enlightenment

The Christologies of the Enlightenment resolved some of the problems of the authoritarian community and then created others. However, the gains were much greater than the losses, since it is the critical rationality which we owe to the Enlightenment that enables the possibility of the constantly changing modern critical research paradigm. The Christologies of Herder, Schleiermacher and Ritschl reflected the individuality of their authors and portrayed the man Jesus as a model of compassion and kindness, bringing a state of blessedness or reconciliation to the individual in Schleiermacher's case, and exhorting communal social action towards the construction of the kingdom of God in the case of Ritschl.

We have to wait for the liberal theology of the nineteenth century, with its emphasis on a humanist Christology 'from below' in Schleiermacher and a concern for the social ethic of the kingdom of God in Ritschl, for the precursors of a social and political Christology that sides with the marginalized. Here, too, the dimension of identification, mutuality and reciprocity is strictly limited.

We are likely to conclude that, although some factors belonging to a human rights culture were present at the Reformation – notably the stress on individual conscience – other factors, especially the appeal to ecclesial and civil authority, militated against it. The situation is very similar to that with natural law in the earlier period. In both cases there is an underlying assumption of theocracy. It would be centuries before the Catholic potential for human rights theology through a re-imagined natural rights perspective would be opened up. Calvin worked out an impressive understanding of liberty and democracy under the sovereign freedom of God and he was conscious of the need to care for the poor (Witte, 1996). But in practice there was little freedom for dissent in Geneva. The Protestant potential was to be unlocked, at least in part, through the work of Grotius in particular. But if you were a seventeenth-century Scottish gipsy imprisoned in Auchtermuchty, it would have been unwise to hold your breath, whether your captors were Catholic or Protestant. Study of local contexts suggests that tolerance was usually a fragile plant:

> The development of a modern liberal society has taught us to admire tolerance above almost every other principle of social interaction. But in the early modern period it was only ever a loser's creed: and one which, if Calvinist church leaders in the Dutch Republic were anything to go by, could easily be abandoned when yesterday's persecuted minority became the day's dominant elite. (Andrew Pettegree, in Grell and Scribner, 1996, 198)

Although the Enlightenment marked a break with authoritarian tradition and signalled a nascent interest inhuman dignity and individual rights, this was a process that was still very much in flux. The Enlightenment is rightly criticized for its limited vision and its authoritarian consequences. The negative effects arose essentially because Enlightenment notions of toleration, freedom, justice and equality were limited to particular interest groups and did not go nearly far enough.

Increasingly, theological pleas were made for tolerance and religious liberty. In *England's Present Interest Discovered* (1672), William Penn wrote, 'I ever understood an impartial liberty of conscience to be the natural right of all men' (cited by Witte, 1996, 42) although even Penn found it necessary in certain circumstances to advocate coercion (Murphy, 2001, 232).

It is too easy for us today to look back at the Reformation and be scandalized at the state of human rights concerns during this period. It is worth reminding ourselves of how much attitudes have changed even since the nineteenth century. Clear progress was made in terms of a conscience about human rights in the twentieth century, but this was only partial progress, as the century's record of 100 million people killed by their fellow human beings eloquently testifies. The roots of human rights culture are many, varied and the property of no particular tribe. They may be seen as essentially contested, or may be reflected upon in a kind of wide reflective equilibrium, with a view to focus upon practical issues. Christology is concerned with the practical delivery of the love of God at the point of greatest need.

The Nineteenth Century

It is not, of course, at all easy for us to imagine the world-view of a culture other than our own. To cite a classic snapshot of an unfamiliar culture, Boyd Hilton's *The Age of Atonement* (1988) provides an illuminating picture of the interplay between religious, political and economic ideas in nineteenth-century Britain. He argues convincingly that concepts of atonement played a huge role in public life in the first half of the century, to be succeeded by emphasis on incarnation and a more optimistic attitude to social reconstruction in the later decades of the century. The providential rule of a God who in his inscrutable providence dealt out prosperity and disaster in equal measure, in economics, in health and sickness, in politics, was an established part of the image. Evangelicals, like economists, believed in a 'hidden hand'. Unlike economists, they believed that the hidden hand held a rod. Moderate evangelicals were assured that the rod was wielded justly, in response to human behaviour (Hilton, 1988, 114). The poor were poor and the rich were rich through the hand of providence. There was a strong consciousness of the all-pervasiveness of sin: sin inevitably brought punishment, and human life was a search for a means of atonement. Notions of atonement were especially relevant to theories of crime and punishment. Some evangelicals were enthusiastic supporters of the death penalty.[3] This whole world-view has almost disappeared from contemporary Britain, and it is very difficult for us to re-imagine it. On the other hand, vestiges of its legacy remain, and reappear in sometimes surprising contexts.

The link between Christian faith and support for capital punishment was strong in the churches for most of the modern era, especially in the nineteenth century, with some notable exceptions. Harry Potter's masterly *Hanging in Judgement* (1993) offers a detailed case-by-case analysis of the extraordinary Christian enthusiasm for execution, clothed in the minutest details of religious ritual. Execution became the occasion for the saving of souls, with scant regard to any other human consideration for the prisoners. Potter charts the debate in England on the death penalty up to its abolition in the 1960s. Until almost the last minute, Church of England bishops were among the most enthusiastic supporters of the death penalty. We may note that the churches have now almost universally moved against the death penalty, and that the record of individual Christians, notably Helen Prejean, in the battle against capital punishment in the United States has been exemplary. But against this, as late as 1990 the general assembly representing sixteen million Southern Baptists voted for

---

3   However, Hugh McLeod has recently argued that the Christian record on the death penalty is not as black as has often been assumed. Cf. 'God and the Gallows' in Cooper and Gregory (2004).

its retention on biblical grounds, and Atlanta jurors are still (2005) encouraged by biblical citation to decide for capital punishment.

The Twentieth Century

By the end of the nineteenth century the more liberal theologians were placing a great deal of trust in education as an instrument for the creation of a better society. In 1902 Adolf Harnack delivered an address to the German Evangelical Social Congress on 'The Pursuit of Education' (Harnack and Herrmann, 1907) in which he laid great stress on the education of women. However, there were, of course, limits to Harnack's view of women:

> I can only regard as a grievous mistake the theory that, because woman is the equal of man as regards human value, it straightway follows that the same course of instruction and the same occupations should be thrown open to her as to man. (ibid., 129)

The great supporter of Christocentric theology in the twentieth century was, of course, Karl Barth. To what extent may his Christology be seen as a Christology for human rights? There is a fine balance to be struck here. On the positive side, Barth's theology of grace was a profound apprehension of the freedom of the gospel and the unconditional love of God at the centre of creation. Everything has to be related to Jesus Christ. The human dignity of all persons, male and female, in the image of God is affirmed. There is continuity between Israel and the church – anti-Semitism is affirmed. In Christ there is neither slave nor free man. Political freedom is affirmed. Every sort of totalitarian political ideology is idolatry.

Since Jesus Christ died to redeem all humanity, talk of capital punishment is tantamount to blasphemy. War is always sinful and pacifism is almost always the Christian option. All are profoundly equal in the sight of God – social justice is important. The Christological argument for human rights in writers such as Moltmann is heavily dependent on Barth's theology.

On the negative side Barth demonstrates a much criticized adherence to patriarchal biblical patterns in the relationship between women and men. It is hard to find explicit reference to civil rights, discrimination against ethnic minorities or world poverty. It may seem that Barth is trying too hard to avoid the concerns of liberal Christianity. It has been suggested, in relation to 'the Jewish question' in the 1930s that Barth concentrates on looking at the issues theologically, rather than politically, and therefore fails to do justice to the horrors that were becoming a daily occurrence. Judaism becomes Jewish history within the *Heilsgeschichte,* and the political reality is masked.[4]

There are no references to 'human rights' as such in the *Church Dogmatics*. But, again, Barth was later to regret that there was no mention of the persecution of the Jews in the Barmen Declaration (1934), and that he did not modify his comments on

---

4   Cf. *Church Dogmatics*, 3.3. 310f; cf. also Haynes (1989).

the gay issue. And, of course, he famously refused to take the oath of allegiance to Hitler and lost his academic appointment in 1935.

In my view, human rights are a classic example of an issue that Christian theology, and especially Christology, still needs to articulate. It may sometimes be inadequate to develop a Christology *of* human rights, in the tradition of classical liberal theology, but it is not enough to leave the human rights dimension as implicit in a Christ-oriented theology. That way lies the danger that the imperative may be masked. My suggestion in this study is for a theology *for* human rights, grounded in Christology but explicitly articulated in relation to practical social outcomes.

Bultmann[5] shared entirely Barth's Christian distaste for National Socialism, but did not see the Christ-event as relating directly to temporal affairs. We find an interesting contrast in the attitudes to human rights issues reflected in the Christologies of the eschatological theologians, Moltmann and Pannenberg. Moltmann connects the crucified Christ directly to human rights issues and to emancipatory themes, while Pannenberg, linking Christology to the orders of creation, provides outcomes of a much more conservative nature.

Moltmann's work provides a striking example of the strengths and weaknesses of the correlation of Christology with issues of social justice. There is no doubt that the emphases on liberation and justice in his *Theology of Hope* and *The Crucified God* provided a refreshing and valuable stimulus to the development of liberation theologies in various parts of the world. On the other hand, there was some validity in the criticism that his social doctrine of the Trinity could lead to his preferred arrangements for political organization becoming hypostasized into God, so potentially and paradoxically creating an opening towards totalitarianism. This danger is clearly a warning to those who seek, as I am doing here, to relate Christology to human rights issues. There is always a gulf and an asymmetry between our interpretation of God's will and the mystery of the divine reality itself. Moltmann is, of course, well aware of the problem, but it is all too easy to close the gap too quickly.

Among leading European Catholic thinkers, Karl Rahner's anthropological approach to Christology leads him to place a distinctive emphasis on human dignity. The consequences are rarely worked out in detail, but his theology has inspired many who continue to work on human rights issues from within the Catholic Church. Virtually the same may be said of Schillebeeckx, for whom emphasis on present experience implied a high premium on human freedom. In process theology, emphasis on divine action through the spirit of Christ led John Cobb to privilege human rights issues and indeed to set up a non-governmental organization (NGO), Mobilization of the Human Family (now Progressive Christians Uniting). On the other hand, the role of experience produced little relevant to human rights issues in the British debates on incarnation, with the exception of the work of the leading critic of incarnation, John Hick, who argued with considerable justification that the

---

5   'Were I a non-Aryan or a not purely Aryan Christian I would be ashamed to belong to a church in which I could only listen but not speak' (Bultmann cited in Knight and Paris (1989, 268)).

triumphalism of traditional Christologies led inevitably to a Christian elitism. In fact, the humanist Christologies pursued by the liberal British tradition unquestioningly supported a positive attitude towards human rights issues – although, interestingly, the explicit connections were not made. As in the patristic debates, concentration on Christology for its own sake would not necessarily lead to human rights-oriented outcomes, and it becomes necessary to dedicate specific attention to this crucial dimension.

Such specific attention comes almost immediately in the proliferation of the emancipatory theologies, very often outside the European theological guild and focused firmly on issues of marginality. To this development we shall have to give detailed attention. The impact of the emancipatory theologies will probably fade as mainstream theology again becomes doctrinally conservative, but it seems equally likely that the emancipatory challenge will finally put human rights issues at the forefront of Christological concerns, even for these theologies which pursue quite different methodologies.

I conclude that, while it is entirely legitimate and often necessary to develop Christological models for their own sakes, it is equally necessary to make explicit the salvific motif in Christology, which includes, par excellence, the whole range of human rights issues, since salvation as human transformation is given in the image of God in Christ.

Christology and Rights in Social Context

The above sketch may illustrate the contours of Christological discussion of human rights. To be constructive it needs to be set in the framework of larger issues in the relation of church to society. Here I want to refer to two studies of these issues, Max Stackhouse's *Creeds, Society and Human Rights: a Study in Three Cultures* (1984) and Ernst Troeltsch's *The Social Teaching of the Christian Churches* (1931) – the latter in some respects dated but still a classic study.

Stackhouse began from the ancient and medieval roots of human rights, suggesting that the deepest roots of human rights are to be found in the biblical conception of life. 'Decisive for all human rights thinking is the notion that there is a pattern of righteousness which can be known by humans in empirical life but which is not the same as empirical life.....(Stackhouse, 1984, 31) This is the reality of God. This perspective could create a sense of superiority to other nations. But, in the hands of the prophets, it suggested that there is a universal moral order, rooted in the righteousness of God. In Christianity, the vision was broadened and gave new hope for the future. It proposed dignity and respect for individual persons and created a community of discipleship. It also created a conflict with political authority, for God's kingdom was not of this world.

Theology developed further: 'In the doctrine of the Trinity which emerged, the very character of God, and therefore the character of all that is really real, is understood as persons in covenanted relationship under a more ultimate integrating principle' (ibid.,

39). Islam was repulsed and papal authority strengthened. Individuals gained rights, which were later to be largely taken over by states. Conciliarism sought a universal ethic which collapsed between a new authoritarianism and a new movement for individual liberty. Between evangelical Lutheranism, imperial Calvinism and especially a liberal–puritan synthesis, the basis for human rights concerns, at least in North America, was laid. This was played out in the realms of technology, the professions, the mass media and the family. It affected politics and economics as well as the churches through the Social Gospel and modern Catholic ethics, creating recent church participation in the human rights movement. Stackhouse compared this development with the structures of society in Marxist East Germany, as it then was, and in India. He defended the liberal–puritan synthesis as both preserving freedom and being rational, pointing out that it maintains that 'all are children of God, all are equally loved by God, and all are sinners'(ibid., 274.) It also affirms transcendental reality and reconciling community. The churches, according to Stackhouse, must support structures that will effectively deliver human rights.

Stackhouse found the theological roots of human rights in the religion of Israel, in faith in the reality of God and the law of God, a code for universal justice, to be observed in an ever-expanding community of believers. He traced the influence of the community, now the Christian church, through the centuries, showing how its values interact with related Enlightenment values and create a covenantal civil society in America.[6] He concluded that, although the liberal and individual-oriented view of rights from Locke and his circle and the American puritans gave a vital impetus to the development of human rights talk, the earlier roots in Judaism and the Christian tradition were also highly significant. Equally, reflection on human dignity and conscience was not confined to Western thought. Once again, the specific interaction of Christology with human rights is very limited.[7]

---

6   James I. McCord made a telling observation on the American scene in the Preface to *A Christian Declaration on Human Rights*, edited by Allen Miller (1976), an excellent study collection by WARC:

> During the Bicentennial Year much has been made of the Calvinist contribution to American beginnings and independence. But this was a revolution that was essentially conservative in nature and that tended to be limited to the rising middle class. The challenge today is to broaden the basis of liberation to broaden the basis of liberation to include the poor and the powerless, ethnic minorities, and women.

In the same volume Moltmann comments:

> By fundamental rights we mean these rights and duties which belong essentially to what it means to be truly human, because without their being fully acknowledged and exercised, human beings cannot fulfil their original destiny of having been created in the image of God. (Miller, 1976, 132)

7   Appended to Stackhouse's study are some human rights documents, including the excellent United Church of Christ *Pronouncement on Human Rights*. This contains a solid section on 'biblical and theological foundations of human rights'. Although it does mention Jesus Christ, it has almost nothing of an explicit Christological dimension. This is one of the puzzles which the present study is intended to address.

Christology and the Philosophical Background of Human Rights

I now want to invite a brief synoptic survey of the philosophical development of ideas of human rights. As we have seen, much more can be found – for example in the Middle Ages – than Protestant scholars tend to notice. Once again, what emerges strikingly is the astonishingly meagre material on Christology, the centre of Christian theology, on this broad development.

We have noted the development of notions of justice and righteousness as norms for conduct in Israel. Similar ideas developed elsewhere – in China, in India and, crucially for the European tradition, in Greece. There are seminal notions of goodness and virtue in Greek literature from Homer onwards, and an increasing identification of a universal justice with the will of God from Aeschylus. Notions of good and evil, of merit and responsibility, pervade the literature. There is civilized behaviour and there is the behaviour of the barbarians. Sometimes the barbarians behave like civilized people and the civilized people like barbarians – these incidents evoke special comment.

For Plato, a desirable society must be oriented towards the achievement of the good, and justice is a supreme attribute of the good. To live as human beings should, in order to achieve their potential, is to live according to reason, and reason leads us to seek for justice. Justice is the basic theme of Plato's *Republic*. It has long been noted, however, that Plato's political suggestions for achieving justice are aristocratic and could lead to totalitarianism. Yet the stress on the need for justice, and the role of a dialectical process of reasoning in seeking to define it, has been an important step in political philosophy. For Aristotle, too, man is a political animal, who achieves fulfilment in seeking the highest political good, justice. Aristotle's reflections on natural law and natural justice have also gone some way towards creating an intellectual climate in which rights issues can arise – although, in practice, they were compatible with a society which kept slaves and could act with striking brutality towards other states that appeared to threaten their interests. For the Stoics, the human aim was to seek for a life in accord with the rational law of nature, which includes respect for others.

This legacy is mediated to Roman philosophy, largely through Cicero, and greatly influenced Roman law. Cicero's notion of *humanitas* influenced the development of Christian humanism through Augustine and beyond. The groups to whom this virtue was attributed and to whom it should be extended remained narrowly elitist. The Roman legal tradition, influenced by Stoicism, could speak of a *ius humanum*, and even of a universal moral order, *cosmopolis*.[8]

The corpus of Roman law continues to influence European law and countries throughout the world affected by it. The determination of justice was at the core of this whole corpus, although its provisions for justice were often restricted to

---

8   Cicero, *De Leg*.1.7.23; Seneca, Ep.28.4 – quoted in *RGG* 4 sv Menschenrechte. For human rights in the ancient world *Der Neue Pauly.Antike.7*.1258ff. Menschenrechte is useful. Cf also the superb and comprehensive articles in *RAC* on *humanitaet* (Henry Chadwick), *humanitas/(philanthropia* (Otto Hiltbrunner) , *Demut (humilitas)*, and on torture (*Folter* and *Folterwerkzeuge*).

selected bodies of elite citizens until very recent times. This legacy was taken up and developed by Augustine and Boethius, and taken into the Middle Ages. The Christian Fathers added the notion that human fulfilment is only found in the union of the soul with God. Talk of humanity, with its implications for rights, was focused largely on the spiritual welfare of the soul. This had distinctive consequences, often limiting concern for bodily well-being. The biblical and classical traditions came together in the masterly synthesis of Thomas Aquinas, who provided an enduring analysis of natural law and human moral duties, but also in Vitoria and Las Casas. A major step was then taken by Grotius who determined that national laws should respect the natural right to self-preservation possessed by individuals. From this platform the modern development of liberal rights theories blossomed: Hobbes and Locke, Rousseau and Burke, Kant, Mill and Bentham. More corporate documents would include the Bill of Rights of 1689, the Declaration of Independence of 1776 and the French Declaration of the Rights of Man and of the Citizen (1789). To this we can add the powerful critique of individualism from Karl Marx, and then we are into contemporary writing.

Positioned halfway between Castellio and Locke, the work of Grotius provides a good illustration of the scope and limitations of the Reformation on human rights. Like Aquinas, Grotius was concerned with society as a whole, but more specifically with the relationships between sovereign nations. Like Castellio, he was concerned with freedom of conscience. Like Locke, he was capable of thinking of individual liberty. What is interesting is the nature of the balance between a large number of factors which would eventually, but through a fairly indirect process, lead to the development of modern human rights theories and the beginnings of a human rights culture.[9]

Grotius was focused on law. Law, one might think, is the basic cornerstone of rights, not just in their conception but in their enforcement. Law is necessary, but not always sufficient. In this respect, one might consider modern regimes in which law was meticulously followed but at the same time completely subverted, as in the Nazi period in Germany. In the face of political chaos Grotius sought to establish a new code for civilized conduct. His proposal had many strands, and it reflects some of the many factors which have gone into the making of modern rights notions.

Grotius put trust in natural law, following the classical tradition of Cicero and the Stoics. He laid emphasis on rationality – an important ingredient of all reflection on justice – and on the need for promises to be kept. Current cultural and political notions became transformed into natural law, and by extension into God's eternal law. This tendency for the accidental truths of cultural history to be turned into eternal truths of reason, even divine reason, is a perennial hazard of natural law theory from Cicero to Bonhoeffer and beyond, but natural law theory played an important role in the developments of rights. Grotius developed a theory of social contract, involving

---

9   There are good accounts of John Knox's and Grotius' political thought in O'Donovan and O'Donovan's *From Irenaeus to Grotius* (1999, 685f, 787f).

the voluntary and irrevocable granting of sovereignty to rulers by popular choice. Here, again, local culture created absolutes.

Perhaps significantly, Grotius, like Las Casas, wrote not about human rights in abstract, but about issues from which rights questions arise – notably war. What mattered to him was the legality of wars. Space will not allow analysis of the text of *De Jure Belli ac Pacis* here, but it made a significant contribution to existing theory. Although Grotius may have ceded too much to the power of nation-states, he did make some suggestions of the need to enforce civilized international standards. In a sense, his advance was negative: there could be no just war in the name of religion. We shall not find him writing a treatise on human rights. But we can find rights issues tied to specific political issues. There may not be theory, but there are goals and suggestions for their enforcement.

In all this huge corpus there is scarcely a single mention of the central figure of the Christian religion, of whom it was said, in the Fourth Gospel, 'I am the Way, the Truth and the Life'. In reflecting on this situation we must remember that the commonplaces of 1776 in America – truths we hold to be self-evident – were inevitably only the seditious notions of the marginal groups in the ordered, closed society of medieval Christendom. When John Ball mused that '[w]hen Adam delved and Eve span, who was then the serving man?', the penalty was certain death. At the same time, we have to record that the extension of the democratic process in the Enlightenment period was also very limited. Life for the lowest orders in society continued to be cheap, and the eighteenth century in Britain saw a huge rise in the number of capital offences, mostly executed on the poorest people.[10]

It might also be just conceivable that cooler heads may have reckoned that direct doctrinal reflection tended to make for more heat than light, and that appeal to other traditions – Roman law – would provide a safer basis for consensus than much contested Christological reference.

This entire stream of tradition has been strongly criticized for privileging a liberal, Eurocentric view of rights, to the disadvantage of other cultures and minority groups. There has been much wrestling with this dilemma, together with a proliferation of advocacy on behalf of a wide range of the rights of minority cultures, including individual and group rights, economic rights, the rights of women, of gays and lesbians, of environmental rights[11] and animal rights, rights in relation to torture and

---

10 Unfortunately, too, recognition of one area of human rights does not necessarily lead to awareness of others. For example, blacks may be patriarchal, while whites may be against racism but homophobic.

11 The marginalizing of such groups is classically illustrated in Schussler Fiorenza and Haering (1999). Schussler Fiorenza contrasts a democratic ecclesial self-understanding with kyriocratic Roman authority.

The Bible may still be read in ways which discriminate against women, gays, blacks and other traditionally marginalized groups. Cf., for example, Bruce Winter on I Cor 6:9 in Lane, (1997).

There is an excellent account of human rights in church history by Martin Brecht in Baur (1977, 39ff). Surveying the history from Lactantius to Las Casas and beyond, he makes the point that, in England, the crucial points were not so much natural law as Magna Carta and civil rights. Defenders of rights were often soon forgotten in the communities in which they worked – for example, Roger Williams (1603–84) and John Wise (1652–1725) from Massachusetts, defending democracy in church polity. In the

ethnic cleansing, imprisonment and capital punishment. The last 50 years have seen a plethora of charters under the aegis of the United Nations and similar bodies. In these, too, there is strikingly little reference to Jesus Christ: the tendency is to argue that rights issues are best supported by leaving out reference to religion.

An examination of the role of Christology in relation to human rights might lead us to look again at Troeltsch's massive *The Social Teaching of the Christian Churches* (1931), which combines theology and sociology in examining the influence of Christianity on culture. The argument is well known. Troeltsch begins from the development of the Pauline communities, as a kind of Christian patriachalism. The advent of the state-church brought the development of Christian natural law theory, which governed the role of family and property, state and economy. Natural law provided the notion of natural justice within a theocracy. Christian charity was channelled through the monastic institutions and seen as conducive to the salvation of the individual soul. With medieval Catholicism came the reality of a unified Christian culture, based on the centralized papacy. Against this trend came the development of Christian sects, small communities of the elect, and also a mystical movement, based on private, individual spiritual experience within the larger society.

Existing social structures could now be seen as in harmony with natural law. There was little incentive to social reform, except among fringe groups, the sects. The sects avoided compromise with the world. The church entered into partnership with culture, but created an authoritarian institution. Mysticism fostered an individuality which comes closest to the mindset of the modern world.

Luther emphasized grace rather than the law, but Protestantism remained a church rather than a sect. There was a continuing tension between the two spheres of creation and redemption, of the law and the gospel: Christian ethics were operative in the private sphere – natural law in the public sphere.

Calvinism combined an asceticism with a business ethic, and accepted that God had given people different levels of social position in his inscrutable providence.

Mysticism stressed immediate personal religious experience, with a freedom from official religious structures. The church had to be open to change and transparency.

As Troeltsch made clear in other writings, Christianity must make more modest claims; it should respect cultural relativity without being completely relativist. In his emphasis on spirit rather than a reductive Enlightenment appeal to pure rationality

---

same volume Wolfgang Wischmeyer, 39ff, on human rights in the early church, highlights the possible cumulative effect of the reading in the liturgy of the Pauline passage Gal. 3: 26–9, stressing that, in Christ, there is neither Jew nor Greek. Susan Heine, 85ff, notes the very limited nature of human rights in the French Revolution, citing the decapitation of Marie Olympe de Gouges, in Paris on 4 November 1793, for supporting the Rights of Woman. John Nurser, 163ff, notes the role of Christians, especially Fred Nolde in the UNDHR, and makes a plea for a revisioned 'Christendom'.

Cf. also the collection edited by H. Schmidinger, *Wege zur Toleranz: Geschichte einer europäischen Idee in Quellen* (2002). Here is material on Salvienus of Marseilles (ibid., 440), who could say in *On the Rule of God*, 2 that the barbarians are heretics, but 'they err through love of God' (ibid., 31). There is also useful comment on Maimonides, Wolfram von Eschenbach and the Ring parable, Ficino and Mirandola, Juan Louis Vives, Meister Eckhart, Johannes Tauler, Grotius's on war and peace among the churches (1642) and on Castellio.

he followed in the tradition of Schleiermacher, although, in equating the values of his own side in the First World War with the spiritual dimension and the values of the other side with rationalism, he was curiously vulnerable to contemporary propaganda. However, Troeltsch was more than simply a deluded romantic. The need to combine the critical rationality of the Enlightenment with a Christian transcendental dimension remains a central issue in Christian engagement with human rights issues. Troeltsch's distinction between church-type communities, sect-type communities and mysticism has been criticized, but it did open up the sociological study of church bodies.

From our survey so far it may seem that the churches' record in human rights issues is, at best, ambiguous. However, although nineteenth-century Christians could support slavery, many Christian groups were strong anti-slavery advocates, notably the Evangelical Christians in Scotland and in England. In the USA, besides Las Casas, protests against slavery went back to the protest on 18 February 1688 in Germantown, Pennsylvania, by a group of Quakers including Francis Daniel Pastorius. Christian groups protested against inhumane prison conditions, and were involved in the setting up of the Red Cross organization and the Geneva Convention on the Conduct of War and the Treatment of Prisoners and Non-combatants. A significant number of Christian people defied the prevailing ecclesiastical trends and dangerous unpopularity to become conscientious objectors during the First World War. Christian faith led some theologians, both conservative and liberal, to oppose the Nazis – Barth, Bultmann, von Soden, among others – although there was, of course, a huge amount of complicity with tyranny. The 20 July 1944 plot to assassinate Hitler centred on Dietrich Bonhoeffer was also motivated to an extraordinary extent by Christian conviction. In England Bishop Bell and others protested against saturation bombing. (Similar sentiments at the General Assembly of the Church of Scotland were quickly stifled.)

There was, however, one sphere above all where the influence of Christian conviction was to make a decisive difference to human rights culture. In his book, *For All Peoples and All Nations*, John Nurser has shown in detail how Christians such as Fred Nolde, now largely forgotten even by the churches, had a decisive effect on the creation of the United Nations Charter of Human Rights. He traces the actualization of their inclusive vision, which finally became too inclusive for many official church bodies. From the creation of the World Council of Churches in 1938, as a result of the ecumenical conferences in Oxford and Edinburgh in 1937, there was a continuous series of ecumenical committees and conferences aiming 'to write the peace', as John R. Mackay put it in 1942, and to avoid the mistakes of Versailles. Through a commission to study the basis of a just and durable peace (CJDP) from 1940, through a Joint Committee on Religious Liberty, through the Churches Commission on International Affairs and through the UN Conference in San Francisco in 1945 a small group of ecumenical activists succeeded, with much support from Eleanor Roosevelt, in persuading the United Nations to adopt its Universal Declaration of Human Rights on 10 December 1948. As a result of Nurser's book it is no longer possible to overlook the decisive role of Christian action, although, as he acknowledges, this form of liberal Christianity went out of fashion in the 1960s, when it became too easily associated with 'Western values' and Cold War rhetoric.

The real significance of Fred Nolde's achievement is accurately expressed in a David Little's Foreword to John Nurser's book:

> The connection of Nolde and his associates to these developments reveals an important new wrinkle in the annals of religious peacemaking. Here are individuals, themselves strongly motivated by religious commitment, supporting and contributing to a set of standards, deemed indispensable for the establishment of peace and justice around the world, that do not necessarily depend on any particular religious or other point of view. Rather, they depend on a shared moral basis taken to be universally common to all people, a basis Nolde described as 'secular' – or perhaps 'pluralistic,' in present day parlance. The ultimate, somewhat paradoxical assumption is that religious people may best contribute to peace, and at the same time most successfully express their own deepest commitments, when they surrender proprietary claims in favour of sharing common grounds with others, and thereby create maximum space for freedom of fundamental belief, religious or not. (Nurser, 2005, xi)

Nurser reaffirms this aim in a telling quote from Nolde:

> ...the declaration is intended to affirm that man has the right to believe as he sees fit; it is not intended to declare what man should believe. (Nurser, 171, n. 27)

It is part of the purpose of the present study to acknowledge the vital continuing importance of that liberal tradition in a new geopolitical era, while linking it to an explicit Christological dimension. It seems to me that it is important in relation to human rights culture to emphasize the unconditional Christian commitment to all humanity – to the outsiders and not simply to those within the churches – while drawing strength for this continuing and difficult programme from the heart of Christian faith.[12]

The year 1948 was a turning point. In the second half of the twentieth century Christian input to human rights concerns continued, with varying degrees of effectiveness. This is most obviously seen in numerous commissions for social justice and for justice and peace in most churches. The World Council of Churches (WCC) continues to be engaged with human rights at various levels, from UN and government levels to supporting the work of NGOs. Through the Churches Council for International Affairs it contributes to the UN Human Rights Committee (UNHRC) on a standing basis. From the 1970s, because of its human rights concerns, the WCC came under deep suspicion in conservative political and Christian circles. The issues involved – matters of nuclear war, the environment and global economic development – all had human rights implications. The churches became explicitly concerned with human rights talk in the 1970s and 1980s.

---

12 I have discussed the Christian realist group around Henry van Dusen in my *John and Donald Baillie: Transatlantic Theology* (Newlands, 2002). There is further material on these issues, referred to by John Nurser, in the J.A. Mackay Papers in Princeton Theological Seminary, Special Collections.

However, as these themes were seen to be inextricably connected with geopolitics, perhaps tainted with secular associations and often uncomfortably related to internal church tensions concerning power and authority, enthusiasm for human rights culture waned. Changes in theological fashion, together with an awareness of the problematic nature of a simple endorsement of the values of Western universalism, led to a concentration on more internalized ecclesiology. Corresponding with this there was an increasing nervousness about the role of human rights concerns in American, Middle Eastern and Asian politics.

Is it possible to develop the best elements of human rights concern in relation to Christian faith while remaining mindful of the lessons to be learned from the last 50 years? That will be our central concern in succeeding chapters.

Christology and Human Rights – Gathering the Fragments?

Where, then, are we to look for further evidence of engagement between Christology and the development of human rights? Possible sources might be discussion of justice, the law and the new law in Christ, in the early church, in the Middle Ages, in Reformation debate on the relationship between the laws and the gospel, and in discussion of the treatment of various groups of marginalized people – heretics, Jews, other nations, prisoners, the disabled and so on. The largest source of such discussion is likely to be biblical exegesis, and we shall address this in the next chapter. We might also expect to find relevant data in modern theological writing on justice and human dignity around the concepts of the image of God, reconciliation and the kingdom of God, in theologians from Schleiermacher through Ritschl to Troeltsch.

Reflecting on the historical development it would appear that the proliferation of notions of religious tolerance and of equal respect was among the most important steps towards the growth of a culture of human rights. As long as people were convinced that there was one God-given way of thinking and action, and that their particular group themselves adhered to this, there was little chance of real progress. Despite the huge amount of Christological reflection, the notion of a Christ who is the instantiation of vulnerable, self-giving love was often overlaid by imagery of Christ the judge, who discerns and approves correct thought and consigns the errant to damnation.

Why this lacuna? A snapshot of at least part of the problem may be found in Jaroslav Pelikan's *Jesus through the Centuries* (1985). Through prose, verse and painting we are conducted through classical images of Christ as the epitome of the good, the true and the beautiful, the rabbi, the fulfilment of history, the light of the gentiles, the king of kings, the cosmic Christ, the incarnation of the divine, the son of man as the antidote to evil, the crucified and atoning Christ, the monk who rules the world, the mirror of the eternal. There is a rediscovery of the full humanity of Christ through Francis of Assisi and through the *philosophia Christi* of Erasmus. But we have to wait almost for Martin Luther King for the use of Jesus' prophetic opposition to the economic and social injustice of his time, for transformation in the ordering of social relations, public and private, and for the explicit relationship of Jesus to all humanity, inside and outside the church. This picture is perhaps an exaggeration, but it does indicate the comparatively low profile of imagery explicitly related to human rights issues in the Christian tradition. Christendom was saturated in imagery of Christ as king and Christ as judge. Apocalyptic imagery could fuel critique of establishment, but this could easily turn to violence. Paradoxically, fixation upon the passion of Christ could foster violence as much as inhibit it, notably justifying harsh penal systems and anti-Semitism. *Damnamus* remains a central motif from Athanasius to Luther.

Hijacking history on behalf of our preferred understanding of contemporary issues is an unwise move, although we cannot avoid creating our own personal reading. We have to try at least to look at human rights issues in the past as they were, rather than as we might like them to have been, and in the present as they are today.

What sort of Christianity might hope to avoid some of the pitfalls of the past and provide a constructive future? That, too, will be a necessary part of the enforcement and delivery of human rights solutions. I have attempted to address this in terms of the notions of generosity and intercultural conversation. My own research project has a consciously liberal Christian trajectory that many Christians will find unacceptable, and this has to be recognized. However, although a liberal project has a very serious commitment, it does not regard itself as producing a final perspective. It is open to interaction and to learning from other perspectives, wherever dialogue partners can be found. It hears the voice of the voiceless.

We may reflect, too, that the silenced are often remembered only by chance. The Glasgow poet Professor Edwin Morgan makes this point with some elegance. On Janet Horne, the last woman burned as a witch in Scotland in 1727, he comments:

> Dear God were you sleeping
> You were certainly not weeping
> She was not in your keeping.

On the contemporary face of the persecuting tradition he writes, in 'The Trondheim Holocaust' (in Morgan 2001, 59, 63f):

> We entered by the gate of fear
> We exited without hope, as smoke
> The chimneys pointed at the sky
> In silence, unaccusing, unaccused. ('The Yellow Triangle')

> Who shall chronicle our suffering?
> We have no lobby and no voice
> Where is our home, where is our country?
> Is that why our destroyers destroy? ('The Brown Triangle')
> We were the lowest of the low.
> Further down you could not go

Nature itself, they said, abhorred us.
How should the Third Reich reward us? ('The Pink Triangle')

An open, porous vision of Christian faith will have affinities to mysticism, in so far as it eschews doctrinal absolutes and infallible authorities, whether of sacred texts or sacred communities. It will continue to respect those who differ on these issues, while seeking to advocate alternative perspectives. As a Christian vision it will continue to be centred on Jesus Christ as the way, the truth and the life, but in an inclusive manner. It will be open to dialogue both with other Christian cultures and with non-Christian and non-religious visions. It will be democratic without being either majoritarian or exclusively defined in terms of Western culture, be it Protestant, Catholic or secular. As a Christian vision it will understand rights as a servant of the gospel rather than as an alternative gospel. It will hope to work with all who seek to promote human welfare through justice, reconciliation and unconditional love.

CHAPTER 5

The Hermeneutics of Rights in the History of Interpretation

The Christological Tradition

The Christological tradition relating to justice and equity is firmly embedded in biblical interpretation. Justice and equity may be interpreted in the language of rights. Other sources of rights language, too, occur in the Bible. There are numerous narrative episodes in the Old Testament, and in the parables, teaching and especially the life of Jesus, which might give rise to reflection and practice in a human rights direction. But there are also many biblical passages which militate strongly against human rights consequences – injunctions to genocide and the observance of numerous instances of cultural discrimination. These strands live on in the history of interpretation and may militate against the apprehension of rights concepts.

We have already noted the influence of biblical notions of justice and righteousness in encouraging awareness of human rights. All are made equal and given identity in Christ, and this gift is to be made available to all humanity. Yet as many studies have shown, biblical imagery was often as much a factor in inhibiting the development of humane attitudes, for example, as it was in facilitating them – the cases of capital punishment and slavery being just two examples. The role of biblical Christological passages advocating unconditional love and forgiveness was not especially prominent. Christ as absolute monarch and implacable judge was at least as influential as Christ our fellow sufferer in identification with those at the point of greatest need.

Postmodern thought has familiarized us with the socially constructed nature of our understanding of the self and of community. This makes the tracing of an unchanging self-understanding in history difficult, if not impossible. Biblical interpretation is influenced by all the social developments that we illustrated from Troeltsch in Chapter 4. Yet there are threads of continuity in the cultural tension between nature and nurture in human history, and this applies to all aspects of society. Some of these threads may be traced through the history of biblical interpretation.

At some future date, when all historical texts can be examined on a powerful database, it will be possible to make exhaustive analyses of the traditions of biblical interpretation. There is a huge treasure of medieval writing which remains practically unread and unexplored. Who reads Godfrey of Admont, Ambrose Autpert, Notker the Stammerer and St Gertrude (see de Lubac,1998, I, 170)? This is itself sometimes an indication that sections of the Christian community have been marginalized – hence the importance, for example, of recent retrieval by feminist and gay writers of significant historical texts. But even a brief selection from well-known episodes will shed significant light on the issue of human rights. Different selections of text are popular at different periods in church history. The history of interpretation is much influenced by the development of allegory, in variations of a twofold distinction between a literal and a hidden spiritual sense, or a fourfold distinction culminating in the medieval grouping of historical, allegorical, moral and eschatological senses summed up in the popular jingle: '*littera gesta docet, quid credas allegoria/ Moralis quid agas, quid speres anagogia*'.

The Good Samaritan

One much-used story is Jesus' parable of the Good Samaritan – a story, we might think, of quintessential significance for human rights issues. Gerhard Ebeling has usefully traced the history of this parable's exegesis, and he has demonstrated some remarkable similarities in the tradition of exposition (Ebeling, 1991, 496f).

Origen comments that this parable does not refer to any human beings. The robbers are those of whom Jesus said, 'All who came before me are thieves and robbers'. Jesus was wounded by their faults and sins. According to Ambrose, the man descending is Adam, going from paradise to this world. The robbers are the angels of darkness, trying to turn into angels of light. In Augustine's view, Adam is the man in descent. The robbers are both the devil and his angels, who rob him of immortality. The blows he receives are sins. He is left half-dead, with knowledge of God still oppressed by sin. For Nicholas of Lyra, man again descends into sin, and is wounded by sin and loss of grace. For Luther, too, we are all wounded by sin from Adam. The robbers are demons, and we are half-dead – living bodies with dead souls.

The interpretation of the priest also follows a continuing theme. For Origen, the priest and the Levite represent the law, which is ineffectual. According to Augustine, the priest and the Levite are the ministry and priesthood of the Old Testament, which do not produce salvation. For Nicholas of Lyra, the priest and Levite are unworthy priests who are concerned only to extort money, not to bring salvation. For Luther, too, the priest and the Levite are Abraham and Noah, who see the necessity of preaching the word of God, but cannot bring salvation.

As for the Samaritan, for Origen he is the one who does not sleep but guards Israel – namely Jesus, of whom the Jews said ' You are a Samaritan, you are possessed of the devil'. For Ambrose, too, the Samaritan is Jesus. Augustine picks up on Origen's interpretation: Samaritan means 'guard', and this signifies Jesus. Luther sees the Samaritan is Jesus who brings salvation not because of our merit, but through his mercy.

The bandaging of the wounds is treated in a similar manner. Christ takes away the wounds of sin, then, by lifting the wounded man on to his horse, carries our sins on his body. Luther sees the inn as the church, the true Church of Christ which is to come. The two coins are the gift of the Father and the Son. The extra payment is the gift of eternal life. For Calvin, as for Luther, Christ is the Samaritan but, significantly, he stresses the ethical imperative of care for ones' neighbour, the concept of which includes all humanity. In doing so he anticipated the nineteenth-century liberal interpretation of the parable as an example of the values of the kingdom of God for the practice of the church.

The image of God

Another avenue into the tradition can be found by looking at the exegesis of a concept rather than a story. Here, the standard relevant example is the *imago Dei* concept. Throughout the tradition man is seen as made in the image of God, with reference to the narrative of Genesis 1:27. From Irenaeus onwards, much is made of the supposed difference between image and likeness in developing the doctrine of sin, and in the question of the natural knowledge of God. There is less emphasis on the New Testament imagery of the renewal of the image in Christ. It is true that Augustine interestingly sees the image of God as essentially Trinitarian. But this is then related to the *vestigia trinitatis* in the soul, of memory, intelligence and will. Calvin, again, is distinctive in stressing that Christ is the most perfect image of God. But, despite his emphasis on the divine freedom, it does not occur to him to see the image in Christ in a context of social or political liberation. Christ's role is within the framework of the predestination of the elect within the faithful community. This Christology effectively serves to qualify the much more ecumenical and universal perspective that we saw in Calvin's exegesis of the Good Samaritan parable.

We have to wait for the liberal theology of the nineteenth century, with its emphasis on a humanist Christology 'from below' in Schleiermacher and a concern for the social ethic of the kingdom of God in Ritschl, for the precursors of a social and political Christology, siding with the marginalized. Here, too, the dimension of identification, mutuality and reciprocity is strictly limited.

It may seem surprising that there are not more Christological references in the exegetical tradition on passages which would seem to demand this. On the other hand, an appeal to Christology of itself may not lead to reflections bearing on human rights issues. Calvin's concern for those outside the faithful community, as he understood it, was highly selective. Much depends on the Christological perspective.

The classical interpreter of the Bible in a Christological framework in the twentieth century is, of course, Karl Barth, and even he does not refer to Christology where one might expect him to – for example, in most of his famous discussion of the *imago Dei* imagery in *Church Dogmatics*. Indeed, he instinctively recoils from any suggestion of the liberal Christology of the social gospel, and his Christological reflection is centred on traditional notions of incarnation and atonement, sin, judgement and election. On the other hand, his use of the parable of the prodigal son is a triumph of Christological reflection on God's solidarity with the abandoned. In his ethics, too, Barth is constantly conscious of the transformative impact of the Christ event. He can suggest that it is nonsense to speak of capital punishment being retributive justice when Jesus Christ has been nailed to the cross for the sins of the world. Here Barth's discernment is much in advance of the views of many liberal democrats in the United States half a century later. Nor should we neglect classical writers on Christology in the development of a cumulative case for human rights issues, even if we have to refocus the discussion. It would be interesting in this context to reconsider the interpretation of the prodigal son parable, and indeed the interpretation of the parables in general.

Barth speaks neither of human rights nor of holocaust, but it would be inaccurate to think that he had no interest in the issues. One of the benefits of the explosion of human rights discourse is that it has provided a catalyst for a necessary focus on rights issues as such, even though the language alone, without a developed human rights culture, has not stopped the perpetuation of horrendous abuse.

Another illuminating text for our purpose ought to be the interpretation of the Johanine parable of the true vine. Here, membership of the Christian community is clearly bound to the display of the fruits of the love of God in Christ.

In reflecting on the history of interpretation we have to remind ourselves that the entire commentary enterprise often takes a very different shape from modern works. For example, the whole of St Hilary of Poitier's commentary on St Matthew's Gospel is centred on the movement from the law to faith. This often takes the form of an unflattering comparison between the Jews and the gentiles or the church and the synagogue. The text bears witness to the history of God's actions in transferring salvation from the Jews to the gentiles. The pivot of this movement is Jesus Christ, who reverses the effect of Adam's sins. There are scarcely any other themes.

Augustine's biblical interpretation, both in its hermeneutical rules as set out in the *De Doctrina Christiana*, and in the practical fruits of exegesis, became hugely influential in the West. His notorious suggestion of taking literally Christ's injunction in the parable to compel the unwilling to enter his community was to be a landmark in justifying the persecution of heretics – a salutary reminder that appeal to Christ in exegesis does not automatically produce solutions compatible with the development of human rights.

Biblical texts have been interpreted very differently in different periods. Henri de Lubac's foundational studies in medieval exegesis give a remarkable insight into the sheer variety of interpretation. They also highlight how the preoccupations of medieval Christians were very different from those of many modern Christians. The vast majority of de Lubac's huge reservoir of sources is concerned to wrestle with issues in the story of salvation and the divine mysteries. There is strikingly little reference to areas relevant to human rights concerns, even where we might hope to find this. Also illuminating are studies of the interpretation of texts in series of sermons – for example, Wilfred Werbeck's analysis of Nicholas of Lyra's meditations on the Psalms.

Luther very often gave a Christological interpretation of Old Testament as well as New Testament passages, in accordance with his dictum that the purpose of the biblical text was to show forth Christ. As twentieth-century exegesis was to show, this paradigm was also to become problematic when it led to a Christomonist view of scripture.

The Sermon on the Mount, the Magi and the Lord's Prayer

There is an enormous literature on the interpretation of the Sermon on the Mount (see Kissinger, 1975), and, inevitably, much of the discussion focuses on Jesus' attitude to the law. Jesus fulfils the law. Does this mean that he abolishes it, reinforces it, or adds a nuanced interpretation to it? The ambiguities in the text, perhaps deliberate on the part of Jesus or his early followers, lend themselves equally to conservative and liberal interpretations. For liberals, this is an invitation to regard the details of Old Testament prescriptions as superseded in favour of unconditional love. A classic example of this approach is taken by Adolf von Harnack in *The Essence of Christianity*. But this did not prevent him from taking a stance in favour of the Great War. For conservatives, this is a careful balance in which the law is reinforced and reinterpreted in the light of the love of Christ. So, classically, Calvin. This did not prevent the burning of Servetus.

Most interpreters of the Sermon attempt to relate the teaching of Jesus to the Pauline understanding of justification by grace. Grace is prior to works, although works may be the fruit of grace. Here again, exegesis is integrated with a specific theological perspective, and the question of which is best remains a matter of debate and advocacy.

Even this brief historical sketch demonstrates the great diversity of biblical interpretation, reflecting, as it does, the theological and social cultures and conventions of its period. As in the biblical texts themselves, we should note, too, that the absence of specific words relating to human rights issues does not mean that the substantive issues are absent.

The Wider Biblical Tradition on Rights Issues

Support for human rights issues

Most discussion of the New Testament naturally tends to focus on Jesus Christ. But the New Testament is built upon the Old Testament, which contains a considerable volume of material that is not only relevant to rights issues, but also of great significance for Christianity. It is also, of course, of basic significance for Judaism, which, as we shall see, has had a considerable input into the development of modern rights theories and institutions. The Old Testament is read by many rights theorists as providing a universal framework for moral law under God, and for a basis in respect for human well-being. This position is developed, for example, in Protestant theology by Max Stackhouse, in Catholic theology by Michael Perry, and within the Abrahamic tradition importantly by Islamic writers, too. It can be seen as a basis for a theological understanding of natural law. Opponents of universal values are not inclined to support such arguments, on the ground that they fail to respect particularity.

What emerges from this synopsis is that in the biblical narratives there is a considerable body of very diverse sorts of material which can be used in support of human rights issues. Opinions will differ sharply on the nature of the arguments advanced, but there is an important agreement that the goals of God's purpose for the world include a future of love, peace and justice, in which violence and coercion are evil and torture is banned. It will be argued in this book that a significant Christian contribution to these goals can be made on the basis of a web of connections to form a cumulative case, which is strengthened, rather than weakened, by constructive tensions that acknowledge the ambiguities and the need for careful reflection on individual issues as they arise. It will also be emphasized that the eschatological future of God includes openness to mystery, signalled in the mysterious and open nature of relationship focused on the Trinitarian mystery of God.

Obstacles to human rights issues

It must also be acknowledged that there is also a considerable body of 'texts of terror' which militate sharply against human rights in the biblical material. I shall argue that this material is to be regarded as evidence of the earthen vessels in which the biblical treasure is contained. It is not a mystery to be accepted and somehow included in the Christian agenda but, rather, an obstacle to be overcome in the developing tradition of research and interpretation.

Biblical texts have been used effectively to oppose most advances in modern human rights. Racism, slavery, the emancipation of women and gays, the extension of suffrage, anti-Semitism and xenophobia – all have been vigorously supported on biblical grounds.[1] These arguments have been strengthened by reading the Bible

---

1   For anti-human rights Christologies and anti-Semitic theologies see Sasse, Elert and Hirsch.

For pro-slavery theologies, see cf. Haynes (2002) – see also the review in *Reviews in Religious Theology*, 10(1), February 2003, 32f.

There is now a growing corpus on the history of anti-gay theology. See Jordan (1997, 2001), Herman (1997) and especially the History on the Paul Halsall website at www.fordham.edu/halsall. There are deeply conservative survey articles in reference works – for example, D.F. Wright and M. Banner in TRE. There are also useful collections for and against gay liberation.

There is little material on either side on concern for people outside the church. Edwin Morgan's short poem on Alan Turing and the Clause 28 debate in Britain is apposite.

W.M. Swartley (2003) is an instructive discussion of homosexuality in a Christian context. Dr Swartley seeks to examine the various sides of the argument with fairness and compassion. His own viewpoint is conservative, involving 'an acknowledgement that we are dealing not only with individual persons, but also with cultural systems that work against God's pattern for human life'. The volume discusses biblical texts and contemporary practice, analyses Western culture and searches for a model of congregational discernment. The tone is eirenic throughout, stressing that all human beings are loved by God, while not affirming sexual practice outside marriage. The bibliography is much fuller on the conservative than on the progressive side of the argument, illustrating just how difficult it is for Christians to maintain any sort of 'objectivity' on this subject. The judgements made and the quotations selected on the secondary literature underline this issue. Compassionate conservatism is a welcome advance on the

in line with prevailing cultural assumptions. But the texts themselves, embedded in their particular culture, have also been a prime source of opposition to human rights and therefore to the oppression of millions of people through the ages. All the major world religions have sacred texts composed over a thousand years ago. When interpreted literally, they have enormous consequences that, from a liberal democratic perspective, are obviously repressive. There is a real crux here, and it is absolutely central to human rights issues. Christians who believe, as many millions do, in the scriptural texts as the literal inspired word of God have great difficulty in negotiating the hard texts of biblical prohibitions and injunctions. They wish to take these texts seriously and have to find ways of doing this while still considering the more progressive alternatives. In fact, on issues such as the emancipation of women and the abolition of slavery many conservative Christians have come round to doing this. But there is no single automatic line of development here, and in particular instances – for example, the Southern Baptist church in the United States – the more literal stance is reinforced. There is evidence that, both in Christianity and in Islam and contrary to the expectations of nineteenth- and twentieth-century scholars, literalist interpretation is sharply on the increase. This implies a continuing long-term task of dialogue, advocacy and persuasion for progressive Christians.

It must also be noted that Christian groups that campaign against human rights issues are nevertheless quite willing to use the language of rights to defend their right to discriminate against people of whom they disapprove on religious grounds. Human rights rhetoric is used by all sides in religious debates, as it has been in the political realm – for example, in defence of 'Asian values' by right-wing politicians. Here is a conflict of rights, in which decisions on the most pressing rights need to be made. But perhaps the willingness to use the framework of rights language for debate is itself a fragile step towards a greater awareness of rights.

The situation in the premodern church was clearly much more complex. On the one hand there was scope for allegorical and metaphorical interpretation; on the other hand, as we have seen, specific texts could become hugely significant, regardless of their cultural and historical context, and were then inevitably read within the parameters of a feudal and closed society. Of course, it would be anachronistic to expect Christians to have insights beyond the plausibility criteria of their times, but the biblical text gave divine support to many activities that nowadays might be regarded as insupportable.

---

ferocities of the past. It does, however, rather lend itself to a measure of irony. One can perhaps imagine such an approach to the burning of witches. No more stern sermons and condemnations: 'Good afternoon, madam. And how would you like us to process you today – well done or medium rare? And shall I add some gunpowder to speed things up a little, or would you go for honey mustard? I do hope you'll find the temperature comfortable for you today, and if there's anything else I'll be happy to assist in any way.'

Nevertheless, it cannot be assumed that conservative theologians always oppose human rights issues. Cf. Hilton's distinctions between extreme and moderate evangelicals on some aspects of slavery and punishment (Hilton, 1998).

On balance

In concluding this survey, we have to ask why Christians have often been sceptical about human rights ideas. They have been associated, in part quite correctly, with the Enlightenment; they have also been suspected of exaggerating the value of human autonomy. But, as we have seen, the picture is more complex. The Enlightenment has not always been a friend to human rights – consider Hume and Kant on blacks and how little they have to say about the poor. The moderates in eighteenth-century Britain were not liberal if judged by present-day. The number of capital offences rocketed, and even Bentham took a hard-line view of the value of punishment. Neo-liberal 'Enlightenment' values in the United States today have led to the institution of draconian prison regimes.

We have to take account of the fact that, in Christian evaluation of human rights issues, the traditional doctrine of sin has played a major role. Certainly, sin is a theologically important concept. It is sometimes conveniently forgotten that Christians are usually as sinful as others and often act contrary to the love of God. In the past, people were made to feel guilty about sins of non-conformity – Auden in the twentieth century is a fascinating example. Prisoners, especially women, were shamed and humiliated – made to feel miserable sinners. Unmarried mothers were branded by the sin of fornication. Blacks were taught to know their place and not be 'uppity' and so on. Jews were allowed professions that Christians were not to touch. Concepts of sin and providence could mask the reality of human rights abuse: Hilton (1988) cites reaction to the Irish famines in the 1840s. Poverty was often considered as a manifestation of sin, either hidden or revealed. Orlando Patterson (1998) noted the connections between poverty and racism, and, even today, it is usually the poor who are tortured.

Attitudes to slavery are a useful indicator of human rights sensitivity in the Christian tradition.[2]

---

2   Cf. Garnsey (1996, 85ff); also Wilkinson (1979): Ginsburg (1995); 'Natural Law and Particular Cases: Antigone'; and Patterson (1995).

Ironically, racism prompted both Northerners and Southerners to go to war. (Patterson, 1995,171)

In Chapter 4 we noted that Gregory of Nyssa viewed slavery as a sin. Most other Fathers do not – Augustine, Ambrose being notable examples. There is little or no reference to Christology as emancipatory in texts. After all, Christ took the form of a slave. So Christians should accept humiliation and so on (as in K Wengst 1988), and slavery is part of God's judgement on human sin. This was still the prevailing attitude in the United States more than a millennium later. E.D Genovese in *A Consuming Fire,* comments that: 'Southerners grounded the proslavery argument in an appeal to Scripture and denounced abolitionists as infidels who were abandoning the plain words of the Bible'(1998,4).

It is important to remember that there was a very strong theological defence of slavery in the nineteenth century, a widespread lack of legal status for slave marriage and family connections, and laws against slave literacy. A US Presbyterian committee in 1863 on slavery stated that '[l]ike the existence of God, it is taken for granted from the beginning to the end of the Bible'(Terrell, 1998, 43). In 1859 a certain Isabella Lucy Bird Bishop stated: 'Slave-trade, which vitiates alike public and private morals, this the pulpit protects and fosters' (ibid.). In slave society the uncertain status of slave marriages highlighted the absoluteness of white authority and assisted whites in the reification of class lines.

Orlando Patterson, in an essay on 'Freedom, Slavery and the Modern Construction of Rights' (in Hufton, 1995) notes the complex interplay between theology and slavery in the Southern states just before the Civil War:

> Forced to accommodate to the northern notion that all men were equal, covenanted[3] children of God, this honorific ideal of freedom was dramatically transformed and democratized, generating the belief that all men are, legally and politically, created equal. Inherited privileges and powers of birth for a few became inalienable rights for many through the simple replacement of the earthly, aristocratic father by the law-giving, godly creator. (Hufton, 1995,155)

The influence of John Locke helped to create contractarian ideology in the United States and, in the South, conflicts between federalist and anti-federalist groups: 'Ironically, racism prompted both Northerners and Southerners to go to war' (ibid.,171). Slavery was part of the fabric of the ancient world. Such objections as existed appear to have been to particular aspects of slavery in individual circumstances, rather than to slavery as such. Much of the modern spotlight on slavery focuses on the experience of African-American slaves in North America and the Caribbean, who, as we have seen, were able to receive Christianity from their captors and transform it. The problem was complicated by the fact that St Paul seems

---

3   Rabben (2002, 24–5) draws attention to James Ramsey, a Scottish clergyman who in 1784 published *An Essay on the Treatment and Conversion of African Slaves in the British Sugar Colonies*. His biographer, Folarin Shyllon, calls it 'a damning indictment and exposé of British West Indian Slavery'. Ramsey declares that:

> Slavery… is an unnatural state of oppression on the one side, and of suffering on the other, and only needs to be laid or exposed in its native colours, to command the abhorrence and opposition of every man of feeling and sentiment.

not to have objected to slavery (cf. Blount, 2001), and this was, of course, a major factor in Christian support for it.

It has been said that the Civil War was not fought by either side to free slaves, but to consolidate their economic interests. Christians were much involved both in slavery and in campaigning for its abolition. Although slavery was widespread in Africa before the arrival of Europeans, the early colonists developed it hugely with the export of slaves to America, and there were black people employed in European households in conditions of virtual slavery. During the Second World War both the Nazis and the Japanese made extensive use of slave labour, often using it as a delayed form of the extermination process.

From the outset in the United States, slavery was entwined with racism, and indeed this is usually the case: slavery and xenophobia are interlinked. In Greece and Rome it was almost always foreign peoples who were enslaved, and regarded *ipso facto* as inferior beings. In the United States the abolition of slavery did not lead immediately to full civil rights, but only to an emancipation in which new and more complex forms of legal restraint ensured that the violation of human rights continued. Here, the legacy of slavery has proved to be enduring and is by no means fully resolved.

In the contemporary world slavery continues to flourish, usually in impoverished societies in which powerful nations have little incentive to intervene. It is usually concealed in exploitative working conditions and in cultures where there is little scope for individual choice. There is probably no panacea for the problems posed by such situations, although an attempt to reduce economic inequalities would help create a culture in which slavery or quasi-slavery would be harder to manage.

Punishments

Theological justification of prejudice could be just as strong in Britain as in America. Tim Gorringe in *God's Just Vengeance* (1996), speaks of the 'social blindfolds' that affected society. He quotes Wesley in favour of a strong prison regime, noting the idealist character of almost all Western theology and the contrast between 'ordinary lives' and eternal realities. (I am reminded of Lessing's famous ditch here.) As he notes, there was much stress upon retribution and satisfaction theories. In the eighteenth and nineteenth centuries prisoners were often seen as scapegoats, and connections were made between foundational Christian texts and violence.

Gorringe explores the Old Testament tradition, of taboo, command and law, and pollution rituals. There are endless examples of human rights abuses in the Old Testament – although not in all Judaism (we may recall the frequent puzzlement over this in the rabbinic tradition). In Deuteronomy there are mutilation and punishments based on a culture of shame. He says of the Cross: 'Thus a story which was a unique protest against judicial cruelty came to be a validation of it' (Gorringe, 1996, 81).

Gorringe notes Huizinga's underlining of a connection between the church, chronic insecurity and punishment. According to Luther, Christ takes on the punishment for our sins. Calvin stresses propitiation and appeasement: 'Where

Calvinism spread, punitive sentencing followed' (ibid., 140). There were a few contrary voices, notably those of Grotius and Blake in his writings against war and in his emphasis on forgiveness. Calvinism tended to defend atonement theory (see R.W. Dale on punishment) although a more liberal approach is found in J. McLeod Campbell's view of vicarious penitence in place of vicarious punishment. As for prison chaplains, Oscar Wilde wrote that they were useless.

Gorringe concludes (echoing Potter, 1993) that the Church of England's stance in the penal debates of the nineteenth century was 'depressing indeed. From start to finish the bishops proved staunch supporters of hanging and flogging'(Gorringe, 1996, 211). Today a new retributionism has echoes in theology. There is still much evidence of this today, especially in the United States (cf. Prejean, 1993, 2004). For Gorringe, the church must act as a community of reconciliation.

In surveying this unpromising tale we must recall that, for centuries, endless inhumanity was a central part of the cultural mix. Wars of religion, famine, punishments and the destruction of religious heritage were, and often still are, common on all sides of conflicts. Today we instantly think of poverty, HIV and the arms trade, and this is why human rights are important. It has to be noted, however, that the churches have usually been dragged only very reluctantly into issues that involve women priests, divorce, marriage of divorcees and so on. In addition, we may reflect that much human rights abuse today occurs as a result of simple neglect – sins of omission rather than commission.

More sinister is the purism of groups like those Germans who stressed in the 1930s – for reasons that were understandable but still not justifiable – that their families had not contained a drop of Semitic blood for centuries, or who make absolute distinctions between male and female, gay and straight, black and white and so on, in order to preserve discrimination.

Not every Christology

Reflecting on the role of Christ in Christological tradition, it would seem that there is a need to stress Christ rather than scripture as such, with Luther and, beyond this, a particular understanding of Christ (cf. Luther and the peasants). Luther stressed that faith without works is dead. Justification is by faith alone. This could lead to a neglect of charitable action and an individualistic notion of salvation.

Perhaps it is necessary to concentrate on experience in the community today (church and world, rather than just experience in church as sect). Sometimes a liberal perspective is defeated (Remonstrants) but conservatives change (Holland.) Sometimes a liberal perspective is defeated completely (Southern Baptists). Outcomes partly depend on sociopolitical cultural shifts of an unexpected nature. For example, the Quakers have historically played a very important role in human rights, but now that role is shrinking.

Different theologies may fulfil different functions in advocating human rights issues. Liberal theology provides a link to huge numbers of people who now stand outside the formal church but who have a background of Christian culture and use it as a guide. Progressive Christianity becomes especially important as churches become more conservative. Theologies of experience are useful in human rights contexts – consider Schillebeeckx, Rahner and Tracy, even as far back as Erasmus. But the experience should not be itself exclusive: Schleiermacher's vision for women was generous but also very limited; and Bultmann's existential Christology failed to tackle many of the pressing issues of twentieth-century social ethics. Radical orthodoxy supports consolidation within the Eucharistic community, but risks neglecting those outside it – an inward-facing Christ. There may be inclusion in principle but not in fact. Human rights concerns call for an inclusive Christ, an inclusive faith, an inclusive church.

It has become apparent that Christological exegesis was often used to support other texts as primary, and that therefore the Christological moment was lost. It is, however, necessary to avoid stereotyping: some American slave owners were enlightened (and some Roman ones too!). For Christians, the central question is the role and interpretation of texts. In a human rights-oriented Christology, more would be necessary on the kenotic theme of a self-dispossessing, loving God.

In the modern theologies of Barth and Bultmann there is still an emphasis on eternal truths of reason in the idealist tradition. More could have been made there of the Jesus tradition of service to the poor and to outsiders. Priority is sometimes placed on the poor in absolutist Christologies – for example, the work of priests in Anglo-Catholic slum parishes in the nineteenth century – and sometimes not in non-absolutist Christologies. Theology often tends to opt for triumphalist rhetoric and solutions where there is a need for confident argument. Faith is centred on the resurrection of Jesus Christ and salvation rather than Christian ideals and behaviour.

In Chapter 4 we noted the engagement of the World Council of Churches in human rights. This concern can be paralleled in the work of the various member churches. I take the Reformed tradition as an example.

Jill Schaeffer (www.warc.ch/dcw/rw982/02.html) has made a good survey of the World Alliance of Reformed Churches' (WARC's) human rights involvement up to 1989. The original emphasis in 1875 was on the protection of weak and vulnerable churches. By 1879 this had expanded to 'persons and groups suffering from social, economic and political oppression' and to a critique of social and economic structures producing inequity and suffering. The years 1880–81 brought attention to persecuted Armenians and native Americans, 1884 brought mention of indigenous churches and the emphasis in 1888 was on workers' rights and the need to bring political pressure on King Leopold about conditions in the Congo. Slavery and the plight of native Americans and persecuted denominations in Eastern Europe were highlighted in the 1890s. The Alliance was critical of the First World War and held a 'John Hus Day' of reconciliation in 1915. The 1920s brought a critique of white domination in Africa and directed attention to Japanese atrocities against Koreans as well as to poverty and women's rights in Europe. In 1933, with the growth of Nazism, the Alliance protested against 'every form of slavery, oppression, exploitation and spoliation' and at the same time attacked the notion of 'aggressive war'. After the war there was an unusual and curious silence. Condemnation of racism came again at Frankfurt in 1964 and this was soon to focus on the struggle against apartheid in Reformed South Africa, culminating in the *status confessionis* declaration at Ottawa in 1982 and the suspension of two of the Dutch Reformed Church denominations in South Africa. Appropriately, a handbook on torture was produced at this time. In the later 1980s there were to be appeals and interventions on human rights violations in Guatemala, Chile, Taiwan, the Philippines, Sudan and Egypt. Since 1989 there have been further declarations and campaigns on women's rights inside and outside the churches, on sanctuary and asylum, on conflicts in the Balkans and in the Middle East, and there is continuing interaction through the Commission of the Churches on International Affairs (CCIA) with the UNHRC and other bodies. There have also been declarations on environmental ethics and ecological rights.

T.S. Shah, in an essay on 'Making the World Safe for Liberalism: from Grotius to Rawls' (in Marquand and Nettler, 2000) traces the development of concepts of liberalism from Grotius' *Meletius* to Johan van Oldenbarnevelt and the Remonstrants in their struggle with the Calvinists:' Our search will be for a politics that preserves, not resolves, the tension between political liberalism and religious pluralism in its various forms' (Marquand and Nettler, 2000, p137). However, the development of Christology in relation to human rights issues must consider angles beyond the liberal/conservative divide, including the impact of postmodernism. In the *Cambridge Companion to Postmodern Theology* (2003) edited by K. Vanhoozer, there is a useful survey of different kinds of postmodernism, both constructive and destructive. There is a postmodernism of construction and a postmodernism of reaction, anti-modernism. Postmodernism can mean many things.

Equally, it should not be assumed that the secular is always inimical to Christian faith. R.K. Fenn, for example, argues against a civil religion and for a secularity: 'At the heart of the Christian gospel... is a tendency towards secularity'(Fenn, 2001, 160).

In assessing the Christian tradition in relation to human rights issues it is desirable not to rush into judgement. The subject calls for a nuanced approach to many of the hotly debated issues of current political theory. Individualism has value, but group rights are important too. Community is important, but theologians can overestimate the impact of the Eucharistic community on a wider society. There is much talk of the monolithic foundations of the Enlightenment – and rightly so. But sometimes this mirrored an earlier monolithic foundationalism – and perhaps a coming one.

There were, of course, exceptions to most of the prevailing trends as indeed there are today. There is a need to develop pluralistic notion of values, but not against the rest in a polemical way: pluralists can also be dogmatic ideologues. Theology which needs human rights concerns must be porous and open – except to coercion. Classic pluralist Christologies may also be too prescriptive, following in the footsteps of dogmatic liberalism. The trajectory of Christology and human rights can be read as both positive and negative – partly one and partly the other – and it perhaps has a long future, as well as a past.

CHAPTER 6

Christology in Human Rights Focus: Towards a Humane Christology

We return to the need for a Christology which will engage most effectively with fundamental issues of human rights. We have deliberately explored in some depth the negative side of the Christian input to rights issues as it is necessary to face up squarely to failure, if there is to be progress. Arguably, there is a case for concluding that the record is so poor that it is unrealistic to claim that there are any solid grounds for believing that Christian faith can contribute substantially to rights issues. In many situations it is not surprising that people are driven to this conclusion. Indeed, the tradition tends to record those who have followed and upheld the tradition rather than those who have sunk under its weight.

However, the negative side is not the whole story. We have already seen instances of Christian contributions to human rights issues, and we shall now examine the more positive side of the subject. We have focused on rights, but we have to look at the balance sheet under other categories too – for example, the fulfilment of duties and obligations. It is also worth recalling that, in the Christian perspective, the future is always much longer and more significant than the past. Without wishing to hijack the future, we may reflect on the fact that faith sees the incarnation of God in Jesus Christ as the decisive point in a trajectory that goes back to the creation of the universe and goes forward to an unbounded future. The events concerning Jesus Christ may provide grounds for hope which will stretch well beyond the limitations of a particular contingent slice of history and culture, even one as large as 2,000 years.

Not everything in the development of the Christological tradition is unpromising. In principle there is no reason at all why traditional Christologies should be inimical or insensitive to human rights issues. Although many defenders of impeccable traditional Christologies have been insensitive to issues of freedom of conscience, religious liberty and toleration – Augustine, Aquinas and Calvin come to mind, and Rorty cites Ratzinger and Falwell – Karl Barth used Christology to critique the death penalty, and Dietrich Bonhoeffer was largely inspired by Barth in his lonely struggle against Hitler.

Looking at the tradition as a whole we may reflect that what was implicit in the tradition in terms of the unconditional generosity of the love of God in Jesus Christ often needed to be made much more explicit, both in theory and in practice. We find such explicit exposition in the liberation Christologies. Very often these studies concentrate on liberation for particular minority groups within the church, and this is important both from a theoretical and a practical perspective. Charity begins at home, especially in the church. The churches are unlikely to be a catalyst for human rights issues in society so long as they are seen to manifest internal oppression. Yet a huge proportion of human rights abuses in the contemporary world take place in society outside the church, and it is crucial for the Christian faith to engage with these problems. In this task the internal issues can often be instructive, but the massive global issues need to be addressed directly.

In the events concerning Jesus Christ we see the incarnation of God in humanity. Jesus is totally divine and totally human. The texture of this language remains open, for it is the language of faith in the divine mystery. In the past it was sometimes taken to mean that humanity belongs to God, so that a man could be killed for the sake of God by those in whom the administration of God's authority was duly vested. At other times it was thought that humanity simply is God. But classical Christian faith believes that God has given himself into humanity in such a way as to invest unique value in every individual human being. To be human is not a trivial fact, – the kind of logic that Hannah Arendt detected in the Nazis. To be human is to be made in a myriad of different ways in the image of God in Jesus Christ. There is no monopoly of the image, or indeed of the theoretical understanding of the image, in a particular cultural shape. But there is a web of connections which spells out the central characteristics of the humanity of God in Jesus Christ and its implications for our humanity. These exhibit both positive and negative features, ruling some things in and other things out. To explore this web we may look at the chaotic but unregimented plethora of biblical imagery in the first instance. This should, in turn, stimulate us to explore beyond this imagery, but in the same spirit or research tradition.

Human Rights and the Events Concerning Jesus

The narratives of the New Testament present us with a collage of pictures of the ministry of Jesus. I use the word 'ministry' advisedly, because that is how the writers see the position. How far we can extrapolate a life of Jesus remains very unclear, although the ministry – and the ministry as a passion narrative in particular – was clearly determinative for his life. Jesus appears as a kind of icon of the divine presence. He exemplifies the values of the reign of God – love, concern (especially for outsiders), scandal to the religiously orthodox. Of course, these values have been masked at various times by cultural preferences and we, too, select values that speak to our own cultural situations. Yet it seems perverse to deny that critical research has uncovered significant elements of the picture and will continue to do so.

Torture and the cross

Jesus was crucified on a cross. The gospel narratives are passion narratives. How does this image fit with the outstanding human rights concerns of the modern world? This seemingly naïve question produces some startling results. In a world of ambiguities, some things stand out unambiguously. For example, the Christian vision endorses Michael Ignatieff's (2004) view that torture is never the lesser evil.

Torture is directly contrary to the shape of the love of God. This affirmation may be helpful in contributing to shaping a human rights culture in a religious setting. It also requires an immediate acknowledgment that torture in a theological context has been common in Christendom down the ages. Any Christian contribution to debate about torture can only be on the basis of repentance and an awareness of vulnerability to abuse.

It should be noted, too, that psychological torture can be as devastating as physical torture. Here again, the Christian contribution will inevitably be chastened and humbled by the memory of Christian abuse – abuse which is reported to continue in many guises.

Torture does not feature directly in Jesus' teaching. We have no record of him criticizing the penal practice of his day, in the way that modern human rights activists might, or of questioning the common practice of crucifixion in the way that one or two Roman writers did. Of course, we have only a very limited sample of all the things he must have talked about, but arguments deriving from silence are of little value. Torture impinges on Jesus directly only at the end, when he is himself scourged and crucified. This appears to have taken place in his environment more or less as a matter of course; later cultures similarly immunized themselves against barbarity, as evidenced, for example, in the manner of executing traitors in medieval Europe. The value of a life is little when seen against the interests of the state.

Theologians have wrestled with the significance of God participating in Jesus' crucifixion, as both permitting and suffering torture and death. The event has prompted awareness of the contrast with Jesus' own teaching on the value to God of each human life. It has also, in curious ways, reinforced the continuation of torture, as thousands have been tortured under the sign of the cross.

Theological studies occasionally mention torture, but rarely explore its details in contemporary practice. Torture is hard to comprehend, but its reality needs to be made explicit:.

> It was unhurried and methodical. If the victim was a woman they went for the breasts, vagina, anus. If a man, they favoured genitals, tongue, neck… Sometimes victims twitched so uncontrollably that they shattered their own arms and legs. Patrick Rice, an Irish priest who had worked in the slums and was detained for several days, recalls watching his flesh sizzle. What he most remembers is the smell. It was like bacon. (Donnelly, 1993, 42)

> Pain and interrogation always occur together because the torturer and the prisoner experience them as opposites…. For the torturers, the sheer and simple fact of human agony is made invisible, and the moral fact of inflicting that agony is made neutral by the feigned urgency and significance of the question. For the prisoner, the sheer, simple, overwhelming act of his agony will make neutral and invisible the significance of any question as well as the significance of the world to which the question refers. Intense pain is world-destroying. (Scarry, 1985, 29)

> Atrocities are both perpetrated and suffered. There is no such thing as an atrocity that just happens or an atrocity that hurts no-one. (Card, 2002, 9)

The scenarios described above have been repeated in numerous modern instances, the actions of the Gestapo being just one example. Yet merely establishing a position is not the end of the matter. If torture is deeply inimical to Christian values, then there is a clear imperative to actively resist torture wherever it occurs. To do this requires expertise and information, organization and finance. It is important for Christian communities and Christian theologians to study the persistence of torture and become actively involved in action to stop it.

Such a strategy will have all sorts of complex political and economic ramifications. To avoid these is to avoid a main imperative of faith, and to turn the gospel into an anodyne entertainment. But persuading large numbers of Christians to walk over the bridge into active resistance against torture on a global scale has proved to be elusively difficult.

In addition, dealing with the aftermath of torture is never simple:

> Truth alone is never enough. Sometimes, though, it may make inroads against power. In any case, the task of human rights advocacy is to speak the truth to power, in the name of past and present victims and in the hope of preventing future victims. (Donnelly, 1993, 55)

Donnelly cites workers' rights, women's rights and racial discrimination as other single-issue human rights concerns. Jesus' concern for justice and for human dignity can be deployed in support of those who suffer in all these areas. The labourer is worthy of his hire. Women are treated with unusual respect and interest in Jesus' presence. Samaritans and strangers are instruments of the effective reign of God. We shall return to these issues again.

So far as the development of torture is concerned, Malise Ruthven's *Torture* (1979) provides an excellent historical survey of the development of the theory and practice of torture, from the ancient world, through the Middle Ages, to Stalin's Russia. He shows how the most elaborate rules for its administration were developed – different degrees of torture in different cases – while emphasizing that the rules were very often exceeded as brutality and sadism took over. In medieval Europe torture was routinely used to elicit evidence of deviation from Christian orthodoxy and was perpetrated out of devotion to the executed God. Women suspected of witchcraft bore much of the burden.

Human rights monitoring of torture already has a substantial history. Amnesty International's 1975 report not only provided an accurate guide to the contemporary situation, but also examined the legal definition of torture: 'Torture is the systematic and deliberate infliction of acute pain in any form by one person upon another, or on a third person, in order to accomplish the purpose of the former against the will of the latter'(Amnesty, 1975, 35). The report goes on to state that:

> It is directly linked to politics, as governments may see the use of torture as necessary for their survival. It is also the most sensitive of all political issues. Though a state may admit that it holds political prisoners, it will never admit that it uses torture. The confrontation between the individual and the limitless power

of the state, between the torturer and his victim, takes place in the darkest recess of political power. (Ibid., 242)

As we shall see when we consider the situation 30 years later, this remains a prophetic observation.

The ministry of Jesus, as far as we can speak of it, covers no more than the three last years of his life and is, above all, a passion narrative. The death of Jesus is a focal point of his significance both for faith and for human rights. The context of his arrest is the perception that his teaching and action constituted a threat to the political and the religious order. This could be argued to be a reasonable perception, given the radical basis of his message. In the event it was heightened, as so often in such circumstances, by exaggerated accusations and personal betrayal.

Martin Hengel has convincingly shown the deep cruelty of the practice of crucifixion and the widespread use of this form of execution:

> At relatively small expense and to great public effect a criminal could be tortured for days in an unspeakable way. Crucifixion is thus a specific expression of the inhumanity dormant within men which these days is expressed, for example, in the call for the death penalty, for popular justice and for harsher treatment of criminals, as the expression of retribution. It is a manifestation of trans-subjective evil, a form of execution which manifests the demonic character of human cruelty and bestiality. (Hengel, 1977, 87)

It is true that a number of Roman authors protested against the barbarity of crucifixion, but usually only in respect of its application to Roman citizens. Historical tradition has ensured that the death of Jesus is perhaps the best-known instance of martyrdom in human history. But the historical reality may have been nearer to the situation of many twentieth-century martyrs who were simply wiped out with mindless cruelty, with perhaps the accompaniment of an extra measure of sadism and torture in the proceedings.

As we saw in Chapter 2, torture in Latin America, usually involving Christians torturing Christians, has been powerfully analysed in relation to Christology by William Cavanaugh. Cavanaugh stresses the importance of the church as a community around the Eucharist as an antidote to the atomization and isolation which torturers create. Mark Taylor's *The Executed God* (2001) and Jurgen Moltmann's *The Crucified God* (1974) have both, in different ways, effectively argued that the cross of Jesus Christ is God's response to evil and torture, participating in the outrage as a victim in solidarity in order to overcome it. The whole passion narrative raises the most serious doubts about the compatibility of the Christian faith with the death penalty – a point already pressed by Karl Barth, but widely disregarded in the United States, where 12 Southern states in the so-called 'Bible Belt' conducted over 80 per cent of all the judicial executions carried out throughout the country.[1]

---

1   Cf. the eloquent and courageous witness of Helen Prejean, in her *Dead Man Walking* (1993) and *The Death of Innocents* (2004).

In reflecting on torture we encounter against the intractable problem of radical evil – a mystery which would take us well beyond the bounds of the present study. Richard Bernstein quotes Hans Jonas on the Holocaust:

> What about those who could never inscribe themselves in the Book of Life with deeds either good or evil, great or small, because their lives were cut off before they had a chance, or their humanity was destroyed in degradations most cruel and most thorough such that no humanity can survive? I am thinking of the gassed and burnt children of Auschwitz, of the defaced, dehumanised phantoms of the camps, and of all the other, numberless victims of the other man-made holocausts of our time. (Bernstein, 2002, 198)

Bernstein contrasts the different reactions of Jonas and Levinas, who lost much of his family to the Holocaust, the first reaction to re-emphasize the ontological differences and the continuity, and the second to highlight ethical issues and the character of the Other. He concludes by stressing the absolute need for global collective and personal responsibility for deeds of good and evil. But he also saw a kind of inscrutable transcendent mystery in evil: 'There is always a gap, a "black hole" in our accounts…We have learned "after Auschwitz" how insightful Kant was about the ultimate inscrutability of the moral choices that individuals make' (ibid., 235).

In the face of monstrous evil Christian faith understands itself in the light of God on the cross. But here is the classic instance where any sort of Christian triumphalism is the last thing that is required. James Keenan gets it exactly right:

> In fact, I think the Christian urge to translate or interpret another's suffering can be almost as violent as the act of silencing… The Christian emphasis on the act of interpreting in the face of suffering should give way, I think, to the Jewish emphasis on listening….
> To assist the one suffering we need to remember the empathetic quality of pain that helps us to acknowledge the depth of the other's suffering. When we become aware of the narrative of pain within our own bodies, we become familiar again with the desire to give voice to our own pain, hopefully assisting us to learn to listen to another's own 'silent' narrative of suffering. (Keenan, 2004, 79–80).

Here is Christomorphic solidarity without hubris, humane sympathy without the tight limitations that Richard Rorty feels bound to ascribe to our humanness.

In a perspective of Christian concern for the particular and the possible, the labyrinthine politics of international human rights negotiation, sandwiched among the tensions of geopolitical interests, inevitably become the subject of active engagement. It is pointless to have an abstract pious concern for rights if this is never embedded in the issues of conflict resolution which alone will deliver effective outcomes. This will necessarily impinge on choices in national politics. Human rights advocacy cannot be done in a hermetically sealed space of 'theology and rights'.

Jesus, poverty and civil liberties

It becomes more difficult to relate the ministry of Jesus directly to other aspects of human rights, especially positive rights. In contrast to the church's dubious record on torture, there is a huge popular stream of piety throughout the ages, which acknowledges the need to address poverty wherever it appears. For 1,000 years, from the time of the Cappadocians onwards, Christian monasteries made a huge effort of charity which must have had significant effects, although these are difficult to document. But this effort was always constrained by the doctrine of the duality of church and state, which meant that the monastic effort was more of a first-aid programme than a means of tackling the social structures that exacerbated poverty.

What of Jesus' attitude to poverty? Clearly he regarded the poor as at the point of the greatest need of the love of God. The poor can mean many things. Economically privileged people can be poor in the sense of lacking health or happiness or social acceptance and so on, and none of these factors is irrelevant. But the main target audience of Jesus' message seems to have been the economically impoverished. Now, it may be argued that the culture in which Jesus lived was a simple one, in which the massive problems of millions of hungry people in an overpopulated planet were utterly inconceivable. The means of delivering sufficient food in our modern world involves complex logistical and economic issues. But the imperative remains: letting people starve to death – as happens everywhere today in huge numbers – is clearly outside God's purpose for the world.

There is little in the New Testament on civil liberties. There may be five loaves and two fishes but there is no mention of freedom fries. There is, however, a significant section of Jesus' teaching which relates to the law. Jesus both affirms the Jewish law and radicalizes it around the commandment to love. The relationship between Jesus and the law and between the law and the gospel is important and has perhaps been most systematically explored in Lutheran theology. Yet nowhere does Jesus come across in the New Testament as primarily a lawgiver. Strikingly, he does not produce a code of legislation with detailed penalties for its infringement. Instead, the legal dimension comes to light mainly in reaction to the attacks of the rabbis on his teaching and healing ministry. It is within the framework of his practical action that the theoretical questions come to expression. The ultimately adverse reaction which his ministry provokes leads to clashes with the law and to his death.

Jesus appears not to have preached *social revolution* against the ruling foreign power. He does not appear, like a modern Amnesty worker, to have led campaigns on behalf of *individual victims* of Roman injustice. He does not appear to have demanded a complete break either with the religious authorities of Judaism. Despite this, his life and teaching came to be seen as a perceived threat to authority, and on that basis he was executed as a subversive.

Although Jesus does not campaign for social justice in any modern sense, his perspective is not totally eschatological either. Rather, he points to the values of the kingdom, which is to come and which is linked with his presence now. In the presence of God, there is a new sense of discernment, where the divine love will rewrite all human scripts for thought and action. If Jesus had been able to use the language of human rights, we might imagine him situating the language within the sphere of devotion to God, the way of discipleship. The presence of God prompts concern especially for the marginalized. In that sense we may see Jesus as an icon of human rights action, and God as the transcendent source of the power of effective action. In the crucifixion this momentum is tested to destruction and crushed. After the resurrection, the power of human rights action in divine perspective is delivered within the influence of the spirit of the crucified and risen Christ.

Resurrection and rights

Central to a Christian contribution to human rights is the faith that, in Jesus' case, crucifixion led to resurrection. The resurrection of Jesus Christ is a dangerous doctrine. It has led, and can lead, to all manner of unpleasant triumphalism and to an unrealistic assessment of the bleakness of death. Doctrines of the resurrection have created bitter disputes which continue to the present day. But the resurrection is an affirmation of the hope of love, a hope that, through solidarity in suffering, God may nevertheless bring light out of darkness. This vision of effective outcomes of love out of weakness has sustained the lives of millions of oppressed human beings and will no doubt continue to do so. Christian faith experiences the spirit of Christlikeness as a power which facilitates persistence in the face of unpromising circumstances. This is a factor not to be underestimated at times when the possibilities of effective human rights enforcement seem remote.

Christians view the resurrection in different ways and will doubtless continue to do so. However we view God's participation in the life of Jesus – as incarnation, as inspiration or whatever – here is the affirmation that the creator of all life has participated in human life and death and has brought about a new creation within the created order. In one immensely significant respect the power of death is destroyed: it does not separate humanity from communion with God. However technically inconceivable this perspective may be, it is not unthinkable and remains a powerful affirmation of the unique value of human life in the face of people who work to destroy it.

We have already noted a tendency to selectivity in attention to human rights, and this applies also with Christian communities. None of us is likely to be immune from selectivity. But it may be hoped that the development of a conscience about human rights as an urgent task will lead to a reduction of blind spots in our various interpretations. If that is possible, then humane theologies of human rights should become increasingly influential.

The Compassionate Imperative

Where do we find significant further directions for Christology in the light of these human rights concerns? Traditional conservative Christologies may be influential in enabling communities to resist in the face of active persecution. More liberal or pluralist Christologies may be better equipped to facilitate dialogue between different faiths and between communities of faith and those of none. In a human rights context, the aim should not necessarily be to produce one totalizing perspective on Christ, but to encourage effective practical discipleship in cooperation between Christians of differing persuasions. The present study, concerned with Christology as a contribution to human welfare in general, is written from a liberal or open perspective.

We may look at life, death and resurrection from the perspective of Jesus as a person. We may also reconsider the Christological centre from the perspective of the traditional doctrines of atonement and reconciliation. Of course, for the Christian faith what Jesus achieves as reconciler derives from his simply being who he is. His presence, then, in a particular context and now universally has a transformative influence on faith just by being there. Human lives are deeply influenced by the presence of others. Their presence is cashed out in their actions, in sympathy, in actions of kindness and effective intervention on behalf of others, sometimes individually and sometimes collectively, in intimate presence and perhaps socially at a distance, through bureaucratic action, scientific advance or whatever.

It is this transformative source of renewal and new creativity which doctrines of reconciliation have attempted to express through the scope and limitations of biblical and non-biblical imagery throughout the history of the churches. Here, we shall attempt to characterize reconciliation through the language of human rights. This will not, of course, supersede all other characterizations, but it may help us to articulate more precisely the connections between Christology and rights.

In the culture into which Jesus was born there were, as indeed there still are in most human cultures, violations of human rights. At the time Jesus lived whole groups of people were *de facto* enslaved by the Roman empire. The empire contributed in many important ways to the development of modern society and, indeed, to notions of law from which human rights law may be derived. But there were also serious negative features, deriving from the nature of the empire as an institution designed principally to benefit the mother state of Rome, and therefore largely insensitive to the needs and aspirations of peoples of the client states. It is true that these, too, were largely totalitarian societies based on feudal structures – micro-tyrannies within the macro-tyranny of the empire. But Roman economic and political demands tended to increase, rather than decrease, the burden which fell upon the lowest ranks of Mediterranean society. Terror was a major weapon of social control.

Jesus was not a philosopher. But he does appear to have been interested in the basis of ethical judgements. That basis was rooted in his devotion to God and his understanding of the nature of God. We can only search for this understanding through the writings of the early Christian communities and in subsequent reflection upon these writings. Jesus was concerned for the welfare of individuals, especially those at the margins of society. He associated physically with the marginalized and teaches that those at the point of greatest need are the nearest to the kingdom of God. Christian reflection comes to understand unconditional love as the nature of

God, and understands the life and action of Jesus as the definitive characterization in human life of this love.

Christomorphic Discipleship

When we think about discipleship, when we think about spirituality in the twenty-first century, then concern for human rights will become an important dimension of the external side of spirituality. The internal side of the same project will be a spirituality which understands human rights action as undertaken in a framework of devotion to God. An open theology will perceive human rights concerns as part of the concentration of Christian devotion in a Christomorphic framework, as part of an understanding of worship that reciprocates with service. While this should not be understood as the only possible framework of Christian devotion, it is part of the contribution offered by a progressive framework to the whole church and to society.

Because I regard openness as vital, I am persuaded that a classical Christology for the future need not be an absolutist Christology. It must avoid the illusion of finality and remain eschatologically open. An open Christology is likely to be a modest Christology.[2] But it should not be forgotten, too, that traditional nineteenth-century liberal Christologies were sometimes absolutist in their own claims to finality, and that Karl Barth was at pains to stress the provisionality and eschatological openness of all Christological proposals.

The imaginative term, 'Christomorphic' appears to be been first used by H.R. Niebuhr. He is speaking of what it is to be Christian:

> They know themselves to be Christian when they see their companions in need in the form of Christ; there echoes in their memory in such moments the story Christ told which ends in the well-known statement, 'inasmuch as you have done it to one of the least of these my brethren you have done it unto me.' The symbol is not a mere figure of speech. Symbol and reality participate in each other. The needy companion is not wholly other than Christ, though he is not Christ himself. He is a Christo-morphic being, apprehended as in the form of Christ, something like Christ, though another. (Niebuhr, 1963, 154–5)

---

2   R. Haight's *Jesus, Symbol of God* (2001) is an excellent example of a Catholic open theology. He notes that: 'The engaged participatory awareness of faith is not individualistic; the real presence of transcendence to it is experienced by a community along the route of its tradition'(Haight, 2001,11) so, individual freedom is realized within community. He also writes effectively of Christology as empowerment (ibid., 50) and of Jesus' freedom for others (ibid., 83).

Discipleship has a distinctive shape: 'The prophetic dimension of discipleship judges and resists everything that kills, diminishes life and curtails freedom'(ibid., 85.) He notes that liberal theology is often accused of individualism, but this is not necessarily the case (ibid., 316, n.22). There is nothing in its fundamental premises or method that is *per se* individualistic. For Haight, '[t]he salvific character of Jesus' action must then be found in his historical action, his this-worldly comportment' (ibid., 338). Cf. also Wildman (1998) and Bernhardt (1994).

An open or progressive Christology will be open to dialogue – and not simply on its own terms – with more absolutist Christologies, both incarnational and inspirational. It should not be forgotten that much Christology explicitly related to human rights has followed an absolutist pattern in the liberation theologies. It is, in any case, pointless to be open to dialogue with other religions and secular humanists on human rights issues, and then to be unwilling to engage constructively with wide sections of the Christian tradition. This would not be dissimilar to the all-too-common sight of churches in eager conversation with other world religions but not working constructively with other, often very similar, denominations.

We have referred to the Christ of terror, who is inimical to human rights. There is also, of course, the Christ of indifference, for whom rights issues are simply not a matter of serious theological concern. This has occurred classically in Pietism, but also happens in an Erastian concentration on the church and the established order for its own sake. Here again there is need for some care. Many theologians have studied Christology for its own sake and have also been heavily committed to human rights issues. But the field is vast enough to require extensive analysis without exploring this additional avenue.

This study is written from a progressive perspective, in the conviction that this is a true and deeply significant pathway to understanding Christ. It is not considered to be the exclusive truth, but it is done in the hope that this kind of open perspective may help illuminate some of the power structures which inhibit churches from pouring a maximum commitment into rights issues and being major contributors to their realization in society. No attempt will be made here to produce a Christology of epistemological purity in the search for an effective interface with human rights. It seems to me to be only common sense to seek to learn from the rich diversity of Christian thought in this urgent task. Wesley Wildman (1998) has distinguished instructively between absolutist and non-absolutist Christologies, and between incarnational and inspirational in different combinations. There are important intellectual choices to be made in determining which is most effective under what criteria.

Philosophers differ on whether there are absolutes in life. There will be a good case for maintaining some near absolutes, in practice if not in theory. It is always wrong to torture people. Violence, coercion, and manipulation are always wrong, but may, on rare occasions, be the lesser evil. In religion God is absolute – absolute unconditional love. Yet the language of absolutes is very often harmful in religious contexts. It has been the source of endless increased tension and discrimination. Wildman makes this point at the end of his study:

> To be encouraged by the church to resist the temptation to embrace hermeneutically absolutised renderings of reality, of personal development and salvation, of society and history, of ethics and sacraments – that would be a delight and a relief to many Christians, as well as to the hordes who avoid churches because of a praiseworthy, visceral allergy to absolutist blunderings through the mysterious delicacy and inexplicable brutality of life. (Wildman, 1998, 368)

I think that the renunciation of absolutes could be accorded greater weight in considering Christology. It is, of course, true that Christians regard the love of God in Jesus Christ as absolutely decisive in the process of God's realization of his future for humanity. But the method of realization deconstructs various sorts of absolutism. Rowan Williams has described the Christian context as one in which the events of the life of Jesus as 'grasped as the radical self-dispossession of God'(Williams, 2000). He sees this as a counter to undesirable aspects of both liberal and communitarian views of society. God realizes his selfhood precisely by giving himself to the other. There is, then, real selfhood in mutuality and solidarity.

Of course, this can be realized only when the rhetoric of mutuality takes on board an appropriate appreciation of gender and other equalities, as Irigaray has pointed out.

Williams sees the church, with all its flaws, as God's way of creating this Christomorphic community on earth. I am inclined to modify the perspective to imagine the church as a contribution – a pointer with all its pluses and minuses – to the realization of human community. Without making an unduly forced analogy, there should be some correspondence between the self-dispossession of God in incarnation and the self-dispossession of the church in community. This is not a dissolution, for the church gains its selfhood through this process. But it does mean that there is an ongoing process of mutual vulnerability, of fragmentation and reintegration of the fragments. It may sometimes be necessary to risk the unity of the church, valuable as this undoubtedly is, for the sake of solidarity with the marginalized. When Bonhoeffer famously stated that only the person who speaks up for the Jews has the right to sing Gregorian chants he recognized that maintaining the unity of the German church was not the overriding mandate of discipleship in all circumstances.[3] In speaking of a Christomorphic theology I want to underline the importance of God's engagement with history and historicality, and therefore

---

3   The tensions between the claims of internal unity and solidarity with the marginalized are always hard to resolve. It should be acknowledged freely that the issues such as women priests, the remarrying of divorcees, contraception and abortion continue to be divisive. Open theologies, traditional Christologies and conservative evangelical theologies are bound to work together provided that joint projects are purged of discriminatory elements. The late Donald Mackinnon was wont to speak eloquently of the accents of Caiaphas in ecclesiastical diplomacy.

Richard Bernstein's engaged fallible pluralism may again be an appropriate image. Some absolutist Christologies are strong on human rights: for example, orthodox Jesuits in Latin America oppose torture. Some absolutist Christologies support women's rights and other rights – M.M. Adams on gay issues, for example. But there is a need for a Christology which can cope with challenge of axial scriptures and so on .

Some Christologies are selectively pro human rights (for example, Cavanaugh, 1998, discussing Christians against torture in a radical Orthodox perspective). But theology must look to human rights beyond the Christian circle (this was a problem with the neo-Orthodox declaration of Barmen!). Hence liberal Christologies are required which will also relate to an often secular society.

Christology should offer an intellectual contribution to society, as well as an inner-Christian project to encourage the church. Modern human rights may be sometimes fairly seen as largely corrections of perceptions from the scriptures of the axial age.

Cobb and Placher both note how Christians continue to struggle with problems of identity and self-identity – for example, as whites more than as Christians (Placher, 2001a; Cobb, 2002). Local identity

with cultural and political particularity. But I also regard the tradition of mystical communion with God through Eucharistic presence as a vital dimension of a viable theology. For understanding this tension between the prophetic and the mystical I am indebted to David Tracy.

Beginning with the UDHR?

As a kind of unscientific postscript to the initial concept of a Christology for human rights it is instructive to consider just one or two features of the early Universal Declaration of Human Rights, in the light of the basic structuring elements of Christology.[4]

The Preamble

> Whereas recognition of the inherent dignity and the equal and inalienable rights of all members of the human family is the foundation of freedom, justice and peace in the world.

For Christian faith, Jesus Christ is often traditionally understood as the New Man, as the paradigm of the perfection of humanity under God. He is also understood as the cosmic Christ, the shape of the character of God's love in the universe. Jesus' respect for human beings can be seen as a parable or icon of recognition of inherent human dignity. Self-giving, self-affirming unconditional love can be imagined as a pointer to the articulation of recognizing dignity. The image of God in Christ may contribute to understanding the face of reciprocity and mutuality. This is not a limiting or triumphalist image, but an encouragement to humane practice:

> Whereas disregard and contempt for human rights have resulted in barbarous acts which have outraged the conscience of mankind...

There is recognition that humanity is able to distinguish right from wrong, and yet that horrendous barbaric evils occur. There is no 'answer' to the problem of evil. The Christ figure remains a constant pointer to how humans can cope with

---

is clearly good, but under wider identity of humanity under God, for which Christ is a pattern. It is often difficult to think of 'humanity' in the abstract. Here perhaps religion/Christianity can help.

I regard the work of D.M. Baillie and G.W.H. Lampe as important points of departure for progressive Christology, and I learn much from Cobb and Macquarrie, Hick, Rahner and Schillebeeckx, and Moltmann. But there is always much to be gleaned from Schleiermacher, Barth and Juengel, viewed in a tradition and not in isolation.

Christian theologies have often been discriminatory and damaging. On the other hand, there are a huge number of coercive and manipulative people who do not believe in God. Abandoning faith does not always make people more sensitive to the needs of others. They may become obsessed with other, penultimate values and lose the sense of discernment which an appreciation of transcendence is sometimes able to provide.

4   Cf. Eide *et al.* (1992). This detailed commentary covers each article, discussing the debate on its formulation and adoption, together with subsequent legal developments in each area.

evil, by creating selfless love in community. Beyond this, Christ brings a religious contribution to suggest that, in the future of humanity, goodness will effectively replace evil.

The General Assembly Proclaims the Universal Declaration of Human Rights

> **Article 1**. All human beings are born free and equal in dignity and rights. They
> are endowed with reason and conscience and should act towards one another in
> a spirit of brotherhood.

Jesus Christ, in a Christian perspective, provides a focus of particularity, emphasizing that the universal is achieved through the local, through attention to individuals and groups in society. Other figures provide other examples towards a common understanding. Christians will continue to believe additionally that the example of Jesus is reinforced through the distinctive incarnation of God in him.

> **Article 5**. No one shall be subjected to torture or to cruel, inhuman or degrading
> treatment or punishment.

Jesus Christ is understood by Christians as the executed God, tortured by the local judiciary through crucifixion. Torture is the evil against which God participates in death on the cross. The Christian perception is that torture is always evil and always wrong. There are no circumstances in which torture is allowable. To make this assertion is at once to acknowledge how far below their own standards Christian communities have fallen in the past and in the present.

Beyond this, any appraisal of 'cruel, inhuman or degrading treatment or punishment' in the light of a New Testament image of self-giving love is bound to raise immediate and urgent questions about prison conditions and numerous forms of degrading and marginalizing treatment, adding humane imagination to critical rationality.

> **Article 12**. No one shall be subjected to arbitrary interference with his privacy,
> family, home or correspondence, nor to attacks on his honour and reputation.
> Everyone has the right to the protection of the law against such interference or
> attacks.

We need only look at records of ecclesiastical jurisdiction – for example, the kirk session records of the Church of Scotland in the seventeenth century – to see how the praxis of a devout community can become a perfect counterexample and a salutary warning. It is worth stressing the constructive value of the negative, as well as the positive, examples still to be found in churches today.

Enabling Paradigms

We can see that the Christological reference need not be understood as a limiting, but as an enabling and catalytic, paradigm. In Christian history there has been a very strong tendency to prescribe the ways in which Christ should be understood and followed in practical life. Deviation from this norm is heresy, betrayal of the Church and of God. In the light of Jesus' own conduct, however, this can be seen to be a fundamental mistake. The Jesus of the New Testament narratives gives himself to others in trust, to be recognized freely by those to whom he relates on their own initiative. St Paul understands this theologically through the metaphor of self-emptying or kenosis, and through an understanding of the freedom of the spirit of Christ. 'Jesus means freedom' is more than a rhetorical slogan. It is of the essence of a Christological contribution to human rights.

These are perhaps some of the initial reactions which we might have to the juxtaposition of human rights language and Christological language. However, it seems clear that a Christian contribution to human rights will have to go beyond reflection on the continuing power of New Testament imagery. If justice, peace and freedom are to be delivered, then there has to be a renewed concentration on the dynamics of cases of human rights abuse, and perhaps a wider commitment by churches to such bodies as Amnesty International, alongside the work done by church organizations themselves.

There are, of course, specific religious human rights, which it is important to recognize, not least when these involve other people's religion or groups that have been traditionally discriminated against through being taught to be submissive – for example, women and black people in particular circumstances. Yet a Christian perspective will ultimately be more concerned with defending the rights of others than with claiming privilege for itself. That, too, belongs to the pattern of self-giving love.

CHAPTER 7

Christology in Relation to Global Human Rights Strategy

Marginality, Memory and Practical Solidarity

It is time to move the Christological trajectory forward towards outcomes. Faith sees the events concerning Jesus as relevant to the tensions which are perceived to exist between the universal and the local, the religious and the secular, that which is negotiable and that which is non-negotiable.

Jesus was focused on the specific people and situations in which he found himself. Yet, because God was involved here in a unique way, the concern shown becomes an ultimate concern for all humanity as well. Jesus was devoted to God, in worship and service. He was also deeply critical of religious practices for their own sake. This is a faith shared by Evangelicals and Catholics, progressive and traditional Christians. It contradicts a fundamentalist reading of the Bible which appeals to harsh readings of scriptural texts. Jesus came to abolish practices that were contrary to unconditional love. Where necessary he made judgements, but these were always the judgements of the kind of love instantiated by his life and teaching. If he had wished to adopt the stance of a stern and repressive religious figure he could easily have done so. The evidence suggests the opposite.

Jesus was faithful to, and instantiated, an ultimate standard of self-giving, unconditional love in all that he did. Yet he was prepared to examine and modify existing laws, social practices and religious conventions for the sake of the people with whom he was engaged. This balance of discernment between the essential and the non-essential, the changing and the unchanging, is part of the continuing Christian contribution to action towards human flourishing and to making an effective difference to human rights outcomes in local practice. To make this assessment is to interpret the tradition in a particular way, to highlight some features and to discount others. This is how tradition lives and grows. In this case it means revising many of the assumptions about texts, authorities and cultures of the axial period in which the great world religions first arose. That is a risk. A theology which believes in the continuing presence of the spirit of Christ in the world is a theology which is open to change and risk.

The Form of Christ in the World

Christian faith believes that the Christomorphic tradition continues. It manifests itself in the action of God through the hands of human beings who respond to God's invitation to transformation. Let us take a very brief selection of examples of Christian discipleship in a human rights context. The first figure to be cited here is Dietrich Bonhoeffer. Bonhoeffer appears never to have spoken of human rights as such. On the other hand, his support for the Jews is a classic statement of a human rights imperative'. As a theologian Bonhoeffer became increasingly alarmed by a regime which seemed to him to be taking the authority of God upon itself. Close contact with friends in the law courts and in the civil service confirmed this conviction, and drew Bonhoeffer into the conspiracy to assassinate Hitler. In the name of Christ he opposed the persecution of Jews and of all who criticized the government. His Christology led him to critique an ecclesiastical triumphalism which was unconcerned about those outside the church's own ranks. This led him to see, as he put it, the form of Christ in the world and to look for a future involving a kind of non-religious Christianity.

Bonhoeffer's vision of a secular spirituality was not to prove popular towards the end of the twentieth century. But his insistence that the church should be concerned for society in general and not simply for its own structure, and this precisely as obedience to Christ, was echoed in a new theology centred on the kingdom of God, which developed in various different directions. Here was a theology of Jesus Christ in solidarity with the despised and the outcast, and which led Bonhoeffer to political action, prison and death. There was debate after the war about whether Bonhoeffer could be counted as a Christian martyr because of his secular involvement. Arguably, however, Bonhoeffer himself would only have been concerned about faithful discipleship and effective action.

Bonhoeffer did not speak of human rights as such. Indeed, the term was not common in theological circles when he wrote. He speaks of the rights of natural life: 'There is no right before God, but the natural, purely as what is given, becomes the right in relation to man. The rights of natural life are in the midst of the fallen world the reflected splendour of the glory of God's creation' (Bonhoeffer, 151). It is not so much Bonhoeffer's writing on rights but his actions, in the context of his whole understanding of discipleship, that are paradigmatic here.

Another classic figure active in human rights issues because of his Christian convictions has been Archbishop Desmond Tutu. It is worth pausing to recall that many of the most courageous opponents of apartheid were also Christians. Tutu's Foreword in Witte's collection aptly sums up his approach to rights issues

> The life of every human being is an inviolable gift of God. And since this person is created in the image of God and is a God carrier a second consequence would be that we should not just respect such a person but that we should have a deep reverence for that person. (Witte and Van der Vyver, 1996, x)
> We must hang our heads in shame, however, when we survey the gory and shameful history of the Church of Christ. (Ibid., xiv)
>
> I can testify that our own struggle for justice, peace and equity would have floundered badly had we not been inspired by our Christian faith and assured of the ultimate victory of goodness, compassion and truth against their ghastly counterparts. (Ibid., xvi)

Tutu's witness to rights involved active participation against apartheid. In a different context we find a Christian testimony against the violation of human rights in Matthew Shepard, the gay Christian student who was crucified to a fence in Wyoming in 1998. A devout Episcopalian, Shepard has become a human rights icon for the younger generation, as his story has been reflected and absorbed in a huge number of website messages on the Internet.[1] It may be that generations of Christians to come will regard the churches' present stance on gay issues, and above all the message which is sent out to marginalized people outside the churches, with the same amazement that now accompanies our reaction to the theory and practice of slavery. As with the slaves, for many it will be too late.

I have concentrated here on Christian witnesses to human rights violations, against Nazism and anti-Semitism, against racism and apartheid, and against homophobia. But, of course, many outstanding defenders of human rights have not been Christians, and Christians have joined with others in admiring them and encouraging their witness. An outstanding example would be Aung San Suu Kyi in Myanmar. She is also a reminder that many hugely courageous women have fought for human rights.[2]

Collective Horrors

The people discussed above are courageous individuals who have fought for human rights, and for whom, in all but one case, Christian faith has been a defining factor. But human rights violations also affect whole communities and have a social dimension. Perhaps the clearest example of an attack on the human rights of a whole community in modern times was the Holocaust which was, as is well known, the immediate cause of the development of the United Nations' concern for human rights. This atrocity flagrantly demonstrated almost the whole spectrum of human rights abuses and had at its core racism in the form of anti-Semitism. The roots of this evil have been endlessly discussed. For centuries anti-Semitism had been endemic, especially in Christian countries, and then conditions in post-First World War Germany turned it into a potent weapon in Hitler's drive for power. Indeed, anti-Semitism remains a potent factor in world politics.

But the Holocaust was more than a matter of anti-Semitism. Any category of people who appeared to deviate from the Nazi norm was under threat of death: socialists, communists, foreign peoples, gays, gypsies and Jehovah's Witnesses were prime targets. The various categories were divided up in the concentration camps and then exterminated. This use of division was deliberate, and it is particularly unfortunate that, after the war, the various groups tended to commemorate their own dead and not the others who perished with them.

---

1   Cf. especially www.matthewsplace.org.
2   Cf. on Aung San Suu Kyi and others, Peter Paris, 'Global Exemplars', in Stackhouse and Paris (2000, 179ff).

Of course, more people have died in other modern holocausts – in Stalin's Russia, in Mao's China, and huge numbers in Rwanda. But the Nazi holocaust was remarkable on account of its meticulous planning and ruthless execution. It is also important for this study because many of the perpetrators were nominally Christian, and traditional anti-Semitic rhetoric from the pulpits of German churches contributed to the public feeling.

There were, of course, courageous Christian protests in fateful solidarity. But these were a minority, and even the record of the Confessing Church on the issue was ambiguous.

There are other situations where it is not the positive oppression of peoples but the neglect of their well-being which leads to the impossibility of achieving basic human capabilities and a denial of human rights. Most obvious, and in some ways most intractable because of the sheer unremitting scale of the problems, are poverty and hunger.

Almost as devastating as hunger is the problem of HIV/AIDS, predominantly in Africa but potentially also in Asia. The figures are staggering, as we all know. This is a good example of a case in which human rights issues are inextricably linked with international economic and commercial interests, and also with theological concerns. One of these concerns has been the interest in limiting contraception occasionally pursued by both Christian and Islamic bodies. Here there are difficult theological issues which have to be resolved for the sake of human beings who are at the point of greatest need, and where there is a fateful conflict of perceptions of rights.

The number of areas in which there is an urgent need for an increased awareness of human rights remains large. The short but excellent chapters of the Mobilization for the Human Family volume cover 'Religion in the Public Schools' (a particularly American issue), abortion, children, human rights and civil rights, homosexuality and same gender unions, crime and the penal system, drugs, immigration, sweatshops, the globalization of economics, the debt crisis, environmentalism, the global population crisis and the influence of the American Christian Right.

Reflection on the affirmation and denial of rights in the Christian tradition, in relation to individuals and to community issues, may suggest ways of negotiating future rights practice between religious and secular interests in diverse cultures. Here there is an important link to be maintained between marginality and memory. The whole raft of the modern emancipatory theologies addresses positively and creatively specific cases of discrimination. It retrieves the memory of the voiceless and the forgotten and, by honouring these memories, strengthens marginalized communities for the future. Documenting the suffering of women, black people, the Jewish people and other groups has often required considerable courage in the face of deep hostility, not least in the churches. It is a process which still has a very long way to go.

Faith beyond Resentment

How does human rights violation affect individuals? A classic account of the scale of the damage done to self-understanding through vilification, and of a positive response which transcends a negative reaction, is given by James Alison in his *Faith beyond Resentment* (2001). A Dominican condemned by many of his fellow Catholics,[3] thrown out by his order, devastated by his partner's death from AIDS, homeless and unemployed, Alison has nevertheless been able to produce a profound response through reflection on the crucified and risen Christ. He comments:

> The one sure way to prevent church teaching from being changed except in the direction of more closed-mindedness is to pander to the paranoia which undergirds it by playing its game. (Alison, 2001, 84)

Faith creates a new being, beyond resentment and reaction:

> We've been killed, lost a being, and find ourselves being given a new one. No, the amazement is that it is our experience of being killed which both empowers and obliges us to learn to tell a new story at a depth and in a way which actually makes it good news for others. (Ibid., 97)

He speaks of:

> The gradual emergence of a love which is not bound by, or in reaction to, all that whirlwind of anger and spurned love. (Ibid., 121)

The centre of this love is the Jesus event:

> Jesus did not come and give the Gerasenes a lecture on the structure of their society. He didn't argue with them about definitions. He didn't propose an alternative form of legislation. He did something much more three-dimensional.

---

3 Catholics are not worse in this regard than Protestants or indeed other denominations. Orthodoxy attempts to stifle discussion of gay issues in the WCC, while the Coptic patriarch, Pope Shenouda III, in 2003 encouraged the Egyptian government in its drive to remove what he termed the 'visible plague' of homosexuals from the land.

There is unfortunately very little reference to gay rights in 'mainstream' systematic theology. This makes the work of writers such as Alison, who combine classical doctrinal with social themes, all the more significant. James Keenan says of Alison's *Faith Beyond Resentment* that:

No other book today so concretely offers a real demonstration of how the texts can transform us. Alison offers us not a utopia but a liberating cross that leads to a resurrected life. (Keenan, 2004, 102)

Much of what has been written – for example, by H. Thielicke, in *The Ethics of Sex* (1964) – is entirely negative, reflecting the culture of the time. In the case of Karl Barth, the position is interesting. His remarks in CD,III.4, esp 166ff, are entirely negative and have been much used by conservative writers. There is a fascinating critique, using Barth's appeal to the order of nature against Barth himself, by Balboa (1998). However, it does not appear to have been noticed that in an illuminating 1968 letter, Barth stresses twice that these remarks were only made in passing (*beiläufig*), could be reconsidered in the light of newer information, and do not represent approval for 'pharisaical' defamation and 'irrational' punishment (Barth, 1945–68, 541f). We may wonder how much more of the text of the *Church Dogmatics* Barth himself considered to have been written '*beiläufig*'.

> He empowered the demoniac to become a human being, sitting, clothed and in
> his right mind, going home to his friends. (Ibid., 133)

Alison's approach is a remarkable Eucharist-centred strategy for rising above
negative polemics and refusing to be brutalized. But it remains open to others who
are not themselves vulnerable to oppression to bring support in the form of a much
more direct and robust challenge to oppressive behaviour at its sources. This applies
equally to slavery, poverty, racism and to the whole range of attacks on human
dignity.

There is a necessary constructive tension in a Christian approach to power and
force. The primary moment of this tension is the gift of the ability to lose – to lose
on behalf of others. This may be desperately hard to do, yet may have a pivotal
effect on intractable stalemates. But the secondary moment is the need to protect
others from coercion and perhaps genocide, if need be by using force. To stand
aside uttering benevolent platitudes when mass murder is being committed is no
part of an authentic Christian vision. To prevent murder being committed, often for
strong ideological reasons, may require a combination of political, economic and
perhaps military preparation which goes well beyond human rights issues alone,
and underlines the need for human rights issues to be integrated with political and
other action. Human rights concerns are not an occasion for taking a holiday from
geopolitical realities.

In a Different Voice: Elizabeth Schussler Fiorenza

A prime example of the value of emancipatory theology in unmasking human rights
violation is the development of feminist theology. Elizabeth Schussler Fiorenza's
classic *In Memory of Her* (1983) is worth looking at in some detail, both because
of its careful structure and because the exploitation of women remains a major
cause of human suffering today. The book is divided into three parts. In the first
part, 'Seeing–Naming–Reconstituting', Schussler Fiorenza explores a feminist
critical hermeneutics and considers models of biblical interpretation, paying special
attention to liberation theology, notably the pioneering examples of Elizabeth Cady
Stanton and Letty Russell:

> The basic insight of all liberation theologies, including feminist theology, is the
> recognition that all theology, willingly or not, is by definition always engaged
> for or against the oppressed. Intellectual neutrality is not possible in a world of
> exploitation and oppression. (Schussler Fiorenza, 1983, 6)

We then move towards a feminist critical method and immediately to the problem
of androcentrism. Androcentric language mentions women only when women's
behaviour presents a problem or when women are exceptional individuals. There is
a particular problem with biblical translations, often done by men.

Schussler Fiorenza notes that Jesus never seems to demand the submission of
women. On the other hand the Fathers, especially Tertullian and Jerome, consistently

attacked the leadership of women. In the face of patriarchalism, she asks, how is a feminist model of historical reconstruction possible? The early Christian situation was not monolithic but multifaceted. For 200 years, Christianity was essentially a movement among the disprivileged. But what Theissen has called a 'love-patriarchalism' eventually prevailed. Oppression of working-class men may in turn have generated more oppression of women in their culture.

Part II is entitled 'In Memory of Her: Women's History as the History of the Discipleship of Equals'. Here, Schussler Fiorenza examines the Jesus movement as a renewal movement within Judaism. Jesus' movement can be seen as an alternative to the dominant patriarchal structures within Judaism: 'The power of God's *basileia* (realm) is realised in Jesus' table community with the poor, the sinners, the tax collectors and prostitutes' (ibid., 121). Women were decisive for the continuation of the movement after Jesus' arrest and execution: 'Without question the discipleship of Jesus does not respect patriarchal family bonds' (ibid., 146). The author then turns to the Early Christian Missionary Movement, as Equality in the Power of the Spirit. We see from the Pauline literature and Acts that women were among the most prominent missionaries and leaders in the early Christian movement (ibid., 184). This is made precise by examining Galatians 3:28: 'There is neither male nor female.' 'Patriarchal marriage – and sexual relationships between male and female – is no longer constitutive of the new community in Christ' (ibid., 210). Paul is concerned, however, to preserve order and propriety.

Part III is entitled 'Tracing the Struggles: Patriarchy and Ministry'. Schussler Fiorenza describes how the vision of the discipleship of equals created tensions in the prevailing patriarchal culture. Christians were suspected of political subversion and of threatening the social fabric of society. This led to tensions between the patriarchal household of God and the *ekklesia* of women, notably in the struggle against Montanism. Mark's Gospel insists on the necessity of suffering and the call to suffering discipleship – exemplified by the women disciples. Mary Magdalene is 'the primary apostolic witness to the resurrection' (ibid., 332) – a challenge to the Petrine tradition. Mark and John 'accord women apostolic and ministerial leadership' (ibid., 334).

The Epilogue turns 'Towards a Feminist Biblical Spirituality: The Ekklesia of Women'. Conventional images of women must be revised:

> Rather than defining women's relationship to God by their sexual relationship to men and through the patriarchal structures of family and church, a feminist Christian spirituality defines women's relationship to God in and through the experience of being called into a discipleship of equals, the assembly of free citizens who decide their own spiritual welfare. (Ibid., 349)

She concludes:

> In breaking the bread and sharing the cup we proclaim not only the passion and resurrection of Christ but also celebrate that of women in biblical religion. (Ibid., 351)

In Memory of Her is a powerful and deeply erudite example of a critical liberation theology which may serve as an eloquent paradigm for other theologies within the range of emancipatory concerns, and brilliantly illustrates the innovative developments in contemporary theology. It shows, among other things, how a theology can be liberal but within an inclusive Catholic tradition, without the need to embrace the anti-modernism of some other developments in recent Christian thought.[4]

The outcome of analysis of the affirmation and denial of rights in the Christian tradition, in relation to individuals and to community issues, may be used to suggest ways of negotiating future rights practice between religious and secular interests in diverse cultures. How can this be done?

The Human Rights Future and the Christian Future – A New Exclusivism?

Global questions of economic inequality and disputes over such issues as contraception raise the problem sometimes termed as a 'clash of civilizations' and its consequences for human rights. In his bold project, *The Next Christendom* (2002), Philip Jenkins has painted a picture of a Christianity split radically between a liberal North and a much larger and very conservative South. The South differs from the North, especially in relation to issues of social ethics (Jenkins sees the Anglican Lambeth Conference of 1998 as indicating this trend), and could be involved in conflict in various parts of the world with an equally conservative Islam. Jenkins describes this scenario with apparent objectivity, not to say equanimity, and does not really offer any serious solutions to the problem of defusing these potentially very serious tensions. Clearly, however, a new version of global warfare would do little to advance the cause of human rights.

Jenkins's picture may be too apocalyptic. Others have pointed out that Islamic states are very often divided on political issues and that there are also many religious differences (cf. also Markham and Abu-Rabi, 2002). To be Muslim is not necessarily to be Islamist. As Halliday comments on the crisis of 11 September 2001:

> The root cause of this crisis is intellectual, the lack of realistic education and democratic culture in a range of countries, such that irrational hatred and conspiracy theory prevail over reasoned critique. This crisis is reinforced through the inaction and insouciance of much of the developed world in the face of the inequalities and conflicts beyond its borders. Neither of these deep

---

4   Talbott gives a good account of women's rights:

> If human beings had direct insight into moral truths, the development of basic human rights would not have taken millennia. Women's rights are a particularly good example of the bottom-up development of basic human rights, because even the pioneers of rights for men often had a moral blindness that prevented them from seeing that these rights should extend to women. (Talbott, 2005, 89)

He notes the social enforcement of patriarchal institutions (ibid., 95) and enforcement by convention (foot binding) (ibid., 97).

cultural and psychological phenomena can, or will, be overcome in short order. (Halliday, 2002, 216)

However, if there is anything in Jenkins's thesis, it is in the way in which it underlines the need for Christians to agree on practical measures to implement human rights even when they approach the issues from different angles. It should be possible to imagine the importance of the person of Jesus Christ for human rights from a number of different Christological perspectives, and to see that the underlying Christian reality is much more important than the differing methodologies. It becomes imperative, too, to construct Christologies which are able to dialogue with Islam and other faiths concerning the nature of ultimate reality and of God's purposes for humanity, without creating fresh tensions of a destructive nature.

In his forthcoming study, *This Side of God*, David Tracy lays new stress on the hiddenness and incomprehensibility of God, in contrast to the exegetical doctrinal precision suggested in Jenkins's scenario. While Jenkins sees stress on the apocalyptic as leading to new orthodoxies and a search for confessional conformity, Tracy sees the apocalyptic as related to the prophetic and the apophatic, emphasizing the importance of fragments and the dangers of totalizing systems. A Christology which is a Christology of the spirit will value openness and provisionality. We need to be patient, to keep open channels of communication in any direction, and to refrain from making penultimate judgements about the ultimate.

Such an open theology will have commonalities with many traditions – for example, with Orthodox traditions of apophaticism and with Barth's understanding of eschatological provisionality, as well as with classical liberal and mystical traditions, from Cusanus to Schleiermacher.

Reconciliation as Outcome

In the field of human rights, the understanding of Christ as reconciler is likely to be particularly relevant. Of course, reconciliation can often be abused as a strategy for various forms of coercion, and it can be understood in many different ways in different cultures, both ecclesiastical and secular. Here, I see it as a 'thick concept' to be offered for use by different partners in a search for reconciliation in perhaps different, but overlapping, ways. Reconciliation involves a large measure of mutual acceptance, respect and recognition. This is not easy, especially where there has been a history of mistrust and conflict. Christians, as much as anyone else, have occasioned mistrust, and that is a challenge to work at rather than a reason to desist.

Ultimately, it seems to me that progressive theology demands a radical reassessment and retrieval of the Christian tradition. If twentieth-century Christian theology has been predominantly anti-modern and twenty-first century theology is likely to be even more so, then progressive options need to be spelled out clearly in order to provide well-founded and viable alternative ways. This cannot be done here, but some suggestions arising from our discussion of Christ and human rights can be laid out.

Ultimately a Christian contribution to human rights issues must be judged not only on intentions, but on results. There has been much theory on human rights but less concentration on strategies for achieving results. An exception is *Effective Strategies for Protecting Human Rights*, edited by David Barnhizer (2001).

Barnhizer has suggested powerfully that one of the most important things to grasp about human rights strategy is that, most of the time, it is not working. Governments and individuals flaunt human right violations at will, and there is often little to be done about it. He gives examples of the deployment of human rights as a strategic system – in tackling abuse in American prisons, the understanding of victims, women's rights, rights and international politics, genocide in Rwanda and contemporary slavery.

In considering the obstacles to implementation, Barnhizer reminds us that 'the factors include deliberate weakening of human rights institutions by those who fear they might be called to account for their actions' (Barnhizer, 2001, 5). He adds that 'there are severely limited resources available to those who want a strong human rights system. There is also a continuing lack of political will and follow-through' (ibid., 17). There is, he argues, a need for context-specific solutions and strong and predictable sanctions.

A reading of the case studies in the volume underlines the enormity of the task still facing human rights workers. It becomes clear that theory without a human rights culture, including the political will to do what is necessary to secure rights, is entirely ineffective. The challenge for Christian communities is to contribute to the creation of a culture more responsive to the effective delivery of rights.

Christology for Human Rights Reimagined

In seeking for an understanding of Christ which relates to human rights issues we need to try to reimagine our Christological perspectives. What I have in mind is not so much a particular framework as a set of parameters within which a human rights-oriented Christology can best be imagined. The reason for this is that I do not think that only one framework can be said to be the best in all circumstances. Important contributions to human rights have been made by people who maintained very different Christologies: some exclusive and absolutist, some inclusive, some pluralist. Rahner and Barth, Chalcedonian and non-Chalcedonian models – many avenues may be, and have been, taken. We have already noted particular dangers in particular frameworks in the course of historical development – kenosis/ empowerment, atonement/forgiveness/reconciliation – and some of these have proved more susceptible to abuse of particular human rights than others. We need to note the abuses, but may still use some of the concepts with care (as with the resources in other fields, like medicine and law.) The challenge is to try to find an appropriate imaginative shape of Jesus Christ in a rights context.

Many different Christologies can support tolerance, justice, mutuality and reciprocity, although much may depend on the cultural setting in which the individual Christology is placed. In seeking to find an open and porous Christology there is clearly a need to avoid the doctrinaire liberalism that reduces everything to an intolerant norm, or the pluralism which rejects anything that does not conform to its own epistemology. An open theology has no final frameworks, although an open Christian theology is always subject to the pattern of the love of God in Christ. There are, of course, numerous reflections on freedom, justice and equality in modern Christology – for example, Kaesemann, Moltmann, Schillebeeckx [5] and the emancipatory theologians whom we have already met. But there is little on human rights as such. What follows should be seen as a preliminary attempt at a more explicit reflection on human rights issues in relation to Christ.

We all have our own culturally influenced impressions of Jesus of Nazareth, and it is right that we should recognize where we come from. Jesus comes through the New Testament picture to me as somewhat like one of these extraordinary human

---

5   Schillebeeckx's version of an open theology is an exemplary shape for a human rights-oriented theology. There is a good account of it in Daniel Thompson's *The Language of Dissent* (2003). In the Foreword Schillebeeckx himself looks to a church which will address the suffering which afflicts so much of the world's population. He identifies the danger of fundamentalisms and of ethnic nationalism, and calls for a view not only of the church but of faith itself, which will resonate with contemporary culture.

The early Schillebeeckx imagines a 'perspectivalism' between abstract conceptualism and subjectivist modernism. He wishes not to abandon tradition but to make it truly intelligible to contemporary experience. In 1966, after Vatican II, comes a hermeneutical turn to a greater emphasis on the pole of experience. All experience is interpreted experience, within a culturally shaped community. Orthopraxis is the test for correct interpretation. In a third move, influenced by critical theory, praxis is to become a source of interpretation. Knowledge of reality comes through practical mediation. But crucially also, praxis which does not disclose truth lacks content and may enslave people. A proper theological epistemology will be 'critically conscious, orientated to praxis, and ultimately open to the saving presence of God' (Thompson, 2003, 45).

God as creator is always relating to us as a saving presence. Salvation comes in creation through history, as God is experienced as the future of humanity. This appears in human lives as the sacramental experience of grace. Christology is, in a famous expression, concentrated creation. Jesus is one who has a unique experience of the closeness of God. This remains a mystery, but is expressed in his praxis of the consequences of the kingdom of God. This language must be tested by a praxis which identifies with the marginalized. Within the church are the structures of mediation, as sacrament of Christ and of the world (ibid., 74). The church reveals the presence of Christ, but by poor praxis may also hide it. Vatican II is a breakthrough, a rediscovery of faith as self-giving rather than self-assertion, a sign of *sacramentum mundi* involving a 'political holiness'.

Where, then, lies authority? Both hierarchy and laity have distinctive roles within the church. Dogmas may be truth but remain subject to the limitations of language. Theologians stand at the crossroads between faith and modern philosophical thought. The church's indefectibility comes through the renewing power of the spirit. In his later work Schillebeeckx emphasizes the connection between orthodoxy and orthopraxis. Papal infallibility has to be located within the infallibility of the world church. Critical communities within the church become important, against reactionary forces (ibid., 140).

Schillebeeckx came to regard theological dissent and critical communities as sacraments of the future church. Such communities may 'act as a critical leaven for church and world by their alternative praxis' (ibid., 156). There is a need for democracy in the church. Identification with suffering in praxis may be costly, but it remains the Christian vision for humanity. Schillebeeckx is out of fashion, too liberal for traditional Catholicism and too modern for fashionable postmodernity. Yet his call for critical communities of solidarity may become increasingly relevant to Christians beyond Roman Catholicism, as a deeply conservative biblicism becomes a more powerful force within world Christianity.

beings we sometimes encounter, who is entirely generous, selfless, a privilege to know and who sets a somewhat frightening standard of existing. The record is, of course, fragile, and the scholarly consensus is subject to change

Formalizing this impression, I take his central characteristic to be self-giving love, directed in the first instance at those outside the magic circle, as well as the disciples. His humanity as a person in a specific place is vitally important. In terms of faith, this is a pattern for our understanding of true humanity. My suggestion is a shape in the tradition of humanistic Christology. But this shape is also the shape of the love of God, definitively instantiated, in Christian understanding. A Jesucentric image would not suggest insights into the mystery of God. Jesus is an icon of the God who is also perceived through other faiths. In seeking to understand this self-giving God in Christ I am drawn to the humanist Christological tradition of Schillebeeckx, Donald Baillie, John Cobb and Elizabeth Schussler Fiorenza. I see as particularly appropriate the emancipatory Christological reflections of such scholars as Blount. But I recognize that much of value to human rights issues can be found in Christologies in a different key – for example, from Karl Barth, Dietrich Bonhoeffer and William Placher. From this base it is necessary to try to offer a developed Christological model, as contribution rather than conclusion, for further development, but as clearly focused as possible.

Some of what has just been suggested is encapsulated, from a different theological direction, in Alison's *Knowing Jesus* (1993). Here an essentially classical Christological structure and an appeal to Eucharistic spirituality are deployed, not to close doors but to open them unconditionally to people outside the community. Alison makes clever use of the notion of 'the intelligence of the victim', who, through the power of the resurrection, is freed from all pressures:

> The intelligence of the victim comes from a freedom in giving oneself to others, in not being moved by the violence of others, even when it is perceived that this free giving is going to be lynched as a result. This free giving is not a seeking to be lynched, but is completely open-eyed about the probability of just this happening. (Alison, 1993, 45)

As he says a little later:

> The presence of the forgiving victim is inescapably subversive of any society that bases itself on victims, and on all and every human relationship that bases itself on exclusion. However obscurely people perceive this, they are still aware that a challenge is posed to their society, to their relationships. The voice of the victim, the voice of God, cannot be hushed. (Ibid., 79)

But knowledge of Jesus precisely excludes any pretence to victim status on our part:

> We have only one self-giving victim, whose self-giving was quite outside any contamination of human violence or exploitation. The rest of us are all involved with that violence. (Ibid., 92)

Incarnation as Constructive Relationality

Human rights are concerned with the quality of human relations, both individual and corporate, and the need to protect the dignity of human beings. How can the Christological mystery and human rights concerns mutually illuminate each other?

When we place human rights concerns in front of our texts, as it were, the Jesus of the gospels may come across to us as a refugee. Whatever the historical situation, Jesus' early family life is tinged with the tone of fragility and insecurity. Many outstanding Christians have begun life in privileged circumstances, but this does not appear to have been the case for Jesus himself. It is always dangerous to say of people that 'he must have felt this way' or 'she must have experienced that'. Different people react to situations differently. But we are all shaped and moulded by our personal and social relations.[6]

Think of the classical distinction between the person and the work of Christ. In the tradition we have been inclined to see the person as essentially moulded by his direct relation to God, and his work, his relation to others, as a self-giving, reconciling work coming from God's self- dispossession into the human person. We might reflect that Jesus, like all of us, becomes who he is in his social interactions, and that this, too, may be seen as God's action in Christ. What is striking in the narrative tradition is the note of attention to outsiders, not just to impart wisdom but to receive the benefits of human interaction from these outsiders. There is a pivotal sense in which we may say that his work of reconciliation itself constitutes his being as a being for others, and that this is how God was in Christ, reconciling the world to himself. In this distinctive turning to others the dogmatic commonplace, 'he is what he does and he does what he is', may gain a new existential significance for the understanding of the action of God.

The hints that we have of the life of Jesus suggest that he was much dependent on a core of close male and female friends, as well as on casual acquaintances, for support. We might reflect that this highlights those connections between the individual and the social, and the ecclesial and the secular, that the theological tradition has not always been able to hold together. We should note also that this total social embeddedness was not a substitute but a framework for his consciousness of a deep relationship with God. It is this insistence that Jesus' self-giving love was the instantiation of the love of God the creator which raises the fundamental question

---

6   A particular form of relationality is intrinsic to being human. This extends even to our biology. We may perhaps remind ourselves of the extent to which our identities depend on biological as well as cultural factors:

Facial expression and the perception of emotion play a vital role in our visual communication. With the thinning of primatial facial hair, the face emerged as a canvas of self-presentation. Upward through mammalian evolution there was a progressive refinement of the structures of the face and improved neurological control of the facial muscles that facilitated active and increasingly subtle communication. During the transition toward visual sensory dominance, primates developed upper lips that were unattached to the gums, allowing a much wider range of expression. With more than 30 finely tuned muscles of facial expression and vocal control, human beings are capable of a wide variety of communicative expressions of emotions and intentions. (W. Hurlbut in Post, 2003, 311)

mark against centuries of ecclesial exclusivism and underlines God's comprehensive concern for the well-being of every human being.

The life of Jesus alone has never been the sole ground for faith in Jesus Christ. His death was to be understood as a decisive sign of God's permanent solidarity with human suffering through Jesus' suffering to the point of death. And, despite the shape of the narratives as passion narratives, the shape of Jesus Christ is not solely one of martyrdom or victimhood. It is a signal of a successful and transformative new beginning in the face of disaster. This, as we shall see, is also of huge significance for a human rights Christology.

Where does a humane, human rights-oriented Christology go from here? Much of the energy of the early church was soon to be devoted to the relationship between the divinity and the humanity of Jesus as the Christ. This was a necessary discourse but, in its concentration on individual humanity in relation to the being of God, was again a potential distraction from that constitutive human relationality of Jesus, which was also the medium of the action of God. Relationality re-emerged with the Trinitarian discussion; but already the shape of the individual Christ and the Trinity is seriously incomplete. The Christomorphic action of God as Spirit may be grounded in the human sociality of Jesus, which is affirmed as it is fragmented in the cross and renewed in the resurrection.

This has implications for the understanding of reconciliation as salvation, leading to an individualized Christ saving individuals as brands from the fire, pulled out of the *massa peccati*, the multitude of the damned. In a Christological pattern which majors on the social connectedness of Christ, we might see individuals as reconciled by the spirit of Christ from within their social relationships, as God's grace works though the mutuality and reciprocity of genuinely compassionate interaction. Here the springs of Christology and concern for human rights issues inextricably interlock. There is no salvation without affirmation of the strangers in our midst. The Word of God is given to be sacramentalized in communal and social relationships.

Compassionate Instantiation: The Matrix of a Human Rights Christology

Faith without works is dead. The epistle of James has never been regarded as particularly profound theology, and Luther's famous dismissal of it as a 'right strawy epistle' is symptomatic. Yet focus on justification by faith is only one side of the gospel and may become an excuse for an introversion which avoids the challenge of otherness and the physical and spiritual needs of strangers. We may explore further the grounds of faith from a Christological and human rights perspective.

At the centre of Christology is the fact that Jesus begins his ministry in the unglamorous setting of Galilee and preaches to fishermen. He is much concerned for the physically ill and the mentally unstable. He teaches largely in parables or in brief homilies. He expects the advent of the promised reign of God, and he sees this as preceded by suffering. He is concerned for justice, the poor and the compassionate interpretation of law. Violence and injustice are firmly ruled out. Without going into detail we may note the striking absence from this brief sketch of the rich and the powerful, the scholars and the image-makers – of the social milieu of most of the shapers of theology and church in the coming centuries.

The ethical teaching of the Sermon on the Mount and the Lord's Prayer, of compassion for humanity and simple trust in God, sum up this activity. It leads eventually to opposition, arrest as a source of social unrest, trial, torture and execution. Through the retrospective of faith in the resurrected Christ Christians have seen God's action as decisively instantiated his life and teaching, in his encounter with a totalitarian state and an insecure religious establishment, in his trial, torture and crucifixion. As we have seen, a harsh penal process has been viewed in the past as in some sense validated and justified by God. But this is clearly a complete inversion of the situation when viewed from a human rights perspective. On this view, God is bound in solidarity with prisoners and with the tortured, and the cross is a condemnation of all unjust punishment in human history.

The resurrection, however that may be understood, is a sign in the history of faith that God is not only compassionate but is also the source of effective transformation. The cause of compassionate, self-dispossessing love is not a lost cause.

Divinity and Humanity: Salvation through a Slave

It cannot be reiterated enough that a modest Christology need not be a reductionist Christology. Christology is about divinity and humanity, about God reconciling the world to himself in Christ. Christology is about the life, death and resurrection of Jesus in relation to humanity and to God. For Christian faith Jesus is, in a decisive sense, the basic form of humanity, and he is this as the man for others. He is a challenge to all barriers of tribalism and exclusion. For him, humanity means mutuality and reciprocity without barriers. For the rest of us there will always be reservations.

The reason for the difference is the continuous presence of the grace of God in Jesus. This recognition is a post-resurrection recognition, and it leads Christians to affirm true divinity in and through his humanity. Henceforth God acts through humanity for humanity; it is through the transformative humanity of Jesus that we recognize the divinity within him. The trajectory of a humanist Christology recognizes divinity precisely in a humanity that is oriented towards others. We may call this an incarnational or a spirit Christology, depending on which aspects of the Christological shape we wish to emphasize. It will not be an exclusive Christology, precisely because all of humanity is included in the movement of reciprocity which Jesus instantiates. But it will not prescribe one pattern of pluralist framework, for it will recognize that the freedom of complete inclusion is sited in the person of Jesus and not solely in the formulas of one particular school of thought. The human mind and will are seen to be significantly shaped by mutual interaction with other human minds. This may be a way of seeing the impact of the mind of God, who communicates in, with and under human action in a paradox of grace. Christ takes the form of a slave and, in doing so, challenges the exploitation and inequality of slavery.

The Chalcedonian Christology, though a compromise agreement, was inevitably a form of absolutist agreement. It could hardly have been otherwise in the culture of the period. Those who did not receive it were anathema. Whole churches suffered terrible destruction in the wake of their unwillingness to sign up. Yet this does not mean that a modern humanistic Christology need always be incompatible with, or indeed superior to, many of the intentions of those who met at Chalcedon. As we have already noted, a postmodern, pluralistic Christology can be just as coercive as the patterns which it seeks to oppose. A Christology which engages with human rights will be likely to learn from a broad stream of traditions.

This leads us naturally to the question of the nature of reconciliation as salvation. Salvation is freedom from exclusion, inequality and exploitation. But since these traits are pervasively present in our own tribalistic prejudices, salvation is also, importantly, freedom from ourselves.

Salvation is salvation from exclusion, an introduction to that generosity which involves reciprocity. Salvation, to use Miroslav Volf's phrase, is the turn from exclusion to embrace. Atonement is the uniting of humanity in solidarity, and therefore the opposite of theories of penal substitution and punishment-related ritual. Atonement is solidarity in compassion, sympathy and empathy, as God through the cross creates transformation through solidarity. It is, of course, possible to reinterpret traditional satisfaction theories in terms of humiliation and exaltation to stress the solidarity of God with us, as Karl Barth has brilliantly shown in his use of the story of the prodigal son. But the history of the tradition seems to suggest that it may often be safer to start from a theology of solidarity linked to all-encompassing forgiveness, in the tradition of Abelard. Perhaps only the angels can be trusted with some of the biblical imagery, and we are not angels. (Although we must then say immediately that solidarity is not a magic formula either: gestures of solidarity can be read as patronizing, misleading and even threatening, giving rise to classic liberal dilemmas.)

In the classical tradition of Christology Christ is often portrayed as word and as sacrament. These concepts express faith's perception of the continuing presence of Christ to human beings. They indicate the action of the spirit of God as the spirit of the crucified and risen Christ. The Word is understood as a living word, in which a specific message makes its impact in the present as the Word of God. The sacrament is understood as the embeddedness of the divine presence within the material substantiality of the universe. In this way the reality of the self-giving Christ may be articulated in particular words – words of compassion, justice and equity – and in the sacramental embodiment of self-giving within the social structures of society. The cognitive and the social dimensions of the Christ event are summed up in the Johannine confession that Christ is the way, the truth and the life. But this claim as always is subject to the primary focus of a self-dispossessing way, truth and life. That is perhaps always the hardest notion for Christian communities to assimilate.

In this study we have laid stress on what one might term the humanist dimension of Christology, upon the call to discipleship as a human response to the love of God in Jesus Christ. Christians believe that an important consequence of the resurrection was God's commitment of his love into the hands of those who would be disciples. Grace is given in word and sacrament to be poured out in commitment to others. But, in all this, God continues to be ceaselessly active in the created order as the power of kenotic love. Human action is dependent, consciously or unconsciously, on the priority of the divine love. This is the antidote to exhaustion, compassion fatigue and possible despair. The surprising invitation of the divine love as the basis of all discipleship cannot be too strongly emphasized. We love God and our fellow human beings because God first loves us.

We find that the Christological subject matter itself can illuminate and be illuminated by human rights concerns. It would be too much to claim that a Christology should be developed only from this perspective. Human rights are only one area that may stimulate reflection on the mystery of Christ. The suggestion is rather that a connection can be made that enables our understanding of Christ to revitalize our concern for human rights issues – not to lament the past or forecast the future, but to act in our own time.

Strange Forms of Salvation

Finally, in seeking to develop a Christology oriented towards human rights we should not lose sight of the fact that Christian theology can no longer be done purely in the context of an underlying European Christendom. We cannot have realism without accounting for this complexity.

The actualization of human rights in many areas is crucially dependent on constructive cooperation between different faiths. Here there is a huge legacy of suspicion to be overcome. The question of a theology of world religions is not a subject which can be entered into here. But the importance of interfaith dialogue should at least be signalled. Jesus Christ is, and remains, the centre of Christianity. But this need not lead to hegemony, domination and the blind conviction that Christendom knows best. Awareness of cultural diversity and identity, and of the symbolic nature of our language, should help us move forward.

We have seen a welcome emphasis on a Christology of vulnerability. Paul Knitter has conceived of Jesus as universal, decisive and indispensable, rather than as full, definitive and unsurpassable revelation. C. S. Song has characterized Jesus as the clue to the character of God as love, as the God of the outcasts and the marginalized. Emphasis has been placed on a spirit Christology in parallel with a word Christology as a means of opening up dialogue. John Cobb writes of a Christological trace in the creative transformation in political events. Jesus Christ is understood as a decisive, but not unique, access to transcendence, as the Spirit of God works beyond the boundaries of Christianity. God is Spirit, mysterious and hidden. But not every spirit is of God. There is always the danger of self-delusion – we have the Spirit, you have not. Only actions consonant with self-giving love can be of the Spirit of God, which Christians understand as the spirit of Christlikeness. Here there is, of course, a danger of a covert imperialism of the cosmic Christ: the spirit is never a possession; it is given to be given away.

Perhaps one of the most important goals of interfaith dialogue is not to solve all the residual theological issues but to agree on the fruits of the spirit – love, peace and justice. Here, and notably in a human rights context, is the possibility of movement towards a consensus between civilizations. Although there are different approaches there are common criteria – only compassionate ways are the ways of the spirit. The nature of love is disclosed in conversation and engagement, mutuality and respect in relationships, in an encounter which embraces all equally, religious and non-religious alike.

A good example of the level of reflection required in searching for different strands of consensus between civilizations is to be seen in the valuable discussion of the main issues concerning the realities of human rights across cultures in Joanne Bauer's and Daniel Bell's collection, *The East Asian Challenge to Human Rights* (1999). In his essay, Inoue Tatsuo shows how debates between advocates of 'Western' and 'Asian' human rights concepts suffer from mutual misperceptions, notably between an individualist West and a communitarian Asia. For Jack Donnelly, the fact that human rights ideas first emerged in early modern Europe does not prove that these ideas are any less applicable in East Asia. Amartya Sen argues that rights have intrinsic value, regardless of their economic and social consequences:

> One of the most remarkable facts about famines in the world is that no substantial famine has ever occurred in any country with a democratic form of government and a relatively free press. (Sen in Bauer and Bell, 1999, 92)

Charles Taylor considers the possibility of a 'genuine, unforced consensus' on human rights norms. Abdullahi An-Naim and Norani Othman argue that the 'cultural mediation' of human rights is needed if universality is to be taken seriously. Where dominating interpretations about a particular tradition (for example, Islam) need to be challenged, this must be done within the local culture. In other cases, the problem is not cultural factors but structural economic forces, which create very poor working conditions and mass unemployment.

Bauer and Bell note that:

> One important insight that has emerged from our years of dialogue is that the impact of economic globalization on vulnerable members of society has produced strikingly similar social conditions on both sides of the Pacific, such as poverty, inadequate housing, lack of access to health care, environmental degradation, and weakening social security nets. (Ibid., 23)

It is easier for those of us who live and work in Northern Europe to forget just how incredibly bad social conditions are for the huge majority of the world's population in the southern hemisphere, in Asia and in Africa:

The North, with about one fourth of the world's population, consumes 70 percent of the world's energy, 75% of its metals, 85% of its wood and 60 percent of its food. Contrast this with the situation in the South. Over one billion people are mired in absolute poverty. One and a half billion people are deprived of primary health care. About one billion adults are illiterate. What this shows is that a huge proportion of the population in the South do not enjoy the most basic economic and social rights. (Suwanna Satha-Anand in Bauer and Bell, 1999, 195)

What this comes down to in terms of human exploitation is vividly spelled out in Satha-Anand's account of Thai prostitution:

With a total population of 60 million, Thailand has an estimated 200,000–700,000 prostitutes, of which 30,000–35,000 are child prostitutes, according to most NGOs… In terms of sex service operators, the NGO estimate is roughly 60,000, whereas the official figure is 6,160 for female prostitutes and 58 for male prostitutes. (Ibid., 201)

Even this is not the worst position. Within these communities, as elsewhere, immigrant workers are usually at the bottom end of the scale of deprivation. But at least the sex trade offers some protection against the starvation which kills millions of people every year. Although all human rights violations are to be regretted and opposed, the sheer scale of the problem brings home the urgency of the need to tackle these issues in their most intransigent forms throughout the world.

Without food, healthcare and work it is difficult to talk about such issues as political rights, although, as we have seen, hunger and totalitarianism tend to coincide. It remains important in any just and fair society to attend to political and civil liberties. Accounts like the annual Freedom House Survey continue to produce countless instances of the serious curtailment of these liberties in a majority of countries. Simply taking the first entries from the 2000–2001 survey (Karatnycky, 2001) makes the point. There was (and is) serious violation of civil and political liberties in Afghanistan, first under the Taliban and now in the uneven administration of the new US-backed government. In Angola there are crippling restrictions on the press and trade unions. In Antigua a single family owns and controls the television and radio outlets. In Argentina there is still a police culture of excessive violence, and prison conditions are appalling. In Armenia there has been widespread judicial corruption and the use of torture. In Australia there is a huge legacy of abuse of indigenous peoples to be overcome. The list of violations extends to every country in the world, although some of the violations appear perhaps less significant in the face of the massive oppression in the worst cases.

Christological perspectives may have both positive and negative value in contributing to human rights issues. Positively, reflection upon Christ has encouraged Christians to work by themselves and with others in addressing effectively many areas of human rights – individual liberty, torture, political rights such as the right to justice, and economic rights like the right to be free from hunger. This effort has been largely ineffective where scriptural tradition has had a strong influence in inhibiting rights – most notably in the areas of gender and sexuality. Here perhaps we have to look elsewhere for guidance. But Christianity has shown the capacity for change and development – for example, in relation to such issues as slavery and race. We should not expect that today's status quo will be repeated in a hundred years from now. The Christian tradition has potential, in reflecting on the dynamic of relationality and respect for others expressed in the events concerning Jesus Christ, to have universal application even in areas where it has so far largely failed. If it is able to face up critically to its failures it may have a future role in encouraging other traditions, both religious and secular, to confront their weaknesses and make appropriate changes in attitude and action. It may also learn from such dialogue to widen its own base of human rights commitments in the long-term future. At present it may be important to concentrate action within the Christian tradition on human rights issues where there is a large measure of agreement, while continuing to work on areas of disagreement. It will remain open to respond to the Christological vision by working with organizations outside church structures in areas where these are more likely to be effective. In this way human rights action may be seen as part of the consequences of the form of Christ in the world.

CHAPTER 8

Rights Reconsidered: Building a Postfoundational Pathway

Towards Effective Human Rights Strategies: A Culture of Human Rights

We have now examined a number of key factors in the history of human rights and the problems in implementation. Human rights awareness has grown in many different areas: in theology and philosophy, in sociology and philosophy, and especially in law, where theory and implementation often go closely together. This reflection has grown along with developing human rights activism through many organizations. As discussion has developed so has the complexity of the questions, and there is widespread debate about the nature and the sources of rights. At the same time there has been a developing consensus on the need for human rights abuses to be stopped and on the general ineffectiveness of measures to stop continuing rights violations throughout the world.[1]

I shall try now to outline a postfoundational pathway to human rights. This will not be an overarching framework, but an attempt to relate the approaches from different disciplines. The idea of redesigning rights may seem vacuous. Designer rights are not to be touted like designer clothes, remodelled by planned obsolescence for every intellectual fashion. Too many people's lives are at stake – people who usually have the luxury of neither designer clothes nor designer ideas. Yet if human rights are to be a vehicle of human flourishing in the future, it is urgently and constantly necessary to refine their construction and improve the effectiveness of their delivery. We must try to reconnect the different strands of the cultural web of human rights activity. Negotiating the pitfalls will inevitably involve hazardous journeys into other scholars' fields.

---

1   An excellent overview of the current state of, and prospects for, human rights enforcement is given in Hegarty and Leonard (1999). This is a survey and analysis of the strengths and weaknesses of existing standards, including new dilemmas – for example, evasion of human rights law through derogation strategies. A section on emerging trends considers equality in relation to gender and women's rights, transgender, children's, refugees' and reproductive rights. The effectiveness of NGOs is measured, with practical advice on strengthening them. Attention is given to obvious, but often undiscussed, issues such as the need for men to be fully involved with women's rights. A section on 'Economic Strategies for the Enforcement of Human Rights' (ibid., 181) offers a sharp assessment of globalization, the role of incentives and sanctions, and the role of conditionality and 'good governance' in attempts to secure rights.

Philosophy and Rights

All the above strands have involved philosophical reflection at different points, not least the philosophy of law. Philosophy continues to produce new grounds for refinement, and often rejection, of rights concepts, and it would be unwise to fail to notice. We have already encountered the ocean of philosophical and legal debate, both in a Western and in a global context, through which rights notions have been refined and disputed. At the most general level, most people will probably agree with David Forsythe's comment that:

> Human rights are widely considered to be those fundamental moral rights of the human person that are necessary for a life with human dignity… Even if human rights are thought to be inalienable, a moral attribute of persons that the state cannot contravene, rights still have to be identified – that is, constructed – by human beings and codified in the legal system. (Forsythe, 2000, 3)[2]

Whatever the origins and definition, human beings have to formulate and implement rights. Although some believe that human rights are given by God and others that they simply are part of what it is to be human, by reason, behaviour or whatever, and some stress the cultural relativity of rights more than others, there is wide agreement on the potentially huge benefit of human rights action in society.[3]

---

2   Although most of the literature cited in this study is from the period after 1945, surprising items can be found on rights much earlier. E.P. Hurlbut, a New York lawyer, published *Essays on Human Rights* in Edinburgh in 1847. This forward-looking piece, much of which revolves round the constitution of the State of New York, even has a special chapter on 'The Rights of Woman' (Hulbert, 1847, 52ff). He begins: 'Man was not "born to command," nor woman "to obey."' The chapter is an enlightened plea for property rights for women.

3   Cf. Richard Rorty in his essay, 'Human Rights, Rationality and Sentimentality': 'We shouldn't claim that our reason sets us apart from other animals, but instead we are set apart by our ability to feel for each other much more than animals can' (in Shute and Hurley (1993).

There is a superb colloquium on human rights in the *Journal of Religious Ethics*, 26(2), Fall, 1998, focusing on the fiftieth anniversary of the UDHR. Cf. 266ff. Henry Shue (1998, 266ff):

> Rights can be understood as social guarantees; or better, as systems of social guarantees… Any given right in the system will in practice be much more valuable to some people than to others because the respective circumstances of the individuals vary.
>
> … These guarantees can be expressed as duties not to deprive, duties to protect, and duties to assist. I believe that every right has these three kinds of correlative duties, which range from negative duties to positive duties.

There is a good account of convergence and divergence in human rights in the essay by D. Little, A. Sachedina and J Kelsey, 'Human Rights and the World's Religions', in Bloom *et al.* (1996, 213ff). They speak of 'clear and surprising parallels between the Western and Islamic traditions…. Both traditions share a common framework within which to think about freedom of conscience and religious liberty' (ibid., 236). Cf. also Wilson:

> For their doctrine to be coherent, cultural relativists seem to hold a nineteenth-century notion of culture as discrete and homogeneous, as the product of isolation, and as the basis of all difference and similarity between human beings. Their relativism is predicated upon bounded conceptions

In different circumstances different rights, and often a combination of rights, need to be achieved – political, civil and individual, economic, social and cultural. Even the most specific issues may require action on different levels – at local level, at national and international level, through individual action, through NGOs, including churches, and through governments. It will not always be possible to coordinate simultaneous action, and the process may take time. How can we envisage an effective Christian input as a reconciling presence in such action?

Rights and duties

I want to take as my starting point the recent trenchant critique of human rights by Onora O'Neill in *A Question of Trust*, her Reith Lectures for 2002:

> We fantasise irresponsibly that we can promulgate rights without thinking carefully about the counterpart obligations, and without checking whether the rights we favour are consistent, let alone set feasible demands on those who have to secure them for others. (O'Neill, 2002, 18)

> I believe that human rights and democracy are not the basis of trust: on the contrary, trust is basic for human rights and democracy. (Ibid., 27)

> But if any of us is to have rights, others must have counterpart duties.... Active citizens who meet their duties thereby secure one another's rights. (Ibid., 32)

This critique is anticipated in her earlier study, *The Bounds of Justice* (2000), in which she robustly defends Kantian approaches to justice against communitarian critiques of individualism and Enlightenment. This is a highly pertinent reminder that rights concepts overlap with other basic ideas such as duty and justice. While we cannot provide definitive solutions to ongoing philosophical debates, we can note that a theological approach to rights can seek to work towards consensus on the basic framework of rights and on their implementation without being confined to the language of rights in its narrowest sense. Perhaps we may imagine an inclusive hermeneutical envelope which seeks to learn from different approaches to values necessary for human flourishing. A critically rational view of rights would have to include also cognisance of the criticism of rights which we explored in Chapter 3. An

---

of linguistic and cultural systems, but it falls apart in contexts of hybridity, creolisation, intermixture and the overlapping of political traditions. (Wilson, 1997, 9)

We should not adopt a diffusionist view of globalisation since it does not just imply a process of homogenisation and integration, but involves a proliferation of diversity as well. (Ibid., 12)

Cf. also T.H. Eriksen:. 'The solution, or rather the "good", multiculturalism must arrive at a blend of sharing and difference' (in Wilson, 1997, 63). Wilson also quotes Donnelly (1989):

Donnelly argues that what is being compared with human rights are notions of human dignity, or limitations on the arbitrary sense of power. These are not rights in the strict sense since they are obligations constituted between human rulers and divine authority, not between rulers and ruled. They are therefore not human rights in the sense of being special entitlements to protection which derive from the mere fact of being human. (ibid., 13).

emphasis on duties might also reveal action relevant to rights that did not surface in our earlier chapters on the tradition. Duties of care may be reflected and exemplified in the Bible and in the history of the church, even in cultures where there is little scope for rights talk.

From a very different standpoint, closer to communitarian thought, a rather more optimistic account of Christianity and a more nuanced account of rights has been offered by Jean Beth Elstain, in her article, 'Thinking about Women, Christianity and Rights' (in Witte and Van den Vyver, 1996,143f). Elstain begins from the Pauline affirmation that in Christ there is neither male nor female, and understands the earliest Christian communities as breaking down classical stereotypes of the role of women and including the traditionally excluded, the poor. In a Christian perspective there should be neither sex polarity nor sex unity but sex complementarity, in 'a community that recognizes male and female sociality and friendship' (ibid., 147). She underscores the role of Christianity in the development of rights through the enlargement of the notions of *ius gentium* and natural law. Rights are immunities from the depredations of the more powerful, which would violate human dignity, rather than entitlements. They are not simply means to acquiring power and should suggest a politics of recognition rather than a politics of resentment.

Rights, emancipation and democracy

Jean Beth Elstain writes about the rights of women.[4] This concern is radicalized in the writings of Marcella Althaus-Reid. I have highlighted the role of the emancipatory theologies in underlining the connections between Christology and social justice. It is often said that the churches should spend less time discussing issues such as sexuality, which are seen as merely Western issues, and devote more energy to world poverty. In *From Feminist Theology to Indecent Theology* (2004) Althaus-Reid refutes the criticism that, in turning from the universal scandal of poverty to sexuality, she is betraying the poor. She responds that sexuality is one of the areas in which the poor are kept in cultural subjection and discriminated against: 'A Queer Christology must also be a grounded Christology, reading the life of the poor and marginalized from the economic and sexual hegemonic orders of the world' (Althaus-Reid, 2004, 9). In her view, such a theology is not simply a Western liberal preoccupation; it applies particularly to the degradation of women throughout the world, and it is necessary not only to underline the feminine body as a hermeneutical space, but also to explore the communal memory of women who have suffered: 'Jesus as God incarnate never gave birth, suckled a child, nor suffered the pains of menstruation' (ibid., 45).

---

4   Cf. also Eva Brems' article 'Protecting the Human Rights of Women': 'The history of HR can be read as a story of increasing inclusion. Both the form and substance of human rights evolve with the inclusion of groups that have suffered discrimination in the past' (in Lyons and Mayall, 2003, 105).

Brems tackles the tensions between sameness and specificity. There is a need for a transformation approach and integration – not 'separate but equal' treatment – especially in relation to reproductive rights, sexual violence and slavery.

A true identification with the marginalized will be suspicious of heterosexual ideologies and will explore disruptive options such as bisexuality. Borrowing from Marx, and recalling her family's eviction from their house, she envisages an epistemology of struggle which questions the normativity of traditional systematic theology, using such motifs as prostitution to destabilize familiar assumptions.

She makes the telling point that liberation theologies are regularly subverted by being treated as 'theme-park' theologies, commodified in order to be neutralized. This process must be recognized and then resisted, focusing on a normative liberationist hermeneutic. The object is not to achieve acceptance within the classical status quo, but move from the modern to postmodern. Romanticism is ruled out:

> To say that the excluded are the invisible people in our big cities may be useful simply as a metaphor of disempowerment, but in reality it is their presence and not their invisibility which challenges us. Poverty is obvious. It is not invisible. It looks like poverty and even smells like poverty. (Ibid.,150)

Poor people in Latin America have to be understood within their own world, such as the Bible drinkers who take pages out of the Bible. 'The page is then cut into small pieces, soaked in a glass of water and drunk, for purposes of protection, empowerment or luck in gambling'(ibid., 155). (I cite this particular example from Althaus-Reid to illustrate the gulf between what most of us who write theology are used to and aspects of the global reality.)

Althaus-Reid explores theologically the lives of poor transvestites in the tale '*Matan a una Marica*: They Killed a Faggot':

> We need to read the life of Jesus with the same eyes that we read stories in the tabloids about homosexual people being killed...Jesus' life according to Mark is also signed by a multitude of deaths. These are the deaths of a Queer man....The crucifixion made him redundant. He becomes an unemployed God, a devalued, misunderstood God outside the market. In everything he did, God's abundant presence was there, but nevertheless, for society, he was a failure. (Ibid., 169)

But death precedes resurrection. In conclusion she affirms that:

> I belong to a community of people who still dare to believe that God is fully present among the marginalized, exceeding the narrow confines of sexual and political ideologies. (Ibid., 176)

A human rights-oriented theology will have much sympathy with theology from the margins. Sometimes it may seem that *only* the emancipatory theologies can offer us a constructive approach to the values of equality and justice that are central to a Christian engagement with rights and rights violations. Yet it is never wise to restrict strategies for addressing complex issues to single-focus perspectives. A Marxist analysis which tends to dismiss all liberal tradition as simply a tool of the market and an epiphenomenon of global capitalism is particularly susceptible to this problem. I do not myself see any credible way of cutting the Gordian knot of complexity and the need for careful differentiations.

This is swiftly confirmed, in my view, by a glance at Jeffrey Stout's philosophical study of geopolitical problems involving rights and religion. In the discussion of rights, especially in communitarian thinking, considerable doubt has been cast on the notion of democracy as a reliable support for rights. This is a common aspect of the critique of liberal, post-Enlightenment values. In his *Democracy and Tradition* (2003) Stout defends democracy as a rich and living tradition, involving the activities of, and conversation between, a wide variety of citizens with differing views, each holding the other responsible in the creation of communal ethical agreements.

Democracy is a tradition of huge significance for social development:

> It inculcates certain habits of reasoning, certain attitudes towards deference and authority in political discussion, and love for certain virtues, as well as a disposition to respond to certain types of actions, events or persons with admiration, pity or horror. (Stout, 2004, 3)

This is 'a pragmatic conception of democratic sociality' (ibid., 5) He quotes Rebecca Chopp:

> Democracy is never just a set of laws about equal and fair treatment. Rather it is an ongoing interpretation of itself, an ongoing production of new practices and narratives, of new values and forms of social and personal life that constitute a democracy. (Ibid., 6)

He affirms that:

> If democracy is nowhere fully realised and everywhere in jeopardy, we all have much to learn from particular cases. (Ibid., 15)

> Character creates an attitude of what Whitman called piety. Piety can be constructive, but it can also be destructive – he cites Baldwin and West in criticism of aspects of Black National piety. Democracy gives rise to a hope, 'the hope of making a difference for the better by democratic means.' (Ibid., 58)

Stout then turns to the role of religion in political discourse. John Rawls and Richard Rorty have questioned the legitimacy of religion in public reasoning. But religion need not inhibit conversation and may be a factor in the construction of positive, rather than negative, freedom. Secularization in the form of the questioning of infallible religious authorities does not necessarily lead to an equally doctrinaire secularism, *contra* the arguments of Radical Orthodoxy. Likewise, the new traditionalism of Alasdair MacIntyre, and the appeal to virtue ethics by Stanley Hauerwas misunderstands the liberal tradition. A positive step might be for the liberals and their critics to converge on 'a form of pragmatic expressivism that takes enduring democratic social practices as a tradition with which we have good reasons to identify' (ibid., 184). Not everyone may agree, but '[t]he fact that not everyone embraces our norms is no reason to think that such norms cannot include unconditional obligations'(ibid., 195), such as avoiding torture.

Stout traces connections between the emergence of rights talk and the emergence of modern democratic culture (ibid., 203ff). This involves reciprocity between rights and responsibilities. Aligning himself with Annette Baier, he sees rights 'as an alternative to begging on the one hand, and to certain kinds of coercion, such as torture and religiously motivated warfare, on the other' (ibid., 206).

Democracy involves the ideal of a common morality: 'Democracy came into the world opposing the representatives of a feudal and theocratic past' (ibid., 225). It involves specific attitudes: 'The line of reasoning that counsels humility with respect to our own beliefs also counsels charity towards strangers' (ibid., 234). Whatever we conclude about God, '[o]ur grasp on the objectivity of obligation is firmest in these ordinary contexts where we fully understand the point of requiring one another to live up to the demands of the decent relationships in which we take part' (ibid., 269). Ethical discourse is a social practice:

> Democratic ethical discourse is social, then, not in the sense that the community of committed democrats functions as an ultimate authority, which no individual can in principle oppose. Rather, it is social in terms of what the individual members of the group do *when they keep track of their interlocutors' commitments from their own perspectives.* (Ibid., 279)

Therefore, 'the only defensible form of democratic community is one in which ethical authority is treated as an entitlement (to deference) that one must earn by repeatedly demonstrating one's reliability as an ethical judge' (ibid., 281). In consequence, 'it is a mistake to think that any community's ethical norms can be reduced to the most general norms accepted by its members....Hence the importance of focusing on discursive *practices* rather than simply on *codes* in comparative ethics (ibid., 285–6).

Stout concludes that:

> Democracy, then, is misconceived when taken to be a desert landscape hostile to whatever life-giving waters of culture and tradition might still flow through it. Democracy is better construed as the name appropriate to the currents themselves in this particular time and place. (Ibid., 308)

It may be thought that we are straying too far here from the highroad of theology. However, I do not think – following Nolde's concern for the fruits of Christian engagement rather than the hallmarks of theological ownership – that we can avoid these issues.[5]

---

5   Traditional liberal notions of justice and democracy have long been the subject of severe criticism. Derrida has written of 'The Mystical Foundation of Authority'. He speaks of justice as the indestructible condition of deconstruction. Justice for Derrida is a messianic concept – unattainable (perhaps somewhat like Reinhold Niebuhr's notion of the relevance of an impossible ideal.) But, as Richard Amesbury notes, Derrida seems both to deny the relativism of the concept of justice and at the same time to be unable to offer any specification which would make justice recognizable. Cf. Derrida (1992); Cf. also Critchley (1999). I am much indebted to Richard Amesbury for this understanding of Derrida.

The Ingredients of Consensus?

It is widely recognized today that there is not, nor is there ever likely to be, a single agreed perspective on human rights, at least in its theory. But with all due caveats and definitional variations there is an increasing consciousness, except in totalitarian regimes, *that the cluster of human rights values will include tolerance, acceptance, mutuality and reciprocity, liberty of conscience and equal respect.*

There is a future prospect of approaches towards a *modus vivendi* (cf. Plant in Storrar and Morton, 2004) in the manner of Rawls's proposals, or an overlapping consensus. It is beginning to be possible to compile an agreed list of basic and necessary goods as ground for agreement. Here, we may borrow the language of wide reflective equilibrium and agonistic liberalism to help us chart rational grounds for such beliefs. To cut a long discussion as short as decently possible, it may be possible, in our search for a wide reflective equilibrium, to contrast an 'essentially contestedness' view of differing perspectives with coherence theory:

> Despite a potential lack of convergence, it is possible, however, to offer standards of justification – standards of *appropriate* coherence – according to which a conception generated by one WRE is superior to one generated by another. (Swanton, 27, following Daniels, 1982)

The problems of balancing liberalism with equality and democracy were much discussed by John Rawls in *A Theory of Justice* (1971) and *Justice as Fairness* (2001) in what has been described by Daniels (in Freeman, 2003) as a complex egalitarianism.[6] Similar problems arise with human rights theory, which must become a developing ongoing research project if it is to be effective. I have indicated the advantages, as I see them, of notions of sympathy and solidarity. These may be necessary, but may not be sufficient. They could be backed up by other principles/ constructions of rationality – perhaps along the lines suggested by Alan Gewirth in his modified theory of rationality (Gewirth, 1982). Hilary Putnam (2004, 102) draws attention to John Dewey's criticism of sympathy and suggests that what is required is transformational sympathy – that is, education into the ethical life in community.

Introducing religion, and in particular Christianity, to the discussion does not automatically resolve the problems but is not necessarily as unhelpful as has often been thought. Perry, in his excellent *The Idea of Human Rights*, argues persuasively for a Christian basis for human rights (Perry, 1998, 3). He quotes Kolakowski :

> Much as the concept may have been elaborated in the philosophy of the Enlightenment in its conflict with Christianity, the notion of the immutable rights of individuals goes back to the Christian belief in the autonomous status and irreplaceable value of the human personality.
> (Kolakowski, 1990, 2140)

---

6   Cf. also Scanlon in the same volume (Freeman, 2003, 150ff). The Freeman volume discusses the very real problems of arriving at a stable account of political liberalism which is compatible with equality and democracy, and makes possible a real *modus vivendi* without privileging particular views.

However, it seems clear that there is a reason for this conflict – the built-in ambiguity in the tradition: human beings who sin against God deserve to be punished and, if necessary, killed. Perry (1998, 49ff) makes an important point in his discussion and critique of Glendon:

> What really matters – what we should take seriously – is not human rights talk but the claims such talk is meant to express: the claims about what ought not to be done or about what ought to be done for human beings. (Ibid., 56)

In response to the question of whether human rights are universal he explores varieties of relativism – anthropological, epistemological and cultural. Are human rights then absolute?

> Even if no human rights are, as moral rights, absolute, some human rights, as international legal rights, should be – and, happily, are – absolute. (Ibid., 106)

Cultivating a Thick Culture of Rights: Tolerance and its Allies

What will it take for another significant step towards wide reflective equilibrium? I want to look now at some supporting webs of human rights connection. The historical roots of rights remain diverse and ambiguous. Bauman (2000) has surveyed intimations of rights in Greece – *philanthropia* – and in Rome – *humanitas Romana, clementia,* Terence's famous '*Homo sum: humani nihil a me alienum puto*'. Although there were traces of universalism, human rights in the ancient world remained narrowly circumscribed, with systematic abuses and violations. On the other hand, it could be argued that nothing in classical Greece and Rome matched the scale of the human rights violations of the 1939–45 holocaust.[7] In this instance it cannot be held that the Christian churches were unequivocally on the side of human rights, although they did play a major role in the development of the UNDHR charter of 1948, and have continued to raise their awareness of human rights issues in the intervening period, though in sporadic and selective ways (Nurser, 2003; Shukpak, 1993, Douglass and Hollenbach, 1994).

The limits of tolerance

Can we enhance human rights culture by encouraging tolerance? After all, freedom from fear of persecution is better than nothing.[8] There has been much debate over the centuries about the scope and limitations of *tolerance*, and about the necessary balances between individual and group rights. David Heyd has described tolerance

---

7. Cf. Wasserstein, 1979, Katz, 1994.

8 '"Freedom from fear" could be said to sum up the whole philosophy of human rights' (quoted from Dag Hammarskjold's speech on the 180th anniversary of the Virginia Declaration of Human Rights, 20 May 1956 (*Simpson's Contemporary Quotations*, 1988, New York: Houghton Mifflin)).

as 'a philosophically elusive concept' (Heyd, 1996, 4), hovering between absolutism and determinism. Bernard Williams has suggested that:

> ...the practice of toleration has to be sustained not so much by a pure principle resting on a value of autonomy as by a wider and more mixed range of resources. These resources include an active scepticism against fanaticism and the pretensions of its advocates; conviction about the manifest evils of toleration's absence; and, quite certainly, power, to provide Hobbesian reminders to the more extreme groups that they will have to settle for coexistence. (Williams in Heyd, 1996, 27)

In the light of the chequered history of toleration, Williams's proposals seem to me to have much to commend them, not least the hint that in a democratic society toleration may occasionally have to be effectively enforced as well as abstractly proclaimed. 'A wider and more mixed range of resources' will be deeply unsatisfying for our purist longings, but it may be the most practical way forward.

David Richards sees the argument for toleration as 'a powerful and explanatory tool in the struggle for a deeper and more complete understanding of what the struggle for universal human rights means and should be taken to mean (Richards in Heyd, 1996, 127f). He sees toleration as part of a continuing struggle against prejudice, exemplified in the parallel battles against racism in the United States and against anti-Semitism in Europe, but applicable also to feminist and gay concerns. Against this, Andrew Murphy, after a rigorous historical investigation of 'myths about religious toleration', defines the scope and limitations of toleration more narrowly, against John Rawls and David Richards:

> I argue that conscience grounds a variety of liberal practices (free speech, press, assembly, principles objection to specific laws) in which individual belief conflicts with established custom or law. While appreciative of the transformed nature of conscience, however, I suggest that a 'conscience paradigm,' still differ markedly from the principles of social equality and equal respect that undergird the more ambitious agenda of contemporary identity politics. I suggest that we ought not to minimise the importance of the *modus vivendi* politics that historically accompanied the achievement of religious toleration. (Murphy, 2001, 272–3)

Murphy notes that blacks and others are discriminated against not because of their conscientious beliefs, but because they are perceived to be inferior as a group.

Although there is a real difference of perception here, it would seem that there is also a considerable area of overlapping consensus concerning the practical issues to be addressed, since there are inevitably connections between individual and group rights. Both are issues of conscience and belief, on the one hand, and matters of social respect and equal treatment on the other. Here, Williams's notion of multiple resources seems apposite. This does not, of course, mean, for any of these writers, unlimited pluralism in toleration. In this theological study the Christomorphic dimension is an indicator of the centre and limits of toleration.

Murphy's historical study of toleration issues in New England and England in the seventeenth century highlights the central role of political as much as theological judgement in the arbitration of toleration, as well as the complexity of a situation in which tolerance was often highly selective. He opposes three 'myths': first, that religious toleration is a self-evident and unqualified good; second, that toleration came about through the efforts of sceptical Enlightenment rationalists; and, third, that toleration provides a basis for multicultural and identity politics. There were genuine reasons, at that time, for tension between conscience and community. Toleration easily dropped when the political situation changed, and the tolerant could become intolerant. Liberal views were combined with the belief that a civilized society could only function within an orderly community, and there was often genuine fear of civil unrest. According to Murphy, toleration leads not to the celebration of difference *per se*, but to a search for a way of living together in peace – a *modus vivendi*. Interestingly for our study, he highlights the religious nature of the argument:

> The arguments made by seventeenth century tolerationists were almost exclusively religious in nature: the true Christian displays humility and forbearance towards those with differing views; Jesus commanded preaching and not coercion; belief is beyond the control of the will and can only be brought about by persuasion; true belief requires the possibility of acting on those beliefs without the fear of penal sanctions. (Murphy, 2001, 13)

Although non-religious views have made important contributions in later times, religious views do not have to be coercive and may make a distinctive contribution in particular circumstances.

Toleration of beliefs, liberty of conscience, concern for equality and equal respect for difference – a raft of issues is involved in the evolving emergence of a human rights culture. Its development is very uneven, involving interruptions and tensions. There is always the danger of the *modus vivendi* breaking down, as we have seen already in twenty-first-century Iraq. The existence of monographs, conventions and treaties is no guarantee of fair and equal treatment *ubique et ab omnibus*. We cannot presume that one instance of an effective human rights regime will set the benchmark for future conduct. Historical studies, such as Murphy's analysis, suggest the need for a constant reinforcement of human rights culture from different directions. Where religion is involved in the political equation, as it often still is, it becomes important that the theological contribution also makes an explicit commitment to human rights.

Where can we find the grounds for a sustained theological contribution to human rights? This book looks to Christology, not in contrast to natural law, human dignity and other elements, but as a central connecting theme. But Christology, as we have seen, can be approached in many different ways.

Murphy's account of toleration reinforces the picture of *complexity* in the development of issues connected with rights, which we have already noted in earlier periods. Among the various figures covered by Cary Nederman in his study of toleration in the medieval world, *Worlds of Difference* (2000) are William of Rubruck and Nicholas of Cusa. Both provide striking examples of approaches to toleration in unlikely contexts. William, influenced by the practice of tolerance among various religious groups in the Mongol empire, comes to see that it is possible to hold firm beliefs and still live in peaceful coexistence with people who think and act differently. Nicholas in his *De pace fidei* allows that different nations may legitimately observe different religious practices. 'Where no conformity in manner can be found, nations should be permitted their own devotional practices and ceremonies' (*De pace fidei*, 62, quoted by Nederman, 2000, 94). We need not be scandalized that different writers approach human rights from different angles. A desire for certainty and uniformity increasingly seems to be an attribute of contemporary religious consciousness. Perhaps this should be resisted.

The promise and the limits of sympathy

A soft perspective on the human rights dimension can be seen in the deployment of the notions of sentiment/sympathy, from David Hume and Adam Smith to Richard Rorty. But sentiment without enforcement may be entirely useless, as the history of abuse in prison regimes throughout history amply demonstrates.

The need for sympathy has to be expanded to include a vehicle for enforcement – otherwise sympathy may be ineffective. James Poling in *Render Unto God* (2002) gives a good example from US prison practice, where sympathy has not produced change.

Rather differently, in her *Religion and Faction in Hume's Moral Philosophy* (1997), Jennifer Herdt explores the notion of 'extensive' sympathy in Hume's philosophy. This is a development of his notion of benevolent intentions, deriving from 'the generosity and capacity of our nature' (*A Treatise of Human Nature*) Hume's *History of England* shows his sensitivity to the dangers of religious fanaticism. Herdt comments on his description of the Crusaders' destruction of Jerusalem:

> They weep over the death of their saviour, but feel no responsibility for the horrible anguish they themselves have just caused. All that human suffering is not really real to them; caught up in religious zeal, the human beings they slaughtered were little more to them than physical obstacles blocking their approach to the sacred places which were infinitely more real. (Herdt, 1997, 115)

We have to cultivate sympathy for the point of view of others, even when we do not share their beliefs and have no dogmatic certainty about our own beliefs. This paradigm of sympathetic understanding provides a way of entering and appreciating the point of view of others, and of avoiding unnecessary conflicts harmful to society:

> Sympathy is not romantic nostalgia. 'The purpose of Hume's sentimental scenes is not to encourage readers to wallow in pity or to re-create emotions from the past, but to rouse them in ways that challenge their unreflective evaluations of character and action. (Herdt, 1997, 195)

The concept of sympathy is linked with Hume's use of 'sentiment' as a source of moral reasoning. This has been explored by Annette Baier in her work on Hume and on moral prejudices (Baier, 1991, 1994). More could be drawn, too, from Adam Smith, through his theory of moral sentiments.

Sympathy may be helpful. But is it enough? Michael Walzer in his *Spheres of Justice* (1983) analysed the complexity of the notion of equality, both in its political and economic dimensions and in its implication for such important areas as education, public health, work, leisure, political office and personal relationships. He concluded that '[m]utual respect and a shared self-respect are the deep strengths of complex equality, and together they are the source of its possible endurance' (Walzer, 1983, 321).

In my view it is possible to learn from Richard Rorty on solidarity and the tradition of sympathy without subscribing to all the implications which he draws. Richard Amesbury has recently demonstrated this in his excellent *Morality and Social Criticism* (2005). Amesbury sets out from Rorty's proposal to replace objectivity by solidarity. He wants to replace human rights foundationalism by a human rights culture based on sentimental education. Amesbury objects that 'his anti-authoritarianism – while ostensibly liberating – ironically renders Rorty incapable of seeing how it could be possible to dissent from the vast majority of one's peers without ceasing to be rational'(Amesbury, 2005, 14). Rorty dislikes the idea of obligations. But '[i]t is difficult to see how Rorty can hope to continue to talk of "a human rights culture" while abandoning talk of obligations that obtain irrespective of whether or not one's peers happen to hold one accountable to them' (ibid., 16). People have felt obliged to rescue strangers in danger – people outside their own communities. Realism without Platonist foundationalism can be reserved as a basis for social action, and Amesbury's approach fits well with an emphasis on the postfoundational.

William Talbott also supports the thesis that sympathy is important but not everything. He notes the importance of empathy as a feeling, but also as more than this:

> The feeling of empathy itself cannot be separated from a judgement about what it is like to be the other person, and that judgement provides the basis for a moral judgement about how the other person ought to be treated. (Talbott, 2005, 66)

He discusses Rorty's theory of moral sentiment, concluding that reason *and* sentiment are at the basis of moral judgement: 'Sentiments themselves are often a manifestation of reason and can essentially involve judgements of what is true and false' (ibid., 170).

Natural law re-energized?

What, then, of natural law revisited? In assessing the influence of natural law on human rights, Julie Clague (in Boswell *et al.*, 2000, 137) has suggested that:

Christianity should consider the language of human rights as a direct descendent of natural law origins – though admittedly Thomas is a more distant relation than some in the family tree that traces the genealogy of rights. And, as in all families, there are a number of skeletons in the closet.

Esther Reid, following O'Neill, but also Brian Tierney, Joan Lockwood O'Donovan, John Finnis and others, find new life in the natural law tradition and discover support for rights in Aquinas. She examines rights in the context of right, goodness, duties, responsibilities. The relation of rights to goodness in the tradition of virtue ethics suggests another strand of moral reasoning which may be called upon in support of the totality of human rights action.

I myself am inclined to think that the value of the natural law tradition in support of rights was very limited up to around 1970. John Langan's use of a natural law tradition is, however, an impressive testimony to its value in current rights thinking.

A rather more optimistic view of the medieval tradition is taken by several Catholic writers. In 'The Spirit of the Laws, the Laws of the Spirit' (2001) John Witte reflects on religion and human rights in a new global era. Today we are in something of a 'Dickensian era': 'We have seen the best of human rights protections inscribed on the books, but some of the worst of human rights violations inflicted on the ground'(Witte, 2001, 79).

Witte identifies the need for a new human rights hermeneutic within religion. Medieval canon law was based, in part, on the concept of individual and corporate rights. It defined the rights of clergy, ecclesiastical organizations, church councils, the laity, the poor and the needy. The Protestant Reformation provided the basis for a further expansion of rights. He concludes that '[r]eligion must be drawn into a constructive alliance with a regime of law, democracy and human rights, or they will be pitted against each other' (ibid., 106).

This more hopeful perspective is echoed by Conor Gearty in his *Reclaiming our Tradition: Rights, Diversity and Catholic Social Teaching*. He outlines three basic principles of human rights: first,, respect for democratic governance and civil liberties (parliament); second, the principle of legality, and concern for procedural fairness,: and, third, respect for human dignity (Gearty, 2003,13).

For Gearty:

> ...the human rights movement is in many ways a visibility project: each generation seeks to see and therefore to respect more of the person before them, more of the needs and demands of their identity...The challenge for the future is to expand the vision of the church, just as earlier generations of activists persuaded the state that slaves mattered, that children mattered, that women mattered. ...But to engage effectively, the Church has to be willing to contemplate a dialogue between adults, a conversation not a sermon. (Ibid., 18–19)

A positive appraisal of rights in the natural law tradition is developed, too, by Linda Hogan (2000). She reviews communitarian arguments against human rights as liberal individualism, and agrees that human rights may have a major role in

Christian social ethics, though not an exclusive one. However, she adds, 'We can recognise that through the centuries Christian discipleship has been enthusiastically lived in dialogue and partnership with the social and political institutions of secular societies.' Early liberalism had a Christian heritage: 'The language of rights emerged in the life of the Christian community...' (Hogan, 2000). Following Jean Porter, natural law can be seen as a Christian tradition of moral inquiry – a perspectival interpretation of a universal phenomenon, in which natural law and the Bible converge. So Christian appropriation of rights discourse is in fact a reappropriation. In contrast, we have thought it necessary to stress in this study the opposite trends of suppression and domination.

Legal Perspectives

So far, we have approached the project of a thick culture of rights through mainly philosophical sources. But we can hardly overlook the fact that most work on rights has come from the legal disciplines. Somewhat inconveniently for the theologian, there is no escape from engagement with the role of law in human rights.

Human rights may often be most effectively articulated in a legal framework. Costas Douzinas puts it like this:

> Human rights have the ability to create new worlds, by continuously pushing and expanding the boundaries of society and of law. Human rights transfer their claims to ever-expanding domains and to new types of (legal) subjectivity, they construct ceaselessly new meanings and values, and they bestow dignity and protection to novel subjects, situations and people. This ability is not a local or exceptional characteristic of human rights but their essence, what human rights are. (Douzinas in Gearty and Tomkins, 1996, 131)

In the same volume R.J. Nayar grounds rights on a conception of basic human needs:

> Basic human needs are those components, qualitatively articulated, which are identified as the universally relevant constituents of what is understood as 'human life', irrespective of the rich diversity of humanity, which when satisfied within specific societal contexts give meaning to a distinctly human life. (Ibid., 171)

In a fascinating paper on the clash of rights, James Kingston (ibid., 455ff) warns against the use of simplistic rights rhetoric on both sides of this issue and Geraldine Van Bueren (ibid., 596ff) highlights the need for demythologizing some of the rhetoric of rights if international human rights law is to be effective. In law, as in theology, we see the need for a constant critical revision of accepted wisdom; in this process an awareness of the benefits of interdisciplinarity in attacking similar dilemmas might bear fruit in numerous directions.

Global justice

We have already often had occasion to mention law in the context of rights. Much human rights activity is inevitably concerned with law – both in the formulation and in the enforcement of rights. Without close attention to the legal dimension much human rights talk is pointless. Yet, as we have seen, the legal discussion brings its own impasses and will not in itself bring about a human rights culture. Here I simply instantiate some of the issues with reference to some pressing problems.

David Forsythe's *Human Rights in International Relations* (2000) concentrates on a particular slice, an important slice of the thick culture of human rights reflection. He notes that the notion of human rights is here to stay in international humanitarian law.

The global application of human rights norms requires delivery mechanisms. These include the UN organs of the Security Council and the International Court of Justice, as well as subsidiary organs such as the Human Rights Commission. Results are monitored through the Human Rights Committee and the Committee on Economic, Social and Cultural Rights, with a view to ensuring international humanitarian law. When Christian theology advocates a catalytic and facilitating attention to the shape of a vulnerable love, it will have to engage with the realities of the work carried out by these bodies, if it is not to duplicate work and act in ignorance of the facts.

In the case of massive abuse, justice can rarely be delivered without deterrents to dissuade intending perpetrators of human wrongs from violent action. Hence there is a need for international criminal courts and the presence of rights standards: 'International law and organisation demand liberalism, but traditional international relations has coughed up realism' (Forsythe, 2000, 48). However, the presence of courts will not in itself prevent abuse, and judicial proceedings at international level are often mixed with diplomatic *Realpolitik*. Victors' justice is not always an equal justice. It would be naïve to imagine that a Christian presence here would resolve the issues. However, attention to forgiveness and reconciliation, with due regard for the dimension of repentance, may contribute to fairness and avoid a cycle of continuing resentment and retribution.

Forsythe examines the application of human rights norms in various regions of the world. He concludes that '[l]iberal democracy, meaning a commitment to civil and political rights, is a necessary but not entirely sufficient condition for achieving a truly rights protective society'(ibid., 136). This leads to a comparison of human rights policy and foreign policy in liberal and illiberal states. State foreign policy is still very important, but increasing attention is being paid to international human rights norms.

We may reflect that any sort of triumphalist religious insertion into national politics would be a return to the bad aspects of Christendom and are to be utterly deplored, not least because many citizens of most states do not subscribe to the Christian faith. But if we are serious about a Christian contribution to human flourishing, then Christianity ought perhaps to have a considered opinion to put forward. This might fittingly take place in the contexts of Forsythe's next grouping – non-governmental organizations and human rights: 'If human rights NGOs had not existed during the past thirty five years, human rights would have had a much less salient position in international relations' (ibid., 177). Here we think primarily of large bodies such as Amnesty International. But church-related bodies such as Christian Aid and CAFOD continue to play a significant part, both in their own right and in strengthening the entire NGO project. A Christian presence is significant on such bodies as Médecins sans Frontières among others: 'as much as NGOs need states – to arrest war criminals etc. – states need NGOs for a variety of ideas and services' (ibid., 188).

Finally, Forsythe's useful survey turns to the enormous impact of transnational corporations (TNCs) on the modern world. Here are companies with much more economic power than many sovereign states, sometimes supporting and at other times abusing or condoning the abuse of human rights: 'The clear experience of the global north is that unregulated capitalism is injurious to human dignity and social justice' (ibid., 200). A mix of incentives and deterrents is necessary to nudge TNCs in the direction of better practice. Here is a classic example of how the decisions of ordinary people working in a whole range of business organizations might have an impact on human rights, often from a great distance, and this may encourage reflection on better practice.

Forsythe ends with a plea for renewed attention to the politics of liberalism in a realist world because '[p]ursuing liberalism in a realist world is no simple task' (ibid., p.236). However, we do not have to subscribe to Forsythe's particular liberal perspective to realize that there are multiple layers of complex human rights issues that are tremendously influential on human flourishing throughout the planet. Policy initiatives deal with the reality of people living or dying, flourishing or being crushed by abuses, and yet these perspectives have rarely been the subject of detailed theological attention, even though theology has itself developed in continuous dialogue with other disciplines throughout the centuries. My contention is that a new involvement in the particularity of rights issues at the theoretical and practical levels may be an effective new way of understanding and communicating the fruits of the Christian gospel in the current century. If this is true, it is a task which has yet hardly begun.

It seems clear that, somewhat as an open Christology acts as a fluid text, so too do the definitions of the structuring elements of rights issues and their interconnections. The roles of nations and states, churches, voluntary bodies and individuals change in developing cultures. These changes in turn affect legal systems, church structures, social and political perceptions. Christians understand God, as the ultimate mystery of compassion, to be active in, with and through all these changes.

Rights against liberties

We noted in an earlier chapter some searching legal critique of the British Human Rights Act. Conor Gearty has suggested (seminar paper, Glasgow University, 11 February 2004) that the Act may have benign or malign consequences in the future, or a balance of both. The benign effect may be that a human rights culture will expand and influence all the work of the government executive. The malign effect may be that human rights work will become a highly legalistic subject which drains human rights of life and becomes simply another career option for lawyers. This becomes a particular problem in a situation where the judiciary may be perceived to have a built-in bias, on class, race and other lines.

Human rights are one tool among others for legislative activity, and expansion of the powers of the Act by the judiciary could actually diminish the liberties of individuals and communities. There is a need for honesty about the application of the Act. There remains value in the critique of absolute rights by Marx and Bentham against a kind of human rights supremacism. Sometimes principles of law may be more useful than rights talk, although, of course, in a country in which civil liberties are not usually protected by the normal operation of the law, rights could become a more effective instrument.

We should note here that tensions between rights-based law and other traditions arise in church law as in other areas of law: for example, in Anglican canon law.

Norman Doe writing on 'Canonical Approaches to Human Rights', notes that:

> The dominant juridical regime among the Anglican churches is that of duties. Within this, the dominant rights regime is that of correlative duties, not of free-standing rights…In short, in practice the canon laws of Anglican churches do not systematically mirror theological ideas about human rights proposed by Lambeth Conference. (Doe in Hill, 2002, 206)

Justice against rights?

It may be thought that I have made it easy to reach an affirmative position on rights by ignoring a decisive segment of the argument, namely the case *against* rights in much writing in the important, though controversial, critical legal studies field. The collection of essays edited by Robin West (2001) is a representative sample.

In her Introduction West reflects on liberal rights theory:

> The justification for rights, and for the particular rights we have, is distinctively moral. The consequence of having a right, however, is legal and political. (West, 2001, xi)

> The very utopian universalism of rights and rights consciousness instils in the privileged the false and panglossian belief that all is normally fair and well with the world, even in the face of glaring and unquestioned material inequality, because whatever may be the case with respect to material well-being, the rights that protect these material possessions are universally bestowed. (Ibid., xvi)

The rights critique argues that we can see that the liberal tradition has failed us when we examine the aspirational strengths and weaknesses of a liberal–constitutional rights culture. Liberal rights are too negative and render us atomized, according to communitarians. They ought to endorse some conceptions of the good over others. Tolerance of alternative perspectives is not enough: affirmation is often required. If it is to be maintained in response that liberal theories can respect our social nature as well as our individuality, then there is a need for positive rights theory. In a revitalized rights theory such values as a right to care would be important:

> When we turn our backs on rights… we turn our backs on a path – not the only path but a path – for transforming universalistic utopian ideals into political realities. (Ibid., xxx)

Morton Horwitz (ibid., 90f) writes eloquently about the use of rights discourse to preserve the interests of the powerful. Rights become a double-edged sword because of eighteenth-century conceptions of rights: radical individualism and little on group rights. There is a need to relate rights to a substantive conception of the good society and to notions of equality (against conservatives). Rights are not just for the protection of property. Some rights have been, and are, damaging – for example, the right to bear arms in the US Bill of Rights. The final part of West's collection examines aspirational rights, their possibilities and histories. Patricia Williams, considering 'Reconstructing Ideals from Deconstructed Rights', highlights a need to suggest the reality of human goods in lifestyles rather than in thin toleration. This viewpoint is echoed by Chai Feldblum in making a progressive moral case for same-sex marriage (ibid., 265ff). Feldblum maintains that a discussion of normative goods is needed and that there may be a specific moral good in an equal partnership between two people. These writers argue that it is not enough to speak of needs, rather than rights (as in much Critical Legal Studies language), and that rights language has helped many minorities. Robin West calls for a 'progressive constitutional faith'.

The Critique of Rights

The resolution of these issues is beyond the competence of theology. But we should be aware of their existence. The rights critique developed by critical legal theorists contains a number of strands.[9] The discourse of rights is less useful in securing progressive social change than liberal theorists and politicians assume. Legal rights are indeterminate and incoherent. The use of rights discourse stunts human imagination and mystifies people about how law really works. In American law, the discourse of rights reflects and produces a kind of isolated individualism that hinders social solidarity and genuine human connection. In this case, rights discourse can actually impede progressive movement towards genuine democracy and justice. We should note that the school of Critical Legal Studies has not met with anything like universal acceptance. Nevertheless, its critique is penetrating and worth evaluating.

Although critical race theorists and many feminist legal theorists acknowledge their indebtedness to Critical Legal Studies, they reject in part or in whole the critique of rights. The existing system of legal rights, they concede, is unstable and often

---

9   My account of Critical Legal Studies is heavily dependent on the account of a Conference on Critical Legal Studies at the University of Colorado and centred on the work of Mark Tushnet Cf. http://socsci.colorado.edu/¬bairdv/Critical_Rights.htm.

manipulated to advance the interests of the wealthy and powerful. But rights can be defended and reconstructed; the critique of rights neglects the historical potential of rights in the real lives of people of colour and women. The argument offered by critical race theorists and feminists to defend and reconstruct rights has several elements.

The establishment of legal rights, even if enforced more vigorously than at present, would not eliminate racism and sexism. But arguments for, and public recognition of, rights for persons of colour and women do help to combat group-based oppression. The impact of rights discourses on social psychology is likely, on balance, to be beneficial to minorities and women. Furthermore, although the organization of human relationships in terms of rights may perpetuate alienation and reinforce artificial distance between people, it at least accords everyone a modicum of respect. And, as a rhetorical rallying cry, rights discourse can both mobilize those who have been oppressed and lend them a greater sense of self-respect and empowerment. Few members of historically disadvantaged groups are deluded by the language of rights into believing that the current distribution of wealth and power is legitimate. The vast majority are able to sustain a 'dual consciousness' – recognizing and capitalizing on the revolutionary potential of legal rights while remaining sceptical of the overall social and political order in which rights are currently embedded.

The content and language of rights are malleable, not fixed, and afford a medium through which even the disempowered can claim equal rights to participate in defining their content. Even if it is only the hypocrisy of the powerful to which they appeal, the disempowered can use the language of rights to demand recognition and, by so doing, contribute to reshaping rights themselves. Using rights talk can get some people in the game who have not even been recognized before as players. Further, for both people of colour and women, social solidarity and close connections with others may be less elusive than protection of personal space and boundaries. Asserting rights as a group can itself enhance solidarity while also assisting individuals in their own personal journey to recognize what they can, and should, demand for themselves.

In her *Making All the Difference: Inclusion, Exclusion, and American Law*, (1990), Martha Minow defends rights while accepting features of the Critical Legal Studies critique:

> Why advance this conception of right, including children's rights, as a vocabulary used by community members to interpret and reinterpret their relationships with one another? It is a clumsy vocabulary; it can never fully express individual experience. Its very claim to communal meanings, its dependence directly and indirectly on official sanctions, and its created past preclude that possibility....[10]

---

10 Minow continues:

Michael Ignatieff advocates a language of needs instead, finding rights language too limited: 'Rights language offers a rich vernacular for claims an individual may make on or against the

Yet when I write a brief, supervise students in their clinical work, or talk to professionals in the trenches, I wonder sometimes whom I am helping and whom I am hurting by criticizing rights. It turns out to be helpful, useful, and maybe even essential to be able to couch a request as a claim of rights – and not just for winning a given case or persuading a particular official to do a good thing but for working to constitute the kind of world where struggles for change can in fact bring about change, and where struggles for meaning and communality can nurture both. There is something too valuable in the aspiration of rights, and something too neglectful of the power embedded in assertions of another's needs, to abandon the rhetoric of rights. That is why I join in the effort to reclaim and reinvent rights... For this task, rights rhetoric is remarkably well suited. It enables a devastating, if rhetorical, exposure of and challenge to hierarchies of power. (Minow, 1990, 306–11)

A Chastened Rights Culture

We may take on board many of the points made. Rights talk is by no means always on the side of justice and equality, and has been notoriously blind in important areas. It is certainly not the only avenue for pursuing the human good. What is important is not to engage in a permanent beauty contest between competing concepts, but to harness the strengths of different approaches in achieving agreed, or at least nearly agreed, goals. This would be consonant with my approach to an interfaith encounter among religions, focusing on the delivery of 'the fruits of the spirit' rather than on the ways to get there.

My strategy is to persist with the language and culture of human rights, not least because they can be shown empirically to have assisted in bringing about a better life for many of the world's most disadvantaged people, while not being complacent about their capacity to produce *ex opere operato* solutions. It is a question not of excluding data, but of building up a richer and more nuanced human rights culture than we have at present.[11]

---

collectivity, but it is relatively impoverished as a means of expressing individuals' needs for the collectivity.... It is because money cannot buy the human gestures which confer respect, nor rights guarantee them as entitlement, that any decent society requires a public discourse about the needs of the human person.'

I, too, have criticized rights rhetoric for its impoverished view of human relationships and its repeated assignment of labels that hide the power of those doing the assigning. And I find something terribly lacking in rights for children that speak only of autonomy rather than need, especially the central need for relationships with adults who are themselves entitled to create settings where children can thrive. Rights rhetoric can, and should, be expressed on account of its tendency to hide the exercise of state authority – even authority exercised in the name of private freedoms. Rights discourse, like any language, may mislead, seduce, falsely console, or wrongly inflame. I have the luxury, as a scholar, of stepping back and criticizing a basic tool of legal practice for preserving assumptions about human autonomy that I believe are contrary to social experience and likely to limit social change.

11   Recent writing also provides robust defence of classical rights theory. Jack Donnelly writes in 'In Defense of the Universal Declaration Model':

I find an ally in the combination of insistence on rights with awareness of limitations in Helena Kennedy's *Just Law*:[12]

> Individual rights have been the great historical counterweight to governmental authority and control; it falls to the judges to decide when rights are infringed, which means that an independent judiciary is a crucial element in any democracy. Rights are indispensable because they act as a restraint on the state even when it is enforcing certain majoritarian preferences. (Kennedy, 2004, 122)

> The introduction of human rights law has presented a powerful tool and a language to remind the state that it has a duty to look after the interests of victims. (Ibid., 208)

New Labour caught the drift of the American communitarian critique of rights:

> But this adoption of American thinking ignores the fact that the European human rights model to which we have signed up is very different from that of the United States, where certain rights are immutable and their impact on the well-being of the community as a whole is detrimental. ...The human rights philosophy which developed in Europe since the Second World War is quite different. It accepts that rights conflict with each other and that a careful balancing is necessary in pursuit of justice. The interests of the community are part of the balancing act. (Ibid., 230)

Kennedy writes about 'The Retreat from Human Rights' and illustrates this using British statistics on prison populations:

> In 1992 45% of all adults sentenced in the crown courts went to prison. By 2001 64% were being jailed. (Ibid., 282)

> Internationally recognised rights are rights, a particular sort of social practice. To have a right to x is to be *entitled* to x and authorised to make special claims to enjoy x should it be threatened or denied....The claim of 'universal' human rights is that all human beings 'ought' to be treated in these ways, not that they are or have been, or that these norms are (let alone have been) accepted everywhere. (Donnelly in Lyons and Mayall, 2003, 21)

Donnelly argues that (a particular type of) liberalism provides a strong normative foundation for the substance of the Universal Declaration model and for its continuing refinement and elaboration in the coming decades (ibid., 26). There may be rights-based, good-based, thick and thin liberalism:

> A liberalism compatible with the Universal Declaration must be strongly egalitarian, must actively embrace an extensive system of economic and social rights, and must reflect a robust (procedural and substantive) conception of democracy. (Ibid., 28)

He takes a sceptical view of group rights, suggesting that it is hard to legislate for a group – women – that covers half of humanity and argues that a better implementation of rights is needed in the existing Universal Declaration and its covenants.

12 Mary Ann Glendon (in West, 2001, 207f), whom we have already encountered, makes the important point that rights differ in Europe and America, Europe adds affirmative welfare obligations and omits property rights (ibid., 211). The United States privileges negative, rather than positive, rights. Joseph Raz notes the difference between the public good (some people in society) and the common good (all in society).

She comes firmly down on the side of rights:

> In fact human rights provides us with a new language for discussing our relationships with each other and with the rest of the world. It offers a language that belongs neither to the left nor to the right, because it is non-ideological, and can speak to all the peoples of the world irrespective of religious belief or world view because it is avowedly secular. Rights have to be given the force of law for that is how we link our dreams to the acts of daily life. Too often we speak of human rights only in terms of how they are violated and not in terms of how they can affirm and legitimise the aspirations of a society. (Ibid., 301ff)

> Contemporary human rights are built upon a careful and sensitive balance between respect for the individual and support for community.... Human rights do sometimes support communities, but it should be recognised that sometimes communities can be oppressive – to homosexuals, strangers, women and those who are different. (Ibid., 304–5)[13]

In recent times the case *for* rights has been made as strongly as the case against. Typical is the collection edited by Kirsten Hastrup (2001). She suggests that '[t]he language of human rights suggests a world in which the resigned acceptance of a globalized world is supplemented by a determined ambition to universalize equality and justice'. In this useful symposium M. Kjaerum deals with derogable and non-derogable human rights, suggesting that different approaches are needed for local implementation in different countries. Daniel Boyarin stresses the need to respect particular identities, seeing Paul's universalism as 'a powerful force for coercive discourses of sameness'. G. Ulrich criticizes Rorty for being deliberately ethnocentric and judges that '[in] general, we should beware of defending human rights as yet another righteous cause that is above justifying itself' (Ibid., 200).

There are problems in both natural law and legal positivism. A global ethics project will involve constructing multiple genealogies for human rights and perhaps legal polycentrism. Ulrich advocates constructivism:

> Conceptually, the constructivist position interprets human rights as both morality and law – thus bypassing the stark opposition between the one-sided positions natural law and legal positivism. (Ibid., 215)

My own postfoundational approach emphasizes goals rather than methods, and therefore has some respect for Rorty's impatience with a traditional foundationalism.

---

13 Kennedy distinguishes a first wave of rights in the eighteenth century from the second wave after 1945.

Rights are not a quid pro quo for good behaviour and the mantra 'Rights and responsibilities' should not be abused. (Kennedy, 2004, 311)

In this book I have tried to argue that whatever we face in the modern world, the sacrifice of civil liberties and human rights is a folly. (Ibid., 317)

Law translates standards of human rights into reality...Human rights is where law becomes poetry. (Ibid., 318)

But a cumulative case will not despair of assistance from earlier traditions, provided that they are integrated into a postfoundational framework. In an incisive critique, 'Solidarity and Dissent: Rorty and the Consequences of Pragmatism' Richard Amesbury (2005) has drawn attention to technical flaws in Rorty's arguments and looks to Wittgenstein to produce a more robust postfoundational perspective on rights.[14]

Rights in Religious and Interfaith Perspective: Beyond the Western Legal Argument

The tension between the religious and the secular runs through the debates about rights in both the East and the West. The ramifications of the problem are clearly brought out in the collection of essays edited by Joseph Runzo and others on the Universal Declaration of Human Rights by the World's Religions (UDHRWR), produced under the leadership of Arvind Sharma (Runzo *et al.*, 2003).

In his opening essay on 'Secular Rights and Religious Responsibilities' Runzo comments that:

> I am suggesting that the notion of rights should not succeed other moral notions such as obligation or role or moral responsibility. (Runzo *et al.*, 15)

> What is needed is the construction of a social ethic which takes account of both the secular and the religious…In particular the secular has a key role as a constructive voice against the dangers of religious egoism, and the religious can add a powerful voice to the call to other-regarding action, which lies at the heart of both the religious and the moral life. (Ibid., 24)

The need for working towards an overlapping consensus is underlined by the leading Islamic scholar, Abdullahi An-Na'im in his essay, 'The Synergy and Interdependence of Human Rights, Religion and Secularism':

> Given the difficulty of agreement on a single foundation for human rights, I suggest promoting the legitimacy of, and popular support for, these rights through an overlapping consensus among multiple foundations, of the usual polarisation of secular versus religious perspectives on this issue. (Ibid., 28)

> The foundation of the universality of human rights presupposes possibilities of internal transformation within each religious and secular tradition. (Ibid., 37)

---

14 Amesbury finds Rorty's appeal to sentiment weak when it is necessary to resist popular prejudice: 'It becomes then a question of "out Rortying Rorty"', 'Rorty gets rid of knowledge to make room for hope. But we need grounds for hope' (2005, 26). 'And so Rorty often loses his grip on principles *internal to our practices.* In fairness to Rorty we may note that in Truth and Progress (the Amnesty lectures) he advocates the rejection of human rights foundationalism and argues that we should instead promote a human rights culture through "sentimental education"'(ibid., 22).

An-Na'im emphasizes the importance of human rights for religion and gives examples of synergy and interdependence in an Islamic context:

> In everyday life, without such human rights as freedom of belief and expression, there will be no possibility of growth and development within the existing doctrine of any religion. (Ibid., 41)

Arvind Sharma regards dignity as a foundation for human rights discourse, and he links human dignity, human rights and human duties. He says of the document *Towards a Declaration of Human Rights by the World's Religions*: 'It is being offered as a fluid text, yet to be fixed' (Ibid., 139). However, it seems to me that the concept of a fluid text is potentially of great importance for the continuation of conversation on human rights, especially as a correlate to an open and porous Christology.

My own study is largely concerned with the legacy of the Christian tradition and Western social developments in rights. But it should be recognized that these traditions have no monopoly on wisdom and innovation. One of the most penetrating contemporary thinkers on rights must be Abdullahi An-Na'im. He writes:

> My view…is that scholars and activists should neither underestimate the challenge of cultural relativism to the universality of human rights nor concede too much to its claims. Rather, it is preferable to adopt a constructive approach that recognises the problems and addresses them in each cultural tradition, as well as across cultural boundaries.
> The proposed approach seeks to explore the possibilities of cultural reinterpretation and reconstruction *through internal cultural discourse and cross-cultural dialogue,* as a means to enhancing the universal legitimacy of human rights. (An-Na'im, 1993, 3)

In a chapter entitled 'Towards a Cross-Cultural Approach to Defining International Standards of Human Rights: The Meaning of Cruel, Inhuman or Degrading Treatment or Punishment' he writes:

> The cultural legitimacy thesis accepts the existing international standards while seeking to enhance their cultural legitimacy within the major traditions of the world.
> It attempts through internal dialogue and struggle to establish enlightened perceptions and interpretations of cultural values and norms. Having achieved an adequate level of legitimacy *within* each tradition, through this internal stage, human rights scholars and advocates should work for *cross-cultural* legitimacy, so that peoples of diverse cultural traditions can agree on the meaning, scope and methods of implementing these rights. (Ibid., 21, emphasis added)

> External imposition is not the only option open to human rights advocates. Greater consensus on international standards for the protection of the individual against cruel, inhuman or degrading treatment or punishment can be achieved through internal cultural discourse and cross-cultural dialogue. (Ibid., 38)

An-Na'im concludes:

First we must try to extrapolate, *as much as possible*, a universal concept through the interpretive reading of existing international standards, while being open to the possibility of revising these standards if necessary...

On the cultural side, each of us must work from within his or her culture to bridge the gap, *as much as possible*, between the present international standards, on the one hand, and the norms and values of the culture on the other. (Ibid., 432, emphases added)

The need for more sensitivity to difference is hammered home by Richard Falk in the same volume. In an essay on 'Cultural Foundations for the International Protection of Human Rights' he reflects on the modern globalized world:

Such a reality posits its own distinctive and opposing social demands: respect for *difference* (culture; to sustain diversity), acknowledgement of *sameness* (international law of human rights; to re-establish normative authority). (Ibid., 46, emphases added)

The rethinking of human rights here proposed also entails a rethinking of culture itself. (Ibid., 53)

Historically, human rights provision for many – North American Indians, Inuits, Australian Aborigines, for example – has been very poor. Even where there is no coercion, the problems of cultural survival may be considerable, as in the case of the Sami people within the Scandinavian state. Issues of cross-cultural legitimacy are not instantly solvable.

This need for internal, cross-cultural and pluralist grounding of human rights has been emphasized by other progressive Islamic scholars, notably by Abdulaziz Sachedina and Reza Aslan:

It is pluralism, not secularism, which defines democracy. A democratic state can be established upon any normative moral framework as long as pluralism remains the source of its legitimacy...Grounding an Islamic democracy in the ideals of pluralism is vital because religious pluralism is the first step towards building an effective human rights policy in the Middle East...As with Islamic pluralism, the inspiration for an Islamic policy of human rights must be based on the Medinan ideal. (Aslan, 2005, 262–3)

We may summarize this section by affirming that there is a strong rational case for pursuing the development of human rights language and human rights culture. We certainly need a heightened awareness of the historical and cultural limitations of particular versions of rights talk. We also need more cross-cultural understanding of the emergence of unfamiliar religious traditions, freed from the inhibitions of extraneous, and especially colonial, frameworks. And the best research traditions need continual development, and benefit from interruptions as much as from continuities.[15]

---

15 There is a good critical discussion and bibliography of Buddhism and rights in Schmidt-Leukel (2004). In an earlier publication (Schmidt-Leukel *et al.*, 2001) he makes an interesting suggestion about

Anthropological Strands

It becomes clear that philosophical, and especially anthropological, issues easily become directly relevant to specific rights matters. Let us take the complex and vexed question of prostitution in Thailand, which was mentioned earlier. Here is a case in which it would be highly undesirable for fools to rush in where angels fear to tread, and where an overtly Christian approach of a traditional nature would be counterproductive. Heather Montgomery has made an excellent anthropological study of this subject entitled *'Imposing Rights? A Case Study of Child Prostitution in Thailand'* (in Cowan *et al.*, 2001). She comments that:

> Discussions should not revolve around universalism versus relativism; rather, they should explore what is best for children given the unique cultural and economic circumstances of their lives. ...The anthropologist is placed in an ideal role to mediate between cultural relativism and universalism. (Cowan *et al.*, 97)

Here, Montgomery is highlighting the fact that central to the issue is an appreciation of the cultural and economic context in which these abuses take place and that an anthropologist is indeed well placed to assist. At the immediate local level there is huge poverty among individual families. The children involved are often from families displaced from elsewhere and brought into towns. It has to be borne in mind that the whole definition of a child is understood differently in different cultures and that prostitution is highly paid, relative to other forms of work. In addition, the children may not themselves always be aware that what is happening constitutes

---

the nature of interfaith dialogue. We enter dialogue with an auto-interpretation, our understanding of our own religion, and a hetero-interpretation, our understanding of the other religion, which is the result of information assessed in the light of our own autointerpretation:

> Thus if interfaith dialogue should serve a better mutual understanding, every partner in dialogue must not only strive for a good understanding of the other's auto-interpretation but of the other's hetero-interpretation as well. In other words, the point is to understand *how* the other perceives oneself and *why*. (Ibid., 9).

We must first listen to the others' hetero-interpretation of oneself, correct one's hetero-interpretation of the other, and then perhaps one may come to modify one's own auto-interpretation. In this dialogue there are many misconceptions to be addressed, notably on the nature of faith, of morality, of God and of incarnation.

Encounters between Christians and Buddhists go back at least to the seventeenth century, and this history has influenced perceptions on both sides, varying from country to country, in India, Sri Lanka, Japan, China and Europe. It becomes possible to see from a Buddhist perspective that Buddhism is more than a system of 'mere morality' and that a Christian understanding of incarnation may not necessarily entail a negative judgement on other religious figures. From a Christian perspective, it is clear that Jesus' 'focus on opennness, truthfulness and unconditional love can be shared with Buddhists in a mutually accepting commitment. It may be that reflecting together on basic human experiences, such as suffering, death and relationship in the present, we may develop communion in the act of communication, building identity in partnership (ibid., 175). This is a valuable insight into one strand of interreligious dialogue, which may have useful consequences for the conduct of other sorts of dialogue, wherever there is a need for greater understanding and more active participation in partnership.

grave manipulation and abuse. There is also a code of honour, through which children may feel good about contributing tangibly to the family income.

In this context, the individual case worker may be able to do something to alleviate the worst abuse by highlighting its nature. But if the family is content with the arrangement, this may produce new alienation. If families are not to starve, alternative sources of support must be found. This requires lobbying at the national and international levels on what are essentially global economic issues. It also requires legal action in foreign countries to ensure that their nationals are inhibited from exploiting the Thai population. However, no country likes to become a focus of international indignation, which itself can be a convenient cover for hypocrisy. This means that concrete action demands attention to these cultural differences which we have already encountered when considering the relation of rights to value systems in the East and West.

In the context of intercivilizational rights, Martha Nussbaum has developed a capabilities approach, by reference to women's rights in India (Nussbaum 2000), which I find attractive. She lists central human functional capabilities, vital to the dignity and well being of each person. These include: life, bodily health, bodily integrity, senses, imagination and thought, emotions, practical reason, relation to other species, play, and political and material control, over one's environment (Nussbaum, 2000, 80). These encompass basic capabilities, internal capabilities and combined capabilities: 'Citizens of repressive nondemocratic regimes have the internal but not the combined capability to exercise thought and speech in accordance with their consciences' (Ibid., 85).

Capabilities have a close relationship to human rights, to political and civil liberties and to economic and social rights. Combined capabilities are rights and do not have the 'Western' tone of rights talk, although rights language is still useful in drawing attention to the role of justification and the importance of liberty in argument for capabilities.

This theoretical framework provides a basis for renewed attention to women's preferences and options in a world that has long systematically suppressed women.

The capabilities approach has the additional merit of strengthening the concern for equality, which is an increasing problem in a globalized world. Tom Campbell, in his 'Globalising Equality – The Equal Worth Project' (in Horton and Patapan, 2004, 23ff) commends the capabilities approach: 'One advantage of this approach is that it can serve to articulate a range of valued properties whose significance is reached when they obtain a certain threshold or degree at which the capacities in question can be said to be exercised' (Horton and Patapan, 2004, 41). He develops the idea of foundational descriptive equalities:

> This takes us to the idea of human rights as a basis for universal obligations and rights, grounded in the foundational fact that the human experiences of pleasure and pain, freedom and dominion, hope and fear are basically the same the world over....

In this context it may seem wise to focus, not on complete equality of well-being properties, but on a conception of equal minimum well-being as a prescriptive goal that knows no national boundaries. (Ibid., 45)

Twenty-first Century Threats to Rights

New forms of the threat of intolerance constantly appear. In the twenty-first century new forms of Christianity are producing new and often unpredicted complications. One of these is the huge rise in various forms of fundamentalism. I believe that there is an urgent need, especially from a rights perspective, to face the challenge of fundamentalism while maintaining constructive links with more liberal evangelical groups on social and ethical issues. In the United States there is a new right-wing Christian rhetoric that is sometimes deeply Islamophobic (cf. Kirkpatrick, 2004; Kristoff, 2004).[16] But there are no apocalyptic solutions, Catholic or Protestant; patience and long-term contributions are needed. In the face of the retreat from human rights it is important to press ahead with rights issues through the dissemination of information, advocacy and action.

---

16 Kristoff's and Kirkpatrick's articles were published in the *New York Times* and were the last in the *Left Behind* series, which has sold over 60 million copies in the United States. This series may be centred around the Rapture and Millennialism, but such sentiments are also clear in right-wing Catholic thought – consider, for example, Cardinal Ratzinger's 2004 instruction to US bishops on refusing communion to some US politicians (cf. A. Sullivan in *Sunday Times,* 18 July 2004).

CHAPTER 9

Christology for Human Rights

Realized Christology: Reconciliation and Forgiveness

The need for an evolving research tradition in relation to rights brings us back to the Christological path. Seen in the light of the rights problematic it would appear that any Christological contribution will be made at different levels. The multilevel impact would encompass:

1 Christology and the philosophical issues – the nature of rights, the uses of rights talk and the basic rights issues;
2 Christology and politics – solidarity with the marginalized;
3 Christ, Christian faith and life – different Christian cultures expressing discipleship differently, but all having a basic common orientation;
4 Christology and enforcement – incarnation, information, advocacy and action.

In the political realities of the contemporary world, these strands are present in different sorts of combination. We have characterized the Christ of faith as the icon of the self-giving, outward-facing love of God. In human relationships, both individual and social, this translates into a catalytic capacity for reconciliation. Reconciliation recognizes damaged relationships, which are intrinsic to human rights violations, and facilitates restoration, restitution and forgiveness. Reconciliation cannot be imposed from above. Its shape cannot be determined by one party to a complex issue. It requires not only patient preparation of the ground, but also an acknowledgement of fault. However, a Christian understanding of reconciliation will not necessarily always demand an overtly 'Christian' outcome. It will be understood as human reconciliation, worked at through faith in Christ and by reflecting on the divine love.

The classic recent example of the implementation of a consciously Christian vision of reconciliation has been the South African Truth and Reconciliation Commission. Here is incarnation into reconciliation. The commission has by no means achieved perfect outcomes, but it has succeeded in bringing a crucial dimension of healing to a deeply divisive and wounded society. Yet, such a strategy would not be directly applicable in a society where there was no prevailing culture of Christian language and values. The challenge will be to consider how the underlying attitude to supporting a generous approach to human relationality can be deployed elsewhere.

Archbishop Tutu in *No Future without Forgiveness* gave an excellent description of the apartheid system itself (Tutu, 1999, 217ff):

> The highest virtue in South Africa came to be conformity, not bucking the system. The highest value was set on unquestioning loyalty to the dictates of

the Broederbond. That is perhaps why people did not ask awkward questions. (Ibid., 222)

He goes on to look at the intractable problems of Rwanda:

> Those who had turned against one another in this gory fashion had often lived amicably in the same villages and spoken the same language. They had frequently intermarried and most of them had espoused the same faith – most were Christian. (Ibid., 258)

He concluded that:

> Forgiving and being reconciled are not about pretending that things are other than they are. (Ibid., 270)

We should reconsider the relationship of reconciliation to forgiveness. In the first instance, forgiveness in Christian theology is the unconditional forgiveness of sin, of forms of relationality which fall short of the unconditional love that reflects the love of God. All other usage reflects this primary use. It is tempting to suggest that, because of the divine reconciliation with humanity through Jesus Christ, the love of God may cut through the complexities of human relationships in an act of instant transformation. The danger is of 'cheap grace'. There may be occasions when it is not appropriate for human beings to forgive others unless and until there is recognition of the damage done and a consistent attempt to make amends for that damage. Instant forgiveness may lead to only superficial reconciliation.

Attention to human rights may produce positive results in the recognition of a denial of these rights and a change of policy to grant rights. The situation may well remain complicated by the consequences of the denial of rights. Where those who were denied rights are long since dead, it is impossible to undo the past. But there can be recognition of wrongs done and symbols of respect. Where the oppressed are still present, there may be justified anger and resentment at the damage done, making relations of true reciprocity difficult. Here, the concept of forgiveness may play an important role, provided that it is not improperly used.

Forgiveness is not initially the appropriate framework for those who have been the deniers of rights. Imagined transgressions on the part of the discriminated against have to be recognized as arising from the pressures of the situation in which they have been placed, and a new basis of partnership must be created. Yet here, too, there may be a significant role for forgiveness. The struggle for rights can produce victims, often unintended, on both sides, and it is here that forgiveness and reconciliation can play an important role, as was seen in South Africa.

In *Between Vengeance and Forgiveness* (1999), Martha Minow offers a profound reflection on the ambiguities of forgiveness, with particular reference to South Africa:

> So this book inevitably becomes a fractured meditation on the incompleteness and inescapable inadequacy of each possible response to collective atrocities. It is also a small effort to join in the resistance to forgetting. (Minow, 1999, 5)

The questions will outstrip any answers. As Ruby Plenty Chiefs once said, 'Great evil has been done on earth by people who think they know all the answers.' (Ibid., 8)

She provides a careful analysis of the aspirations of the Truth and Reconciliation Commission (ibid., 87) and raises the issue of reparations (ibid., 91ff). She notes that:

Forgiveness is a power held by the victimised, not a power to be claimed. (Ibid., 17)

Between vengeance and forgiveness lies the path of recollection and affirmation and the path of facing who we are, and what we could become. (Ibid., 147)

The language of forgiveness and reconciliation may be manipulated. Yet an awareness of forgiveness linked to compassion is a hugely valuable Christian contribution to the complex negotiation of the fruits of human rights in society. Forgiveness has often opened up the dimension of generosity as a catalyst to move complex issues forward. The development of critical emancipatory theology provides some resources for the comparative reappraisal of the history of marginal groups and the impact of contemporary Christologies on their lives. It raises, in acute form, the problem of undoing the past and of retrospective forgiveness and reconciliation – paradigmatically in the tragedies of anti-Semitism and the Palestinian crisis.

More light is shed on the pros and cons of forgiveness in *Forgiveness and Reconciliation* edited by R.G. Helmick and R.L. Petersen, (2001). In the Preface Archbishop Tutu comments that 'We are made to tell the world that there are no outsiders' (Helmick and Petersen, 2001, xiii). Petersen stresses relationality: 'The terms of forgiveness are meant to bring us into relation with one another, not to drive us apart through self-justification or modes of insincerity (ibid., 17). Miroslav Volf seeks to preserve the link with justice: 'A genuine embrace, an embrace that neither play-acts acceptance nor crushes the other, cannot take place until justice is attended to (ibid., 43). He comments that '[t]he step from the narrative of what God has done for humanity on the cross of Christ to the account of what human beings ought to do in relation to one another has often been left unmade in the history of Christianity (ibid., 47). Don Shriver reminds us of our own fallibility: '*We are all vulnerable to collaboration in the doing of great evil to our neighbours:* If Christians bring any gifts to politics, this truth about us all ought to be one of them' (ibid.,162).

In Chapter 8 we explored the contribution of an open Christology to these tangled geopolitical issues. We have to try to see beyond the failures of the churches, past and present, to the continuing vulnerable love of God. George Ellis (Polkinghorne, 2001, 122ff) has written of the importance of kenotic actions in conflict situations: 'They are appropriate when they have the potential to transform the nature of the situation to a higher level' (ibid., 122). They should not be able to be taken for granted by opponents, for then they could not be transformative.

In the same volume Keith Ward writes:

Jesus' life of healing the sick, forgiving the guilt-ridden, befriending social
outcasts, and undermining hypocrisy, is a very good image of the compassionate
and persuasive love of God...In the moment of kenosis, God relates the divine
being to creatures who have a proper autonomy and otherness, which it is the
divine will not to infringe.

There is a very definite cosmic vision implicit in a Christian view of creation
as a cosmic and pleromal process. (Ibid., 166)

Reconciliation is not something that occurs spontaneously in complex conflicts; it
requires action at various different levels, from the general to the minutely particular.
It calls for a cumulative strategy which is neither distracted by detail not marooned
in romantic generality. How may we try to ensure that an effective strategy is not
constantly derailed by uncertainty? We shall not do this by theology alone.

Recognizing God's Love

A Christology for human rights can be articulated in a number of ways. If it is to
enrich our understanding of the goals of human rights, then it should encapsulate
the nature of the Christian understanding of the love of God, as we have sought
to characterize this in earlier chapters. It should illuminate the self-giving, self-
dispossessing nature of divine reality as a pattern for human relationships.

What is it to speak of the divine love? Theologians by no means speak with one
voice on the subject. Dr Muehling-Schlapkohl of Kiel, in an exploration of the basis
of ontological language (Muehling-Schlapkohl, 2000), has recently made this very
clear in his logical analysis of the shape of relationality in the understanding of love
in the theological tradition.

As his starting point Dr Muehling-Schlapkohl uses Martin Luther's perspective
on human and divine love: man can only understand love as he understands himself
as God's creature. Augustine's work on the Trinity is now subjected to rigorous
scrutiny. God is here conceived primarily as an individual. In this he is followed by
Karl Barth, though not by Friedrich Schleiermacher. Eberhard Jungel's attempt to
speak of divine relationship through the language of event is no more satisfactory,
and Lucien Richard's concept is heavily dependent on his particular version of the
ontological argument. Jürgen Moltmann lacks a properly grounded ontology. Karl
Liebner comes too close to modalism. John Zizioulas fails to clarify to what extent
the persons are constituted by love. Wolfhart Pannenberg's view of love as a power
or field may be more productive. Within this group, Richard Swinburne excels in
clarity, but his conception or person suffers from a body/soul dualism and, again, a
tendency to modalism. Some understand God as love in such a way that the persons
of the Trinity have no distinct extensionality; others do not. For all the models, love
is more than a mere attitude: it seems that the unity of God is safeguarded only when
the persons are constituted through love.

Muehling-Schlapkohl then constructs his own model for understanding the
statement that God is love, first considering love as a human mode of relational
behaviour and then considering the individuated Trinity as the objectivity of God.

He argues that God, in his revelation to us, is always experienced and identified as a Trinitarian, relational being. Moreover, faith is not an earthly religion of love, but a God-given religion of love, experienced in the framework of creation *ex nihilo* and in redemption *sola gratia*, based on God's self-relatedness, not on his relation to the world. The unity and diversity of the persons come from the same source and sustain each other in being. As such, the inner Trinitarian relationships can be understood through the metaphor of friendship.

The conscious concentration on inner Trinitarian relationships means that no illuminating comparison with other human portrayals of love, and indeed lack of love, in literature, politics and history is developed. There is almost no sense of conceptual input from the cultural setting. But it does highlight the range of conceptions within the limited field of dogmatic theology alone. Somehow, much theological reflection on the nature of divine love succeeds in inhibiting, rather than facilitating, its essential characteristic of openness and porosity.

James Alison comments pertinently on the use of love as motif in theology:

> I think we would be wise to send the word 'love' to the laundry, and use the word 'like' instead. ....It seems to me that the doctrine of the incarnation of our Lord, the image of God coming among us as the likeness of humans, is a strong statement that the divine regard is one of *liking* us, here and now, as we are. And this means that the one who looks at us is not just looking at us with a penetrating and inscrutable gaze of utter otherness, but is looking at us with the delight of one who enjoys our company, who wants to be one with us, to share in something with us. (Alison, 2003, 107)

Is love enough? In the real world, no wars are just, but some wars may be justified. It may not be very Christian to maintain armed forces just to promote the national interest – conducting diplomacy by another means. But suppose other people – not ourselves – are being persecuted? The gospel (we can say it so easily) is for the marginalized and the oppressed. *Vox victimarum vox Dei*: the voice of the victims is the voice of God. Where there are atrocities, there is suffering, and there is intractable evil in the world. There is also love, often undetectable. Elizabeth Stuart has suggested that '[w]e love because we are loved first. Those who love us first, before we are able to love, spin powerful threads between us' (Stuart, 1995, 58).

Like the resurrection, love so often comes as a surprise – not in solemn pronouncements but in unexpected events and encounters. God likes us. God is there to remind us that violence may often be a hideous reality but it is not the last word. As the martyrs in the Book of Daniel put it, if there is a God who is able to save us from the blazing fiery furnace, it is our God whom we serve and he will save us. But if not, tough. We will stick with it. God likes the whole of the created order. God is constantly trying to persuade us to delight in being liked, to look squarely at doom and gloom and reject it, and to say 'no' to injustice, inequality and disrespect. Every human being is allowed to say, 'God likes us, and we should like ourselves too.' When we try to do something about the dark side of our world, in our own modest ways, we should perhaps try to remember that God is there before us. There may be quite a bit of the apocalyptic still around, but life is totally worthwhile: God likes us all.

Christology in Community: The Way of Schleiermacher

What is missing in a purely theoretical approach to the divine love, and essential for an understanding of the integral connection between Christ and human rights, was, I think, anticipated in an important way 200 years ago in Schleiermacher's Christology. Although I do not believe that any single avenue to Christology is the only viable pathway, my own liberal approach owes a great deal to Schleiermacher, and I therefore want to look in some detail at Schleiermacher's Christological tradition – a tradition that continues to be widely misunderstood.

For Schleiermacher, community and relationality are decisive. If Kant had put away knowledge to make room for faith, it was Schleiermacher who transformed the Kantian moral diet into a warm affection for Christ the redeemer, a man totally engulfed in the consciousness of God and the creator of community. Christ and community, suitably reimagined, was always basic to Schleiermacher's Christianity. Although he was to rebel against the moralism and restricted lifestyle of the Moravian Brethren, he was deeply affected by the life of Christ-centred piety which they taught, and always regarded himself as 'a Moravian of a higher order'. His ground-breaking hermeneutics is intimately related to the Word by which all things were made, centred on the Word made flesh. As contemporary theology has sought to appropriate new dimensions – for example, in Catholic and liberation theologies – I will remain indebted to Schleiermacher for his threefold emphasis on experience, Christology and community, and for his concern with hermeneutics.[1]

In Schleiermacher's early *Speeches*, Christology is viewed in the framework of religion in general and then in the specific context of Christian religion. Jesus is seen as the mediator *par excellence* between the spiritual and the material realm. What Christology meant for Schleiermacher in his middle period is best seen in the *Christmas Eve* dialogue. Here Christ is understood through the transmission of Christlikeness in Christian community. Feeling, rather than rationality alone, is the medium of communication. Here is a transition which others have made in seeking to expand the basis of communicative rationality – one may think of Habermas, for example.

There is here a very high view of the church, as the community in which Christ is mediated to humanity in mutuality and reciprocity. Christ is always understood in his relation to humanity, not as lord but as friend. Schleiermacher speaks here of

---

1   There is an excellent succinct comparison of the Christologies of Schleiermacher and Barth in Roger Haight's *Jesus Symbol of God* (2001, 301ff). Baur judged that Schleiermacher failed to bridge the gulf between the historical Jesus and the Christ of faith. But Schleiermacher had his own subtle way of acknowledging historical problems and still using the narratives as a vehicle for preaching the sacramental word (cf. DeVries, 1996, 71ff).

the church as the source of joyfulness and is not concerned with negative aspects of church life.[2]

In *The Christian Faith* there is an extended treatment of all the main areas of Christology. In his classic definition, 'Christianity is a monotheistic faith, of the teleological type of religion, and is essentially distinguished from other such faiths by the fact that in it, everything is related to the redemption accomplished by Jesus of Nazareth (Schleiermacher, 1928, 11). Central is redemption, and the reality of redemption is firmly related to Jesus. Only Jesus requires no redemption and must therefore be different, in kind rather than degree, from the rest of humanity – and this leads theologians into all the problems of Christology. The creation of the redeemer is an eternal action or decree of God. But in order that a specific intervention of God against the natural processes of history may be avoided, the human race is taken to be originally created in such a way as to have the power of bringing forth, in due time, such a single perfect life. The appearance of the redeemer is complex and unique: it involves both the creation of something new and the development of something originally given.

In the second part of *The Christian Faith*, (paras 86–99), incarnation is historically worked through as salvation – the full working out of what was begun at the creation. So the redeemer takes the form of the appearance in history of the perfect form of humanity. We recognize his central importance by his activity – activity which we see not through the successful working out of the Christian community in empirical terms, but through the inexhaustible power which he gives to those who believe. In Christ the religious dimension of human nature is perfectly completed, so it is necessary to speak of an actual being of God in him. But although he is the perfect

---

2   Janet Martin Soskice captures the spirit of the *Christmas Eve* dialogue remarkably well.

We are very near the heart of Schleiermacher's Christology, and of his hermeneutics. The adult Christians in the story (the community of piety) mediate the gift of divine life to the infant, as they do to each other. This is possible because each is illumined by the light of the Christ child, whose aureole embraces each individual and makes them all one. God, dwelling with them, is present in their loving communion and is their loving communion. Jesus as for Adam, this new baby will come into 'a world' through the love of and communion with other people. (Soskice in Olivetti, 1999, 572)

Richard Niebuhr notes in the Jesus of the *Dialogue*, as compared with the *Speeches*, a 'greater emphasis on the historical necessity of his person as the embodiment of original and true humanity' (Niebuhr, 1964, 35). He sees here the conviction 'that the central figure of Christmas can be approached, if there is any access to him at all, only through the experience of his benefits or of his life as it is mediated in the historical continuity of such human fellowship as is represented here by the circle of family members and friends (ibid., 44). 'Contemporaneity is with Christ as he is reflected and refracted in the innumerable facets of socially mediated experience' (ibid., 45). Niebuhr supports this view from the 1806 sermons: 'It is clear that Schleiermacher does not believe that human words have the power to create relationship to Christ but rather he believes that the relationship is established by Christ himself or by the spirit of Christ.' I regard this comment as profoundly significant for the interpretation of Schleiermacher's Christology. Christ is always understood in his relation to humanity, not as lord but as friend.

There is also an excellent discussion of the dialogue in Verheyden (1975, xxiff). He notes that Leonhardt represents historical theology and criticism, Ernst religious consciousness and Eduard 'man -in -himself': the three strands of theological construction.

form of humanity, he is also a being completely involved in history, conditioned by his times and background. This conditioning stops short only in the innermost part of his life – here there is a firmness which shuts out all temptation. Therefore Christ is also the instrument for the indwelling of God in the whole of humanity. He has the power to transmit this God-filled consciousness to all human beings, yet to do so in the same way as other men influence each other, not by any magical process. God's creative act and the development of the human race are inextricably bound together. The concept of freedom, the subject of Schleiermacher's early dissertation, is central to the Christology. Redemption creates freedom and Christian liberty, and is never coercive.[3]

I have suggested (Newlands, 2006, 187ff) that Schleiermacher makes a shift from a text-based to a person-based theology, from a focus on the biblical text to a focus on the person of God in Jesus Christ, something that is problematic but may be highly significant for the long-term future of theology. I see this as consonant with the mystical dimension of Schleiermacher's thought, with its emphasis on the invisible influence of the spirit of Christ operating mysteriously through the church and the world. It reflects the Johannine emphasis in the Christology. David Tracy, whose work is in many ways the closest contemporary reflection of Schleiermacher, has emphasized the dual importance of the mystical and the prophetic sides of the Christian faith. In Schleiermacher the mystical predominates, although the prophetic comes to fuller expression in his *Life of Jesus*. The central role of the church is preaching – preaching the Word of redemption. However, his engagement with politics, education and social issues indicates that the prophetic strain in Christology also influences his thought, although not in the direct (and, in their own way, also problematic) manner of later social theologies.

Christology leads directly to church and community. We come to faith within the Christian community, through regeneration, justification and conversion. (Schleiermacher, 1928, 476f). The Holy Spirit works through the community and also through the wider society. For Schleiermacher, the Holy Spirit is of central importance. Although he did not have a spirit Christology in the later twentieth-century sense, his was certainly not a Christomonist approach to faith.[4]

---

3   Although he chooses not to use the Chalcedonian imagery of the two natures, he still wants to speak of Jesus as fully divine and fully human, the relationship being constituted by Jesus' unique God-consciousness. This consciousness signals the divine presence and is Schleiermacher's version of the incarnate Logos. Redemption and reconciliation leads to the blessed state of union with Christ. This sense of beatitude, individual and communal, may shut out the effects of bodily suffering and is the quintessential spiritual experience. John Macquarrie has felicitously characterized Schleiermacher's as a humanistic Christology, in the tradition of Irenaeus, underlining his sensitivity to the need to do justice to the intentions of the classical tradition.

4   Clive Marsh has spoken of a Trinitarian Christocentrism rather than a Christological Trinitarianism (Tice, 1993, 87ff), and Ralph Del Colle addressed the question of a Spirit Christology in the same series. Del Colle characterizes the relationship in the following way. Schleiermacher's Christology is 'an exemplarist Christology in which the reality of God present in and revealed through Jesus Christ becomes present in and transformative of the human condition. The theological symbol for such presence is Spirit' (Del Colle in Tice, 1994, 180ff).

Schleiermacher affirms that 'there is no living fellowship with Christ without an indwelling of the Holy Spirit, and vice versa.' (ibid.,124). There is a convergence between the pneumatological and the Christological. This is a position that is perhaps echoed later by Donald Baillie in his famous (and much criticized) use of the paradox of grace in the individual Christian life to illuminate the nature of the union of the human and divine natures in Christ. The church as the sphere of the Spirit is a central agent of divine action – in community, in baptism and in Eucharist. Participation in the Lord's Supper confirms our fellowship in union with Christ (ibid., 651). The sequel to the coming of Christ is the church of the divine vision, the ideal to which we are drawn. It is the community of Christ and the community of friends in which Schleiermacher personally found contentment, kindness and generosity – beatitude. This is an important factor, but it means that there is little or no treatment of the negative aspects of the church.

Schleiermacher's concentration on the church did not prevent him from seeing the relevance of Christology to a wider society, although he saw the church as the crucial link between Christ and society. He was concerned to link Christology firmly to ethics, as the *Introduction to Christian Ethics* makes clear. 'The existence of a special Christian ethics stands or falls with the superhuman conception of the person of Christ'(Schleiermacher, 2002, 53).

Through Christ, and by his own testimony and the testimony of Christians from the earliest period, an active power has entered the church. This power is designated the divine spirit, and this is the moral capacity that is effective in the Christian church. Christ's behaviour is the basis of Christian behaviour.[5]

Schleiermacher preferred to speak of the divine activity rather than the divine nature. The divine activity brings about Jesus' perfect God-consciousness. God is also present in the church, as the Holy Spirit. The same divine activity that was in Christ is also present in the church. (Donald Baillie would argue later, turning the equation, from the experience of grace to the paradox of grace in the incarnation.) Because God is love, the divine essence unites with the human nature in Jesus and in

---

5   F. LeRon Shults has seen in Schleiermacher's thought a 'constructive and regulative principle of reciprocal rationality' which he sees as operating throughout his work and notably in his Christology (Shults in Richardson, 1998): 'Christology is not intended to counterbalance the transcendent ground of the feeling of absolute transcendence. Rather, it is the central test case for the regulative function of reciprocal relationality' (ibid., 192). The work of Christ should be regarded 'as the completion, now only accomplished, of the creation of human nature' (Schleiermacher, 1928, 365). We may note the continuance of this perspective in Schillebeeckx's view of Christology as concentrated creation, in reaction to dualist accounts of creation and redemption.

Richard Niebuhr aptly describes Schleiermacher's work as Christomorphic theology. Other religions come close to Christianity to the extent that they convey a sense of absolute dependence on God and that they create a sense of participating in God's purpose for history. Creation leads to redemption: 'The feeling of absolute dependence is fully formed only in and through the agency of Christ, the Spirit and the Church' (Niebuhr, 1964, 247). Mark Chan has recently offered an interesting characterization of Schleiermacher's Christology as 'a Christology of the heart'. Schleiermacher roots Christology in experience. Subjectivity is transcendental, mediated and intersubjective. Faith, as a response to revelation, comes through inner experience and personal friendship, but it happens within a particular Church tradition, 'inalienably rooted in history and ecclesiality' (Chan, 2000, 188).

the church, as God becomes a Trinity in history. Schleiermacher leaves a challenge to later thinkers to reimagine the tradition not by restoring any particular project to its original pristine state, but by exploring new dimensions. This would doubtless involve issues beyond the European arena to which he addressed himself and take in the emancipatory theologies as a balance to the strain of individual pietism in which he was brought up and which influenced his work. But in counterpoint to this heritage, Schleiermacher's concern, throughout his theological work and not least in his Christology, was for all human beings and for dialogue in the widest possible frame.

Christology is for all humanity. It may be legitimately and properly committed to the delivery of basic human rights for every human being.

After Schleiermacher

Schleiermacher is our entry point to a progressive Christology. But much constructive work has been done in Christology in the intervening 200 years. Divine love incarnated means relationality and community. It raises the question of the limits, if any, of community. But whose community? It has been, and remains, incredibly hard for Christianity, and indeed for other world religions, to understand community as embracing all human beings, in their diversity as individuals and groups as well as in their commonality. In many instances we still exhibit a tribal preference for those who seem to be most like ourselves. In other instances it is often easier for Christians to empathize with people who live far away and who they never meet face-to-face than with their nearest neighbours. 'The last temptation is the greatest treason.'

As Charles Taylor and others have observed, there is a limit to the power of moral exhortation. It is not easy to persuade people to commit themselves to courses of action which they find uncomfortable or costly in terms of time and resources. Embracing tolerance and granting negative freedom may be valuable first steps towards the implementation of human rights. Freedom from fear is infinitely better than being constantly terrified. Beyond this there is a need to positively recognize the goal of achieving the maximum available capacity for human flourishing and to acknowledge a variety of cultural values and personal circumstances.

Joining up the Dots

I do not claim, as theologians have often done, that a Christian perspective will automatically yield an agreed basis for human rights culture. What I do claim is that a Christian construal of human love, as mirroring the divine love understood through Jesus Christ, has a hugely valuable capacity to assist in generating a consistent and unconditional engagement with human rights issues. It has not always done so and may not always do so in the short or medium term. But Christianity, along with other major religions, encourages us to take a very long-term view and to develop aspirations based on future potential.

In other words, the basis for my position here is an application of the view which I set out in *The Transformative Imagination* (2004) and described as the metamodern, deriving from discussions of postfoundationalism and foundherentism.

Accepting the demise of foundationalism, in explicit or implicit form – that is, of the idea that there can be one overarching theory and structure of knowledge – and the advent of non-foundationalism, Wentzel van Huyssteen in his book, *The Shaping of Rationality*, seeks to avoid relativism 'where incommensurability may finally stifle all meaningful cross-disciplinary dialogue'(Wentzel van Huyssteen, 1999, 11). Knowing has experiential and hermeneutical dimensions, leading to a postfoundationalist fusion of hermeneutics and epistemology. Rationality balances 'the way our beliefs are anchored in interpreted experience and the broader networks of belief in which our rationally compelling experiences are already embedded' (ibid., 14). These networks include the 'research traditions' in which communities are embedded, and these ideas are then developed systematically in dialogue with other writers in the field, notably with Calvin Shrag's notion of 'transversal rationality' and Susan Haack's concept of 'foundherentism'.

The metaphor of the metamodern, as I would want to use it, signals postmodernity in an *inclusive* and transformative sense, rather than as a limiting and prescriptive mode. It underlines that the postmodern is, in many respects, very much part of the modern, and is unthinkable without the modern not only as its origin, but also as a continuing force. The metamodern acknowledges both the advantages and the disadvantages of the traditional ontological categories of the European tradition. The metamodern emphasizes all that scholars such as Bernstein and Berlin have had to say about engaged, fallibilistic pluralism and agonistic liberalism. It is, then, not so much a category as a *signal*, indicating inclusivity and flexibility.[6]

My intention here is to describe a Christological component of that unforced or intercivilizational consensus which appears to provide the best way forward towards the delivery of human rights goals.

Transformative Practice

One of the distinctive characteristics of Christology is in its capacity to imagine 'the world turned upside down', a situation where the prevailing status quo is not the only determining factor in our thinking . Exactly to the point is the Korean American theologian J.Y. Lee's recent striking, and perhaps characteristically rarely cited, *Marginality*:

> Marginality and centrality are so mutually inclusive and relative that it is imbalanced to stress one more than the other...By stressing marginality over centrality, we can restore the balance between the two poles... Like the ripples

---

6   Since writing this I have come to value the distinction which Cobb and Griffin frequently make between a postmodernism of construction, which seeks to relate the physical world to notions of Christian transformation, and a postmodernism of deconstruction, which tends to concentrate on individual self-understanding.

in the pond, our lives are filled with many centers and margins; margins are also
created inside of centers.(Lee, 1995, 31)

Lee develops the notion of marginality creatively, aware of the risks in accepting the
perspectives of the majority groups in society:

> The idea of connectedness 'in-between' leads us to a positive and self-affirming
> understanding of marginality 'in-both' worlds. This new self-affirming definition
> complements the earlier self-negating definition, or the classical definition of the
> dominant group. (Ibid., 47)

He relates marginality directly to theology:

> The power of the new marginality is love, which is willing to suffer redemptively
> by accepting others unconditionally as Jesus did on the cross. If justice is more
> important than love in liberation theology, love is more important than justice in
> marginal theology. Justice reacts to injustice but love responds to it; justice often
> demands revenge but love forgives. (Ibid., 73)

He construes Jesus Christ as the margin of marginality and incarnation as divine
marginalization:

> The determinants of Jesus' marginality, class, economic, political, social, and
> ethnic orientations, made him the marginal person par excellence, so the stories
> of incarnation ought to be interpreted from the perspective of marginality. During
> the incarnation, God was marginalised in Jesus Christ. (Ibid., 79)

Lee thinks in terms of a principle of reversal. True discipleship comes through
the new marginal people of God. Creative transformation involves overcoming
marginality through marginality (ibid., 149f).

Students of rights literature are not short of important technical studies in
innumerable aspects of rights language in legal and philosophical studies. But it
is rare to come across imaginative concepts that so decisively upset our instinctive
ordering of things as Lee's work does. It is possible to construe incarnation as a
divine 'wake-up call' to humanity to focus thought and action in unconditional self-
giving, solidarity and compassion. This is not a call to sacrifice for its own sake but
a suggestion that the human good is achieved by concern for the most vulnerable.
It has some similarities to John Rawls's notion of blind choice in matters of justice.
The crucial difference is that we should try always to see ourselves in those who are
most disadvantaged, and this will vary from instance to instance.

Clearly, this is not how Christology has always functioned, and we shall always
fall short of the goal. But it does provide an important focal point of aspiration and
hope – a pointer to the human good which has shown a capacity, Christians believe,
to encourage and facilitate transformation.

Faith understands human love as a mirror of divine love which may be offered
by people of faith to others who do not share that faith. For Christians themselves,
it is immeasurably strengthened by the belief that God is constantly present in

Christomorphic action in the universe, encouraging and persuading towards fulfilment. Traditionally, theology has concentrated on the significance of the Christian perspective within the Christian community, and this remains an immensely powerful vehicle for inspiring action. In addition, it is important to concentrate on the persuasive capacity of Christian beliefs in conjunction with the beliefs of non-Christians. This becomes all the more imperative as the medium term future appears to suggest an increasing polarization between Christian and non-Christian thought and action. A forward-looking Christianity needs to be ever conscious that it is there as a form of Christian witness for the long haul.

Tracing the Rainbow

Progressive Christology, I have emphasized, need be in no sense a reductionist Christology. The eschatological element makes clear that all our theories are only pointers in the direction of the mystery of the divine love. The sociohistorical dimension of faith, with its uncertainties and cultural and temporal limitations, can be honestly affirmed. We do indeed participate in the life of God, but as pilgrims on the way to a mystery – a mystery which will reveal itself in all kinds of ways in the future. Christian truth is true, but it remains a suggestion – a pointer to the Christomorphic future.

Awareness of mystery is not a reason for indecisiveness. Faith remains decisively opposed to evil in all forms, to contempt for human rights and human life. Laws need to be enforceable if rights are to be delivered. The Christomorphic shape of faith points to a *continuing invitation* to reflect on the mystery of God and of the human future in its various cultural dimensions. But the clearing away of injustice is an integral element of the Christian vision, not least where the vision has been clouded by human rights violations in the name of religion or by abusive ideological zeal. The trace of unconditional love gives a sharp refusal to the failure to respect individuals as precious to their creator. An intercultural theology will *prioritize* the most defenceless.

A Christomorphic paradigm is keenly relevant to all discussion of ethics, religion and politics. It sets the priorities as always being related to those at the greatest point of need. This is especially apposite in a political context. It is not enough to reflect on the need to have a better representation of black people or the poor; it is also necessary to devise *strategies for delivering* a greater participation in political and social action on the part of the disadvantaged. In principle, the churches, with their wide coverage of the social and political spectrum, should be able to be vehicles of raising conscience at every level. At present, there is clearly a serious danger that disenchantment may lead, in time, to new forms of authoritarian movements. Abuse of democracy does not take away its proper use.

It is through a conception of *divine action* – for Christian faith, through a sense of the *Christomorphic shape in history*, social, political and personal – that an intercultural theology comes to speak most readily of God. In relation to human rights, in the experience of minority and marginalized peoples, issues of transcendence arise and are pointers for faith to God. We may not extrapolate from our preferred political patterns to the nature of God, to envisage a social democratic triumvirate to all eternity. Yet a God whose nature and actions are less sensitive to the human condition than the best of human thought and action can be neither respected nor worshipped by intelligent beings. For Christian faith, the Christomorphic paradigm is the icon of God's unconditional generosity. This generosity is God's nature. It is both self-subsisting and self-relating. How this is so remains the divine mystery.

The triune pattern expresses God's responsible care for all that is in the cosmos. Creative transcendence points to God *from within* the mystery of suffering and reconciliation in the emancipatory quest. This does not mean that all creation necessarily points to God. Clearly not, for the theodicy problem, and especially the omnipresence of luck, good and bad, and random evil, raises a question mark against all romanticism. The Christomorphic trace enables those who recognize it to cope with the created order and see it as not totally inconsistent with the divine love. Christian discernment is that faith is sometimes effective despite the appearance of things. Most of the time we can see only fragments, sometimes hardly a trace, of a Christomorphic element in the complexities of society. It is the Christian vision which 'traces the rainbow through the rain' and may provide an antidote to indifference, lethargy and despair. This is a *trace* which, from a Christian perspective, we may recognize in other religions and in humanist action, where we recognize the lineaments of the signature of the divine love. Such lineaments are, however, more likely to be found in concrete and coordinated instances of attention to grinding poverty than in sentimental reflection.

The Silent Presence of Christ

Christians have spoken of the unknown Christ of Hinduism and of other religions. By this they have meant that where they see the signs of unconditional love in other religions, or indeed in the activities of secular associations, there they discern the presence of Christ. This is intended as an affirmation of respect and solidarity. However, it suffers inevitably from the danger of covert imperialism, as everything that is good is appropriated to the Christ symbol.

But these Christians have not been entirely wrong. Where there are traces of that kind of generous compassion which is identified with Jesus Christ, Christians are naturally drawn to recognize this, and to discern it in all sorts of places outside standard Christian frameworks, in unfamiliar religious contexts in the society of marginalized groups and in various unlikely contexts. What needs to be said in addition is that people with other religious symbols, or other symbols of value, will naturally recognize the same hallmarks of goodness and will also recognize their central symbols and values in these same activities. For Christians, this self-dispossession does not necessarily mean the kenosis of kenosis in the sense that Christlikeness always becomes totally indiscernible. It is often effective as a pastoral and political trace recognizable to faith as Christian and to other human beings as love. It is true that in difficult circumstances it can fail to be acknowledged as love even by those whom it supports, and in this instance it becomes love undetectable. It is then up to others engaged in a particular context to seek to act within the framework of purpose which they recognize as Christomorphic. A silent presence need not be a passive presence, as people have discovered over the centuries.

Here we have travelled a long way, it may be conceded, from the necessary task of delivering enforceable human rights in the minutiae of individual cases – for example, in employment law. This, too, has its necessary function. The role of the theologian is to attempt to suggest a wider, perhaps more long-term, perspective in which the technical operation of rights action can be understood and re-energized within a cluster of wider horizons of understanding. Although there are inevitably operational demarcations, the boundary between Luther's two kingdoms – the kingdom of God and the state – is ultimately porous, diffuse and dynamically developing. This can be misunderstood as an opening for theocratic interference, but it can also be read as an opportunity for a catalytic facilitating encounter between God and humanity.

Christology *for* Human Rights

I have deliberately avoided the concentration on a Christology *of* human rights. More germane, in my view, is Christology *for* human rights. Direct one-to-one analogies with current issues as Christological moulds are always in jeopardy when they attempt to fit a given mould to a society which is always changing in many directions simultaneously. More helpful perhaps is the recognition that the relation between Christology and human rights will always be a dialectical one, in which the spirit of God is constantly active from above and from below, and that our task is to try to remain alert to its prompting.

Talk of spirit reminds us that Christology can never be as self-contained as we normally find convenient. It should also remind us that we are always thinking of the instantiation of the love of the God who is, Christians believe, the creator and sustainer of all that is. We cannot impose a God concept on rights dialogue which is genuine dialogue, as a given foundation. But we can say that Christian communities and individuals who have worked out ways of living together on the basis of gradually agreed values have drawn strength from the faith that, at the root of all existence, there is a power which is entirely non-coercive and that that power is the power of unconditional love. At least in an informal sense, Christians will say, with Jean-Luc Marion, that before God is being, God is love. They will regard it as significant that human beings – to date, the most complex entities in the cosmos – are the field in which God has become incarnate in the shape of self-dispossessing love. It is as the shape of the mystery of ultimate reality that faith in God through Jesus Christ transforms hearts and minds and societies.

This does not mean that you have to believe in God to be able to access the Christian construal of ultimate reality as love in generous relationality. You may come from a humanist appreciation of social and ethical values without an appeal to transcendence. That distinctively Christian tradition which is centred on the self-abandonment of God does not claim a monopoly on either visions of the common good or construals of God. You may come from another religious tradition, with its own rich resources for accessing and understanding transcendence and compassion. The Christian vision is offered as a contribution, along with other contributions, to the practical tasks of delivering human rights solutions at points of greatest urgency.

There is another paradoxical aspect of the relationship of the divine love to Christian discipleship which often goes unremarked but which should be openly acknowledged here. Some of the most deeply knowledgeable and influential figures in the Christian tradition, past and present, may be at the same time some of the most deeply unpleasant human beings. This is part of the problem of what is traditionally thought of as sin. Piety not uncommonly produces an intransigence and an overwhelming obsession with power, which entirely subverts the considerable gifts which such people bring to Christian life and thought. It can be all too easy to proclaim human rights in the name of Christ and in practice exhibit all the negative characteristics of the traditional bully. If we are to make genuine progress in rights issues, we shall have to name and own up to our inadequacies as a tradition, as well as our constructive resources.

The way, the truth and the life?

What then has become of the traditional affirmation that God is the truth, and that Christ is the way, the truth and the life? Christians in community believe that Jesus Christ plays an indispensable and decisive role in God's purpose for humanity. This is a pointer to mystery – a Christomorphic mystery. It seems to me that all Christians can affirm gladly and doxologically their participation in the life of the triune God in faith. The eschatological element makes clear that all our theories are only pointers in the direction of the mystery of the divine love.

The norms of such a project will be determined by the Christomorphic shape which is the hallmark of all Christian theology and the catalysing contribution to human dialogue about the most serious issues facing humanity. Such norms are crucially *inclusive*. They are sensitive to cultural and political marginality, to the dialogue of world religions, to humanist projects of various sorts. But they are *not infinitely inclusive*. Faith remains decisively opposed to evil in all forms, to contempt for human rights and human life. To take an extreme, but a still all too common, issue, genocide, dialogue might often take the form only of appeasement and be open to manipulation. On a more domestic scale there is need for law enforcement in civil society. Sometimes, as Reinhold Niebuhr famously noted, there is no escape from using the lesser evil of coercion to prevent greater evils being perpetrated on the most vulnerable groups of people. This is part of the fractured nature of the world as we know it.

Rights: Kenosis and Plerosis

At this point we ought to face again the objection that a Christomorphic vision of the self-dispossession of God and an understanding of human beings as owing everything to God and having nothing apart from God ought to make Christians very cautious about rights talk, even on behalf of the oppressed.

In his 2004 essay 'Gathered at the Altar: Homosexuals and Human Rights', Gerard Loughlin cites Conor Gearty's Bray Lecture, and judges that the ambivalence of the church on human rights 'is both further away and closer to the full vision of humanity that Gearty seeks' (Loughlin, 2004, 74). He is clear that '[i]f the church recognises the full humanity of homosexuals outside the church it can do no less when they are inside the church, and yet this is what the church appears to do' (ibid., 76). Loughlin takes as his starting point Thomas Aquinas, for whom everything exists because it is caused by God. We have no rights, except as gifts of God. Human rights discourse tends to forget the God dimension. Without this, rights exist only because they are recognized as such, and rights discourse alone cannot say what it is to be human. The church is the body of Christ, 'where human flourishing is known and celebrated as a social good' (ibid., 80). Failure here is not a matter of rights, but of failure to allow the fulfilment of humanity in the life of Christ. The church should be more harmonious than a body of competing rights, but 'it fails to see who Christ is calling to the altar'. Loughlin concludes that '[i]f the church is correct to be wary of human rights, for what they tempt us to forget, the church may yet learn from human rights how to see the body of Christ more clearly' (ibid., 82).

We may think that although human rights have often been both individualist and neglectful of God, they need not be, and have stemmed partly from Christian sources. There is, as Loughlin himself suggests, room for mutual learning and respect. We may be glad to recognize the Christian contribution both to rights discourse and to aspiration for a vision of love, peace and justice in Eucharistic community, and at the same time remember the hegemonic strand of Christian discourse which may still counter rights and contribute to a despair of transcendence. With Gerard Loughlin we may see, in the Eucharistic dimension, an invitation to generously and gratefully affirm alternative lifestyles rather than purely negative freedom and reluctant tolerance.

But it may also be necessary sometimes to mount a reasoned defence of persecuted minorities within the church. Beyond the Christian community the paramount task is to manifest constructively and in its own right the huge positive potential towards the human flourishing of marginalized groups, who have often learned the true cost of discipleship through suffering.[7] A Christomorphic vision always reminds us that

---

7   The best case for gay rights known to me is David Richards's eloquent and erudite *Identity and the Case for Gay Rights* (Richards, 1999). Richards argues for the integrity of intimate love in gay relationships and their positive connections with wider family relationships. He underlines the dehumanizing effect of homophobia as moral slavery, parallel to, but more radically annihilating through the device of unspeakability, than racism and sexism: 'The uncritical ferocity of contemporary political homophobia draws its populist power from the compulsive need to construct Manichean differences where

Christ suffered 'outside the camp'. Christian community is always an outward-facing community, concerned for the marginalized in society as much as for the marginalized in the church.

The energy of transcendence

For a Christian, Jesus is the man in whom it has indeed become manifest that revolution and conversion cannot be separated in man's search for transcendental experience. His appearance in our midst has made it undeniably clear that changing the human heart and changing human society are not separate tasks, but are as interconnected as the two beams of his cross.

The spirit of Christlikeness encourages response. We have reflected on the Christomorphic trace in history – the recognition which faith sometimes believes to be the action of the divine love in historical and political change. It is right to stress the objectivity of the action of God in Christ, beyond our comprehension and beyond our control. Yet divine action, Christians believe, may sometimes take place in, with and under human action, even our own human action. Changing human society is connected with changing the human heart. Here God acts in mysterious ways, but always produces, in very different sorts of Christians with very different theological perspectives, the same fruits of the spirit – love, compassion, forgiveness reconciliation. In this respect we may think of Martin Luther King, Desmond Tutu and others. This is why we cannot say that one particular theological tradition will necessarily always produce the best results, although we can say that some theological concepts have a poor track record as facilitators of the divine love.

If we have to recognize the element of transcendent mystery in God's action in history, the dimension of mystery is even more apposite in reflecting on the grace of God in human life. Here the connection between the revolution and conversion, between the prophetic and the mystical, is basic. The traditional language of forgiveness and reconciliation in individual lives, and in lives related in community through personal interaction, takes on new life. We are mostly captives of our cultural situation, to the extent that we find it incredibly difficult to act out of turn,

---

none reasonably exist, thus reinforcing institutions of gender hierarchy perceived now to be at threat' (ibid., 164). He finds unusual supports for his case for gay marriage: for example, John Witherspoon lists as a basic human and natural right a 'right to associate, if he so incline, with any person or persons, whom he can persuade (not force) – under this is contained the right to marriage' (ibid., 75). In place of argument about biology, Richards highlights 'the narratives of romantic sexual attraction, quest, passion, and love as well as the narratives of connubial tender transparency and mutual support and nurture and those as well of patience in travail and care and solace in illness and before death' (ibid., 184).

William Talbott comments perceptively on this subject:

> Objections to gay and lesbian marriages are reminiscent of objections to mixed-race marriages. In 1967, the idea of racially mixed marriages evoked the same sort of visceral reaction in some whites that the idea of same-sex marriages evokes in some heterosexuals today. (Talbott, 2005, 136)

This is perhaps a point for both white and non-white Christians to ponder today.

to take unpopular or dangerous initiatives, or to expose ourselves to risk. Yet there are times when some people are able to act on the values of the kingdom, to be vulnerable to the consequences of the world turned upside down. This is where grace in individual lives produces love out of loveless circumstances. This may take the form of respecting human rights where these are violated. Christians understand this phenomenon as the spirit that brings rights to life; this is other than rights talk, but may be expressed through seeking similar goals. Faith may be the motor of mistaken zeal, but it may also produce the fruits of love, peace and justice: the risk is usually worth taking.

In the light of our reconsideration of rights issues we should be able to reconstruct a perspective on the role of Christ in human rights issues. It is clear, not least from the history of Christology, that there is little value in imposing a triumphalist Christology as a solution to rights issues.

Christian faith believes that there is a divine creator of the universe whose nature is expressed in the working out of unconditional love. This love is communicated in many ways, and decisively through the continuing presence in the cosmos of Jesus Christ, manifested through the working of the spirit of Christlikeness in human life.

This whole process is highly mysterious to us, and Christians have understood these events differently at different times. There is, in the understanding of Christ, a considerable measure of agreement on the norms of Christology – on the central strands of what constitutes the character of the love of God through Christ – without agreement on the theory of how this can be so. At the same time, a Christian belief, still unfortunately widespread, that God coerces obedience to his will in ways that violates individual and social rights can be seen to be contrary not only to the central strands of the New Testament narratives, but also to the faithful articulation of the gospel in history.

Historically, some Christologies have been entirely inadequate to support this faithful articulation, precisely because they have obscured the thrust of the gospel towards that concern for the marginalized in society, which was central to the life of Jesus. Here the liberation and emancipatory theologies have performed a crucial service, and 'non–absolutist' Christologies have pointed the way to a conceptually open approach. At the same time, however, the Christian faith has classically drawn strength from an understanding of Jesus Christ as effective not only through his life, but also through his death, which has been seen as making a distinctive difference to the nature of the universe as God's creation and, through his resurrection, as the first transformative product of that difference. This is why faith is quintessentially a trust in God against the appearance of things, often prepared to think and act *contra mundum*. It is important to recall that many Christian actions in support of the marginalized have been sustained through a faith in the efficacy of love through self-giving on the cross and a trust based on the resurrection of Christ.

Christological focal points

None of the classical Christological perspectives, from the most conservative to the most radical, is likely to be as effective in coordinating human rights action as a consensus on the basic Christian norms for human rights action will be. These norms flow from the continuing experience of the presence of Christ to Christian faith in community. The apprehension of the central structuring elements of faith is affected by local theological cultures and concepts. Individual people and communities should be free to contribute in their own ways, and no *single* approach should be understood by either the traditionally liberal or traditionally conservative wings of the churches as *the* authorized way. That is not an easy perspective to actualize.

What is this cluster of Christological norms? They involve the acknowledgement that the unconditional love of God is at the centre of the future of the universe. This love is recognized as being decisively characterized in the life of Jesus of Nazareth, in his words and actions. As the Christian tradition develops, it comes to see this life as focused on self-dispossession and concern for the marginalized, so that the margins become the centre and the centre the margin. This entails care and respect for the most vulnerable in society at every level, as well as advocating a vision of justice and peace as the human future – although, of course, this vision always has to be cashed out concretely in changing cultural circumstances. This tradition meshes closely with the aspirations of the United Nations Charter on Human Rights, which, as recent research makes clear, was much influenced by Christian thinkers in its inception.

But this Christian affirmation of the Charter can only be genuine if it is given to be used freely and be developed by all those affected by the Charter. It is a permissive, rather than a prescriptive, affirmation: it is to open new doors rather than close them. For the churches it also represents a huge challenge to become ever more integrally committed to rights talk and rights enforcement, as well as to engaged conversation with other faiths and secular bodies on rights issues. There is an unconditional obligation on Christian people to embrace human rights norms within a human rights culture and to help to improve upon whatever is currently lacking.

The Christian faith believes that there is a divine creator of the universe whose nature is expressed in the working out of unconditional love. This love is communicated in many ways, and decisively through the continuing presence in the cosmos of Jesus Christ, manifested through the working of the spirit of Christlikeness in human life.

Discerning the Humane

Cultures also need reasons and intellectual support. With the caveat about the need for a catholic and ecumenical approach to justifications, I now want to suggest an approach to Christology and human rights from a research tradition of liberal theology. Mine will be a 'thick' liberal project, with attention to the catholic, evangelical and open elements of a liberal conception. There will quite properly be other Christological justifications.

Threads and traces of theological humanism, of engagement with a loving humane God, in, with and under human thought and action, are to be found throughout the Christian tradition, from the biblical narratives and the Apostolic Fathers, through the Middle Ages to the Renaissance and beyond. With Schleiermacher we find a systematically articulated emphasis on the humanity of Christ as the perfect embodiment of his divinity and, with this the crucial step, a resolve to accept that humanity as humane divinity, rather than as a symbol which is more a concession to our inadequacy than a natural expression of the divine. As such, it resonates with, and for Christians deepens immeasurably, the talk of *humanitas* and *philanthropia* which arose in the early Mediterranean world, and also provides a basis for conversations with conceptions of humanity in other cultures and religious traditions.

What is here envisaged, we have indicated, is a humane Christology which starts from the work of Friedrich Schleiermacher. Of course, although once again it has to be remembered that Schleiermacher was himself hugely indebted to centuries of classical Christology and that later Christologies, notably the liberation and emancipatory theologies, have made crucial advances on Schleiermacher, we are concerned here with the continuing outworking of the whole tradition of the gospel. I find Schleiermacher attractive because he marks a stage in that long, varied and fragmented tradition of humane Christianity with which I most easily resonate and which I am sure will always be an important part of the tradition which many Christians find hospitable to their needs and values.

Christian humanism

You may wonder why I have not yet mentioned Christian humanism. The language of Christian humanism is often close to what I understand by humane Christology, especially in its older forms in the tradition of Erasmus, the Brethren of the Common Life and later writings. More recently it has been associated with 'non–realist' and sometimes 'non-theistic' forms of theology which I find in some ways helpful and in other ways unduly restrictive. I myself see no reason to think that transcendence and immanence are exclusive options. It has been the weakness of earlier forms of liberal theology that, in shedding the depth dimensions of catholic and evangelical spirituality, they have ceased to speak to what is most profound in human individual and social life. A progressive humane Christianity should be able to learn as it develops.

In an earlier chapter we related the life, death and resurrection of Jesus Christ to focal areas of human rights – poverty and hunger, marginalization, torture and the death penalty, respect, recognition and effective resolution. Christian faith may reflect further that these connections are not only human reflections but also traces of the texture of the life of God. It is God, the source of the cosmos, who is committed to economic and social equality, to recalling the marginalized, to rescuing the tortured and the dying, to according respect and bringing this to full and integral completion.

For Christians, God is the ultimate source of effective action. But because he is totally self-giving, God's ultimate fulfilment is not simply for himself but for his creatures. There can be no effective human future without the accomplishment of an effective human rights culture.

I offer this tradition, maybe a little perversely, because it seems to me to be both particularly neglected today and especially important for a Christian human-rights-oriented future. Though apparently forgotten in the rather conservative reconstruction of Christian memory of the present, humanistic Christology is much more widespread than often imagined. Of course there are the obvious sources in various countries: Schleiermacher and Rothe; Catholic modernism and Maritain, Maurice, Adams Brown; and the Baillies, Bonhoeffer and Schillebeeckx. But there are deep strands of humanistic reflection in Rahner and even in Barth, especially in his later writing and some of his letters. There are millions of intelligent, often highly educated, people today for whom religious doctrines, Christian or otherwise, are inaccessible. Such doctrines are often invisible in interreligious dialogue, but they, too, are an important part of a genuinely open conversation about human rights and their enforcement. I regard this constituency, as well as progressive Christian groups, as a potentially important force for human rights in the future.

Salvation: the human rights dimension

In Jesus Christ, Christians have always seen the instantiation of the love of God in its most basic form. The outcome of this divine action was salvation for all humanity. Through interfaith dialogue Christians are coming to learn, slowly and painfully, that an exclusive salvation within an exclusive community for all humanity is a contradiction in terms. From the first fateful inclusion of the gentiles in Pauline Christianity there have been competing pressures within the Christian community to centralize and reach out to the margins. Some Christians are coming to believe that it is possible to combine faith in the centrality of Christ with the recognition that other figures, religious and non-religious, may be pathways to the love of God in other cultures. For classical Christology, Jesus Christ is what he does and does what he is. He brings salvation, fulfilment, peace and the justice of God.

Salvation has been described in Christian tradition in very many ways: as rescue and reconciliation, as the gift of new life, as rescue from a great evil, as atonement, as propitiation, as purifying sacrifice and many other things. I suggest that we may view salvation as including the recognition and enforcement of human rights. Of course, there is more to salvation than human rights. Salvation is not a response to demand or obligation but a new and transformative gift of God, but also a response to human rights culture. Although this has been worked through as a specifically Christian reflection, it can also be conducted, in an appropriately varied form, through other traditions, both religious and non-religious. There may be no ultimate conflict between self-interest and altruism: it is in all our interests to live in a community where there is mutual satisfaction. The alternatives are likely to be unstable, unless stabilized by totalitarian polity, which may in itself lead to greater instability.

As far as I am aware, a formal theological connection between human rights and salvation has not yet been fully articulated, although a valuable beginning was made by Ignacio Ellacuria before his murder in Central America. Ellacuria's work, however, reached only a limited public, and with the weakening and partial suppression of liberation theology in Latin America it has not been developed. Nevertheless, when we reflect on the innumerable references to salvation in churches, books and websites throughout the Christian world, we may begin to imagine how effective a proactive coupling of salvation concepts with human rights could be. Of course, we would still have to test the legitimacy of the use of rights language, open as it is to all kinds of abuse. But the potential remains.

It is not necessary to limit the Ellacuria instance to the political arena. We have seen how Alison, also a long-term worker in South America, used the language of liberation in meditation on the marginalization of gay people, particularly in the churches, and how Cavanaugh related torture to salvation in the Eucharistic community. All this serves to demonstrate that there is a considerable raft of human rights issues in which the Christian salvation motif can be used to open up advocacy and action.

F.W. Dillistone, in his classic work on atonement (Dillistone, 1968), adduced a rich variety of images of salvation, many of which may also contribute to opening our eyes to rights problems. He traced atonement as the unique redemption – creating a new beginning in relationships – and saw the Christ event as the supreme tragedy, underlining the intractable nature of the conflict and the potential for lethal violence within it. Atonement and salvation can be seen as supreme judgement, in which justice issues are brought to the surface and argued out. Salvation is satisfaction, in which there is restoration and reparation. A central model is that of the all-embracing compassion, within which a new culture of relationship may be created. Salvation is all-embracing forgiveness – and we have already seen how important forgiveness may be – properly understood in healing scars. The last image is that of perfect integration, in which there is a firm commitment, throughout the life of Jesus, to the marginalized. This social integration is intimately related to integration with God, to participation in God through clothing the naked and feeding the hungry. Through this participation we are called to *imitatio Christi*. Nor did Dillistone neglect the notion of salvation as sympathy – evident in writers as diverse as McLeod Campbell, H.R. Mackintosh and Richard Rorty.

In all this imagery there is a strand of affirmation of each human being as in the image of God. This affirmation is not simply for the glory of God, but is God's affirmation of the value, in the perspective of his love, of every human being. Although it has often been read as an affirmation of God as the real recipient of value, the Christ event suggests equally that God's goal is fulfilled in the flourishing of every human being. This instantly makes a mockery of human rights abuses, not least when they are perpetrated through a veil of piety or morality.

God Instantiated

We are now brought back to the classic but basic connection between atonement, incarnation and inspiration. A Christology for human rights pays particular attention to the many dimensions of the continuing power of reconciliation in Christ. In the events concerning Jesus we see the instantiation of the person of God in a specific human being, identified with the loss of all human rights, without remainder. This cluster of events can be envisaged through different concepts, notably of incarnation and inspiration, each of which makes its own contribution to conceiving the mystery. It is possible to speak of a bifocal, or even a varifocal, Christology.

Incarnation, which itself may be conceived in different and sometimes overlapping ways, points to the reality of the involvement of God with human bodies. What happens to bodies is important to God, who has shared human embodiment in every range of experience. The consequences of incarnation include the creation of visible communities of Christian faith, who continue in communion with God through word and sacrament, through response to proclamation and participation in the Eucharist, in the tradition of the gospel. This tradition also embodies the ambiguities of the human, yet can still act as an outlet for the divine love. Incarnation simultaneously has a wider connotation, for it is a catalyst for the reconciliation of the whole created order. Where the church is outward-facing as well as inward-facing there is a constructive relationship between incarnation and response. Where the church is purely inward-facing, this relationship is diminished. Incarnation is concerned with all dimensions of human life, personal and social, and with the shape of the cosmos beyond the merely human. It is not a trump card, for it is always incarnation through humiliation.

Further dimensions of the archetypal divine instantiation are expressed by inspiration. Spirit is not in conflict with, but complements, embodiment. The consequence of resurrection is the presence of the spirit of the risen Christ within the created order.

Within Christian community the spirit is always related to the focal areas of word and sacrament. How these are related has been the subject of endless sacramental controversy. What matters here are the intrinsic connection and the central importance of both.

Two thousand years of Christianity has shown that the spirit of Christlikeness is not confined to Christian community. The divine love has been experienced by Christians as active in other religions and in secular spheres, in individual lives, and in social and political developments, sometimes from within the churches and sometimes challenging the churches from the outside. Acknowledgement of such a state of affairs is always a matter of faith, though not of faith without grounds. Grounds for affirming the reality of Christlikeness may be seen in the fruits of reconciliation within the world. While it is not possible for us to conceive of the shape of cosmic reconciliation, faith will see pointers to reconciliation in human history, which has often been grim but which might have been much worse. Christians may understand that the love of God in Christ remains a potent factor in all sorts of diverse individual and communal experience. There remain, then, basic links between incarnation and inspiration, reconciliation, Christlikeness and the action of divine love throughout the cosmos. Here, Trinitarian doctrines may sometimes provide avenues to a degree of comprehension.

There is a basic bond between the humiliated and exalted Christ and attention to human rights in all its dimensions. Christology is for human rights. Christian theology will understand action for human rights not as identical with, but certainly as caught up within, the much wider and more mysterious dynamic of the cosmic presence of the divine love. Because it claims this underlying ground it benefits from immersion in an inexhaustible vision, however unpromising the current outlook in any given area may become.

It would be possible to produce a more comprehensive human rights Christology in which the imagery of human rights culture was taken up in transformation of traditional theological categories. We have already indicated something of this. Jesus Christ may be imagined as God's incarnation of human rights, as subject and object of human rights concern. Here God recognizes the cause of all humanity as his own, in sympathy, solidarity and the fullest possible identification. He reaffirms the value of all human beings, who are destined to be fulfilled through unconditional love. God opposes cultures of violence, exclusivity and discrimination, participating in death to overcome this opposition and subverting it through loving action. Jesus himself, in identifying, becomes a victim of human rights abuse through being marginalized, tortured and murdered. Such a Christology may help Christians appreciate the imperative of human rights action in every sphere. However, the purpose of this study is not simply to produce a Christology for internal Christian consumption, but rather to concentrate on a contribution to human rights culture and enforcement as such.

A Christian apprehension of the love of God has consequences for human rights dialogue and action at various levels. For Christians, faith in the incarnation of divine love provides a permanent motivation for urgency in advocacy and action for human rights. The fact that it has not always done so in the past does not lessen the imperative once it has been recognized. This faith operates at different levels. There is recognition of the example of Jesus as a man of perfect goodness, identified in solidarity with all the marginalized, present to faith as a transformative power. There is recognition that divine action throughout the universe, however hard to understand, is always loving action. God may not always be able to prevent evils on all occasions because of the conditions of the possibility of freedom in the universe. But God is able to act on some occasions, either directly or through human agency. Where human agency produces outcomes in love and compassion, Christians may see here the activity of God and give thanks for what I find helpful to describe as Christomorphic traces of divine action, the spirit of Christlikeness, in the created order. This is the salvific outcome of the dynamic sequence of the life, death and resurrection of Jesus Christ.

Inclusive Reconciliation

Here we must take care, for we are always vulnerable to forms of triumphalism. We cannot say of ourselves that, because we are trying to respond in loving action to our understanding of the divine love, we are automatically agents of divine action. This way madness lies. We can say only that we are hoping, provisionally and to the best of our ability, to follow in the way of Christian discipleship. We have seen only too plainly the disastrous consequences of Christian self-delusion and abuse of power in the past and in the present. But we may hope also to recognize the manifestation of the divine love in the actions of others and regard this as a huge encouragement for the future of God's purpose of love, peace and justice.

For those who do not share Christian faith, Christian theology can offer the example of the life of Jesus as a significant pointer, along with other pointers, to the way towards a community of compassion and justice in society. Here is a human being whose life may be viewed as transformed and defined by constant concern for others in a less privileged position than himself – a concern which has individual, but also social and political, dimensions. In conversation with partners who do not share a religious perspective, Jesus the man can be seen as a humane example of self-dispossession and service. For conversation partners who share a religious perspective in other religions, Jesus may be seen as a major figure among others, who opens up the nature of transcendence within a particular culture but whose significance may be appreciated within other cultures in appropriate ways.

It is possible, then, to envisage the events concerning Jesus Christ as contributing to human rights culture and action at a number of different levels, either separately or in combinations. However the perspective on Christ is understood, the norms which are privileged here will be the norms of unconditional love in their specificity. These involve respect for persons as free persons, free from hunger and economic deprivation, free to move and associate in constructive relationships with other human beings and, above all, free from fear – perfect love casts out fear. Given the immense volume of fear generated in contemporary life, and the neurotic and often violent individual and collective reactions that fear generates, this may make no small difference to human rights enforcement.

Structures for realizing rights projects are already in place in Christian communities, a good example being the Progressive Christians Uniting project directed by John Cobb and others. There are significant resources flowing into the realization of rights objectives in Christian humanitarian organizations – some more theologically conservative, like Tearfund, some more liberal, like Christian Aid, and some more directed from a single church, like CAFOD. All these bodies are accustomed to working alongside other humanitarian organizations operations targeted on famine and disaster relief. But when we consider the huge amount of Christian effort and finance directed towards evangelism today, especially in conservative evangelical circles, it is clear that a direct contribution to human rights recognition and enforcement could become infinitely more substantial and effective. As we have seen when examining the issues surrounding unforced consensus, this only works in an atmosphere of unqualified mutual respect and reciprocity. There is a long way to go. In my view, a Christian community today which declines to make a significant contribution is likely to be seriously lacking in catholicity and apostolicity. A corollary would be the refusal to waste valuable energy and resources on controversies of an ultimately futile nature.

Christians believe that Christology may influence life at every level – political, social, economic, individual and psychological. An open and progressive Christology need not doubt the Christian capacity for contribution to social transformation even if it takes several further millennia before this is generously actualized. It is always useful to consider a transcendent dimension in which the need for urgent action now is not translated into short-term strategic thinking.

Throughout this study we have sought to err on the side of caution in assessing the potential both of a distinctive Christian contribution to human rights issues and of the ability of human rights language and culture themselves to solve the problems that regularly confront humanity. But there is a real positive balance in this accounting. There is no doubt that serious reflection on the Christ event – the coming into the world of this vulnerable, self-giving God – creates grounds for the hope of a transformation into a more just and generous society than we have at present. This is a matter not of sentimentality but of the nature of the Christ event itself.

The history of Christian action is one which calls for humility. How could we have got so much wrong so consistently often? Yet there are still outbursts of transparent goodness produced by the Christian gospel and shared with a wider humanity. This is what Christian faith has understood as the fruits of the spirit. This kind of patient, humble and sustained commitment is a vital ingredient of any successful work in human rights issues. In the first instance, human rights means always listening to what the different sides in a dispute have to say and trying to address these concerns and interests. A dialogue of the deaf is always a confession of failure. It is only when such dialogue is exhausted or impossible that a different strategy may need to be invoked. In the Christian perspective, violence is always wrong but may be sometimes invoked as a last resort to protect communities from physical destruction. To stand aside and watch slaughter take place is not a human rights option, as events in Bosnia and Rwanda have tragically demonstrated.

Progress here will involve a comprehensive renunciation of traditions of cultural and religious superiority. On the one hand it is important to distinguish Christian contributions from the Western or neo-colonial packaging in which they have so often been offered. At the same time, it is desirable to acknowledge honestly the predominantly Western contribution of much Christian thinking. This should not be concealed. Equally, however, the real value of Western Christian thinking and action to the human future need not be disparaged or underplayed. Despite its serious flaws and its only partial perspective, it is also a hugely valuable legacy to build upon.

An Enduring Vision

I have constantly stressed the need for sensitivity to alternative, perhaps non-Christian, perspectives in seeking to make a Christian contribution to rights issues. There will be occasions when it will be desirable to offer an explicitly Christian approach to justice and rights enforcement, but there will be other occasions when the approach will be entirely implicit. This is not a matter of deviousness or hesitation. Loving action in society often takes place anonymously and is all the more effective for this anonymity. Action in the public arena does not always preclude silent and unobtrusive engagement.

How can the Christian vision of Christ contribute to practical outcomes in human rights issues? Consider some of the people we have encountered in the course of this inquiry. Well-known people and countless others often without a name have lived and sometimes died opposing intolerance, prejudice and bigotry, and they have done so because of their Christian faith. Although we have argued the necessity of recognizing and confronting the bleak side of the story of Christ and human rights, there is still a positive story. This is a solid ground of hope. In our consideration of an open Christology we have noted different sorts of theologian, from different theological traditions, whose theology reflected directly on the vulnerability and humility of the self-giving God in Jesus Christ. If the future of Christianity is to involve a strongly conservative and exclusive dimension, as Jenkins (2002) has suggested, it also has solid foundations for a much more progressive and inclusive dimension. There will be scope for dialogue between these perspectives and for contributions to thought and action outside the circle of internal Christian discourse. While there may be no distilled essence of faith in Christ that can be applied mechanically to differing situations, the impact of the God whose being is expressed in the radically self-giving life and teaching of Jesus will continue to open doors of compassion in the negotiation of complex human rights issues in the future. This will be one of the ways in which the Christomorphic pattern of divine action continues to mould human life and action.

A framework for persistence

It may be that for every step towards effective human rights action there is an equal step towards violation. In this case, the solution will not be to give up, but to try harder. I suggest that a Christian contribution – specifically a contribution based on reflection upon Christ – can be continued on several different levels.

First, there is the level of relationality and solidarity with the marginalized and the not so marginalized. Jesus the Christ is who he is and does what he does through his being as being through relationality. I begin with the not so marginalized. We have to recognize that different Christians will have different views of current flashpoints. Where there are deep differences, we have to struggle to maintain mutual respect and communication. Christians who may be deeply critical of one group of marginalized people may be hugely supportive of other groups. We cannot afford to waste resources on unnecessary quarrels. There may be reason to hope that separate support of different abused groups may lead, in time, to an awareness of common grounds for affirmation and respect.

Second, we should privilege groups whose human rights are threatened. Christ is crucified outside the gate, outside the magic circle. Everyone feels marginalized in some ways at different times. Making the imaginative leap into trying to look at issues from this perspective is both possible and necessary. Not all marginalization amounts to denial of human rights, but denial is often the next step. It is incumbent on all Christians to do what they can to indicate solidarity. Where Jews or Arabs are persecuted, it may be important in some situations to stand in solidarity as an honorary Jew or Arab, and in other circumstances as a clear outsider who is standing in total solidarity despite huge differences. Whether solidarity is achieved by secret diplomacy or vocal public advocacy or a combination of both will depend on what is likely to be most effective in specific cases.

Third, one of the most important needs for those who are oppressed, by torture, hunger, racism or whatever, is to retain a sense of self-respect in the face of general vilification. This requires the combined efforts of Christians, both inside and outside the issue. Only women perhaps can fully understand the devastating effect of patriarchal attitudes in church and society over the last 2000 years – an effect not mediated by a uniformly patriarchal Christology. Yet men can take the trouble to immerse themselves in the issues and take steps to remove the barriers which they themselves have created.

It is true that human rights action is a high-risk activity. Bonhoeffer, King, Shepard and Ellacuria all met violent deaths. It is true that Christians have supported human rights abuses with great tenacity. There is no quick fix. But as a community response Christian action has had considerable success in mitigating the effects of slavery, racism and many other abuses over a longer timescale.

Christian action has often taken the form of charitable work in deprived areas by church organizations. Despite their much criticized less desirable aspects, Christian missions have contributed significantly to the alleviation of human suffering in the modern world. Christian NGOs, such as Christian Aid, continue to make a significant contribution to human rights issues, especially economic rights, worldwide. This type of action will doubtless continue to have its own positive impact. Christian action has had to learn, and is learning, about the need for sensitivity to local culture in making its contribution. Anything less is counterproductive. The achievement of sensitive contribution depends on listening carefully to voices which are themselves usually not Christian. This is entirely in accord with the vulnerability and reciprocity which the Christomorphic pattern encourages. But it is not always simple or straightforward. Action without understanding is always counterproductive.

Christological perspectives may have both positive and negative value in contributing to human rights issues. On the positive side, reflection upon Christ has encouraged Christians to work by themselves and with others in addressing effectively many areas of human rights – individual liberty, torture, political rights such as the right to justice, and economic rights like the right to be free from hunger.

On the negative side, it has been largely ineffective where scriptural tradition has had a strong influence in inhibiting rights – most notably in the areas of gender and sexuality. Here perhaps we have to look elsewhere for guidance. But Christianity has shown the capacity for change and development, for example, in relation to such issues as slavery and race. We should not expect that today's status quo will be repeated in a hundred years from now. In reflecting on the dynamic of relationality and in respect for others expressed in the events concerning Jesus Christ, the Christian tradition has the potential for universal application even in areas where it has, so far, largely failed. If it is able to face up critically to its failures it may have a future role in encouraging other traditions, both religious and secular, to confront their weaknesses and make appropriate changes in attitude and action. It may also learn from such dialogue to widen its own base of human rights commitments in the long-term future. In the present it may be important to concentrate action within the Christian tradition on human rights issues where there is a large measure of agreement, while continuing to work on areas of disagreement. The option will remain to respond to the Christological vision by working with organizations outside church structures in areas where these are more likely to be effective. In this way, human rights action may be seen as part of the consequences of the form of Christ in the world.

CHAPTER 10

Making Rights Stick

Non-compliance, Unconditional Love and Effective Enforcement

In his study, *Holy Terrors* (2003), Bruce Lincoln has analysed the deep fusion between religion and culture in what he describes as 'maximalist' manifestations of religion, through analysis of the speeches of Osama bin Laden and George W. Bush after 11 September 2001, the final instructions to the hijackers found in Mohammed Atta's notes, and an interview between Pat Robertson and Jerry Falwell. In contrast to the 'minimalist' understanding of religion as a mainly intellectual perspective which grew out of the European Enlightenment, 'maximalist interpretations infuse every aspect of thought and action with underlying religious significance'(Lincoln, 2003, 76). In my view, the increasing prevalence of such views in many parts of the contemporary world means that religious discourse of different sorts will have to be understood, assessed and taken into account in the practical implementation of human rights in the future. Those who share religious beliefs will have a significant role in facilitating both the conversation about, and nature of, the appropriate enforcement of rights. Lincoln's study is particularly relevant to Christian theology in underscoring the risks of maximalist standpoints:

> Less militant than al Qaeda, perhaps (given that the violence they employ in pursuit of their goals is rhetorical and not physical), the televangelists' religious ideal is equally maximalist, if Christian rather than Muslim. (Lincoln, 2003, 50)

Case Study: 2005

The world in which we now live is not obviously becoming more stable or more peaceful. The 'end of history' envisaged at the end of the last century, as a general triumph of consumerism, has not happened. Addressing the problems of peace and justice is not simply a leisure activity for the underemployed academic. We need to use every resource we can find, religious and non-religious, to facilitate the common good in a pluralist world. A snapshot of the human rights situation today only emphasizes the case for an urgent constructive encounter between Christology at the centre of Christianity and human rights.

As it is unlikely that the tensions between what Lincoln terms 'maximalist' and 'minimalist' standpoints on religion will be resolved in the next few decades, it becomes imperative to look for negotiating strategies between differing perspectives in the face of the common need, whether acknowledged or unacknowledged, for constructive coexistence. This cannot be done in any single way. Different sorts of dialogue may need to take place. For example, the 'scripture reasoning' project between the Abrahamic religions may help build bridges between people who take a high view of sacred texts. Other convergences may be built between people who follow other faiths, or who have more liberal religious visions or more completely secular perspectives. This may eventually lead to different patterns of joined-up dots, yielding webs of connection which may constitute an intercivilizational consensus.

To underestimate the real progress which humanity has made in many places in the development of human rights enforcement would be fatal for such an enterprise. Inaction invites disaster. Yet the events of 2005 demonstrate clearly that there is constant need for vigilance not only in the numerous brutal dictatorships which still tyrannize much of the globe, but in the more democratic societies. The events of 9/11 brought huge worldwide sympathy to the United States, but this was largely dissipated by the aftermath of the Iraq war.[1] The abuses of prisoners in Abu Ghraib in Iraq, the unprecedented use of an isolated area to avoid legal responsibility in Guantanamo Bay and the totally unjustifiable practice of 'extraordinary rendition' to export suspects to countries where they might well be tortured to extract information raise issues which we might imagine to have been long since settled in the United States. Torture, suitably reformulated, has again become a thinkable option.[2]

Discounting hostile commentaries, we find the US Army Criminal Investigation Command cataloguing fatal attacks on civilians. Here is a single instance:

> Private Brand, who acknowledged striking a detainee named Dilawar 37 times, was accused of having maimed and killed him over a five day period 'by destroying his leg muscle tissue with repeated unlawful strikes.'
> The attacks on Mr Dilawar were so severe that 'even if he had survived, both legs would have had to have been amputated,' the Army report said, citing a medical examiner.

---

1   Cf. Donnelly (1989, 268): 'Most Americans apparently believe that "human rights" problems exist only in places that must be reached by flying over large bodies of salt water.'

Attitudes to human rights in the United States have become especially critical since 9/11. Once seen as a beacon of liberty and tolerance, the United States is now often seen as a prime violator of rights. There are certainly two sides to this argument. On the one hand, there are clear abuses of rights, documented in critical reports by Amnesty International and Human Rights Watch. On the other hand, we have seen that infinitely worse abuses are regularly committed in countries where there is no free media and where all is shrouded in silence and oppression. It should also be noted that the United States as a neo-colonial power is probably no worse, and usually a great deal better, than its imperial predecessors, including Britain, Germany, France, Belgium, Holland and Russia.

Mark Taylor in his *Politics, Religion and the Christian Right* (2005) unsparingly documents the dangers of a mixture of right-wing politics and right-wing religion. He traces the growth of a politics of fear and calls for a 'textured liberalism' and a new growth of 'deliberative and civic reasoning'. He speaks of the gospel as 'emancipatory reconciliation':

> Without forfeiting the primacy of the liberation motif, Christian experiences of emancipation, at their best, seek also to make and embrace unities, to reconcile differences....At their best, Christians might contribute a dimension of 'listening love' for deliberative reasoning in prophetic struggle, without letting that love lessen the ongoing or thoroughgoing character of a revolutionary justice and emancipation.(Taylor, 2005, 188–90)

2   Legal opinions of Alan Dershowitz in, Greenberg (2005) and *New York Times*.

American military officials in Afghanistan initially said that the deaths of Mr Habibullah, in an isolation cell on Dec. 4, 2002, and Mr Dilawar, in another such cell six days later, were from natural causes.

Mr Dilawar, who suffered from a heart condition, is described in an Army report dated June 6, 2004, as having died from 'Blunt force trauma to the lower extremities complication coronary heart disease.' (*New York Times*, 12 March 2005)

When such a development is accompanied by manipulation of the media and a rhetoric measurably avoiding words like 'human rights' in favour of 'freedom' and 'liberation', there is cause for alarm. On the other hand, the continuing presence of a sharp critique of these practices in American society is a reliable indication of the underlying strength of American democracy: in other countries, great and small, abuses are often completely suppressed.

The Americans may be the publicly obvious problem. But the corrupt regimes to which they are sometimes opposed are infinitely worse abusers of human rights. The Europeans are hardly a shining example. In Britain, detention without trial threatens to undermine 1,000 years of legal precedent. This is not helped by the conditions suffered by the detainees. To quote, in fairness, the same newspaper as quoted above:

Amnesty International and other groups charged that the conditions at Belmarsh, where the men were locked up for 22 hours a day in tiny cells and never saw daylight, were inhumane. As at Guantanamo Bay, the detainees were never informed of all the charges against them and were not given access to lawyers. (*New York Times*, 12 March 2005)

It is, of course, the duty of the nation-state to protect its own citizens as vigorously as possible from terrorist attack. This may involve violence in the face of imminent threat. However, this cannot become an excuse for gratuitous violence and abandoning the rule of law.

Today, human rights are being violated by means of all sorts of complex routes. In recent years France has consistently offered financial support to corrupt regimes, and Russia pursues a policy of increasing authoritarianism at home and at its borders. Civilians suffer at the hands of soldiers. Soldiers are themselves subjected to a culture of bullying and abuse, from Soviet barracks to the Deepcut scandal in Britain and continuing incidents in the United States. When countries treat their own personnel in this way, what hope is there for aliens? *Quis custodiet ipsos custodes?*

In Western countries there remains a disturbing residue of institutionalized violence in a number of significant areas. In non-Western countries the scenario is often hardly more promising.[3] In Iran, for example, the penal code still prescribes stoning to death for the offences of adultery and prostitution among others:

---

3   A good account of Islam in relation to terrorism today can be found in Lewis (2004). Lewis analyses the basic contemporary issues – especially the poverty and corruption in many Middle Eastern countries.

> The stones should not be too large so that the person dies by being hit by one or
> two of them: they should not be so small either that they could not be defined
> as stones.
>   Regulations updated in 2003 specify that flogging is to be carried out with
> leather cords 1.5cm thick and 1 meter long. (*New York Times*, 13 March 2005)

Some of these problems may be resolved when there is an effective United Nations
Human Rights Commission, of the sort envisaged by the founders of the Charter. At
present there is every opportunity for abusive states to join the Commission so that
they can block criticism of their own countries. In 2005 the panel included China,
Cuba, Sudan, Nepal, Congo, Guatemala and Saudi Arabia, and almost included
Zimbabwe, one of the greatest current violators of human rights. Grasping the nettle
of hypocrisy is a difficult, but urgent, task. Few corners of the earth lend themselves
to romanticization when it comes to human rights abuse today.[4]

In the media there is much talk of humanitarianism. Yet as David Rieff has shown
eloquently, even this expression of a human rights culture has to be deployed with
alertness and intelligence. In his *A Bed for the Night: Humanitarianism in Crisis*,
Rieff clearly highlights the dangers of humanitarianism becoming involved with
politics. Humanitarianism often fails. Human rights concerns produce legal norms,
which are then disregarded. Politics and force are sometimes necessary. A balance
between inaction and unrealistic expectation is crucial. Human rights have a limited
but vital role. He spells out the humanitarian paradox – the hazards of charity – in
Bosnia, Rwanda, Kosovo and Afghanistan. There is a need to avoid claiming too
much success in the real world, but also a need for hope against hope:

> The tragedy of humanitarianism may be that for all its failings and for all the
> limitations of its viewpoint, it represents what is decent in an indecent world.
> Its core assumptions – solidarity, a fundamental sympathy for victims, and an
> antipathy for oppressors and exploiters – what we are in those rare moments of
> grace when we are at our best. (Rieff, 2002, 334)

This kind of discernment, we have argued, is what faith believes the Christomorphic
trace in history may contribute to conflict resolution. Obstacles are not hard to find.
In South Africa reconciliation was often in danger of sliding into impunity. The
culture of a sacramental community of reconciliation may slide from an undesirable
blame culture into an equally undesirable no-blame culture in which confidence in
justice may be deeply eroded (cf. Jones, 2003 – a critical analysis of contemporary
Italian politics). In the face of so many imponderables, faith trusts in the spirit of
God in order to persist at the level of particularity.

---

4   Examples abound. Particularly disturbing is the US use of 'extraordinary rendition' to export
suspects to countries where torture is routine (*New York Times,,* 1 May 2005).
    These problems are not confined to America. The British ambassador, Craig Murray, was compelled
to resign in 2004 after reporting human rights abuse in Uzbekistan. And the treatment of civilians in
occupied countries continues to be as subject to brutality as it has always been ('From "Gook"' to
"Raghead"', *New York Times*, May 2005).

We have seen that there is considerable continuing academic debate about rights issues in legal circles, especially in the United States. There is also a lively philosophical debate, not least about intercivilizational human rights values, as well as a huge amount of practical work being done 'on the ground' by organizations at different levels. While it is neither possible nor desirable to bring all these concerns under one umbrella, we should bear in mind the connections to practical human rights outcomes.

Apart from the necessary political and diplomatic activity of governments, much human rights work continues to be achieved through the efforts of humanitarian organizations such as Oxfam. Some of these bodies – for example, Christian Aid and Caritas International – have a distinctively Christian basis. Here, I want to focus on a body whose basis is nothing other than promoting human rights, Amnesty International. If we want to see the scale of what still needs to be done, it is worth contemplating soberly Amnesty's current list of areas of its work. The organization's website lists armed conflict, children and juveniles, commonwealth, conscientious objectors, crimes against humanity, death in custody, the death penalty, detention, arrest, disappearances, discrimination, economic exploitation, excessive force, extrajudicial executions, freedom of expression, impunity, indiscriminate killings, international justice, investigation of abuses, medical issues, military, security and police transfers, prison conditions, prisoners of conscience, racism, refugees, sexual orientation, torture and ill-treatment, trade union issues trials, and the treatment of women.

Each of these themes indicates a considerable and diverse area where human rights violation continues to occur. As problems are resolved in some areas, new issues continue to appear. Until more progress is made, all talk of the common good is blind to abuses. That is why wrestling with these issues in theory and in practice is anything but a waste of time – we need to hear more, not less, about human rights action. This study, however, deals only with one area – the potential contribution of the Christian faith in the centrality of Christ to human flourishing. If the energy of the huge number of Christian people in the world could be brought to bear on human rights issues, there is no doubt that tangible progress could be made.[5]

---

5   I am constantly struck by the disparity between the huge amount of effort put into human rights culture by disciplines other than theology, in comparison with the comparative neglect by theologians.

A single example will suffice – the interdisciplinary study of *The Future of International Human Rights* (Weston and Marks, 1999). Richard Falk spells out the current reality:

> As with almost all aspects of the human rights subject, the achievements over the course of the last fifty years are extraordinary, but the obstacles to full realisation seem as insurmountable as ever. (Weston and Marks, 1999, 24)

In 'Capabilities, Human Rights and the Universal Declaration' Martha. Nussbaum develops her capabilities approach (which I have discussed at length in *The Transformative Imagination* (2004):

> Instead of asking, 'How satisfied is person A?,' or 'How much in the way of resources does A command?,' we ask the question, 'What is A actually able to do and to be?' In other words, about a variety of functions that would seem to be of central importance to a human life, we ask: 'Is the person capable of doing this, or not?' (Ibid., 41)

Christ and Human Rights: Towards a Summary

We have examined numerous arguments on different sides of the rights debate, in religious and secular discussion. It is time to bring the threads together. It is argued here that, despite many cogent objections, human rights language and human rights culture continue to be useful instruments towards the development of a fair, just and equal society. Both positive rights and negative rights may enhance the human condition for many sorts of people. Religious perspectives and political and social commitments may deepen the cultural foundations of rights talk, making the delivery of human rights values and practices more possible. The enforcement of certain crucial rights may free people from fear. The affirmation of positive rights may encourage aspiration and the recognition of cultural values and particular lifestyles as positive human goods, beneficial to society as a whole.[6]

In Chapter 9 I suggested that Christology may have a multilevel impact on rights issues, for Christology is about engagement – God's engagement with this world. I now want to look at some further avenues towards enforcement.[7]

In 'Voices of Suffering, Fragmented Universality, and the Future of Human Rights' Uprendra Baxi offers a sharp critique of current geopolitical trends:

> I take it as axiomatic that the historic mission of 'contemporary' human rights is *to give voice to human suffering*, to make it visible and to ameliorate it. The notion that human rights regimes may, or ought to, contribute to the 'pursuit of happiness' remains the privilege of a miniscule segment of humanity. (Ibid., 103)

> In the 'modern' paradigm of rights the logics of exclusion are paramount, whereas in the 'contemporary' paradigm, the logics of inclusion are paramount. (Ibid., 108)

> I believe that the paradigm of the UDHR is being steadily supplanted by a trade-related, market-friendly human rights paradigm. (Ibid., 150)

Dinah Shelton in 'The Promise of Regional HR Systems' (ibid., 351f) explores the idea of distinctive, but interconnecting, human rights cultures – European, inter-American, African and Asian. John Dugard, writing on 'Reconciliation and Justice – The South African Experience', notes that:

Reconciliation is hard to achieve and difficult to sustain. For this reason, it is necessary to strive for the rebuilding of the society to ensure that the crimes of the past are not repeated while at the same time continuing the pursuit of reconciliation. This is where human rights come in. (Ibid., 329)

6   Pointers towards the cumulative approach to human rights culture advocated here may be found in very different approaches. Alan Dershowitz, a lawyer, in *Rights from Wrongs,* suggests a bottom-up approach (Dershowitz, 2004, 82). Wrongs provoke rights (ibid., 90). The rights process is always in flux (ibid., 96). Rights do not guarantee the 'right' result (ibid., 141). There are also newly recognized rights:

> Virtually every newly recognized right – whether it be the right to leave a country or the right to marry a person of the same sex- has been invented by human beings based on the wrongs they experienced or observed. This dynamic process will continue until the end of human experience. (Ibid., 191)

> Rights are the product of experience of wrongs. If rights grow out of the experiences and histories of human beings, then they are more a function of nurture than of nature. (Ibid., 86)

7   Weingartner (1994) offers a useful step-by-step guide to working on the ground in human rights issues, including who and how to interview, and how to gather and preserve evidence.

Diplomacy

A Christian understanding of reconciliation takes the pattern of Christ's relationality – a generous and respectful relationality – as grounds for dissatisfaction with the violence that is involved in human rights abuses in which, the vulnerable are exploited rather than supported. An effective human rights strategy will recognize that the situation requires urgent action at different levels. This is far from easy. A romantic view of the judiciary is unhelpful: laws are often either non-existent or unenforceable. A romantic view of solidarity based on a universal recognition of inhumanity would be worse. The tragic powerlessness of the UN contingent in Bosnia was an object lesson in failure by omission rather than commission. A Western Christian intervention, whether overt or more disguised, could be perceived as insensitive and misplaced arrogance. Diplomacy will be required, even though its effectiveness will often be slowed by national considerations of sovereignty, national cultural perceptions and geopolitical calculations that may inhibit long-term larger benefits.

Action only occurs when there is pressure for it. It would seem that a Christian framework of reconciliation could be commended in such, not untypical, situations at many different levels. There is the level of individual action, of action by private groups, of semi-official bodies like church denominations, by governments and international bodies. If a Christian human rights initiative is to be helpful in a non-Christian environment, then it has to be conceived and delivered in terms appropriate for a mutual and reciprocal dialogue. Otherwise, it is likely to make things worse, whether the agency concerned is an official Christian body or not.

Advocacy

Christian action is not solely the prerogative of official bodies. Christian people working in business, in the civil service, in law and in many walks of life can, and do, make significant contributions to human rights issues. Many of the workers in NGOs have reflective Christian and other religious convictions. Collaborative action, provided that it is taken sensitively and with openness to others, is always highly desirable. But, equally, it may occasionally be necessary to appeal to Christian bodies on the solid basis of Christian conviction. We should not underestimate the continuing enormous actual and potential resources which countries with a strong Christian presence will continue to make available for the foreseeable future. It has always been central to faith to believe that God acts through the hands of those who are willing to follow in the way of discipleship. Christ as facilitator of human rights may act in society at many different levels.

Raising levels of conscience

It is not within the competence of the theologian to devise strategies that the officers of NGOs and other specialist bodies in the field are best qualified to construct. But it will perhaps be part of the task of at least some theologians in the future to familiarize themselves with study and action in the area of human rights, to try to contribute to this from a theological perspective, and perhaps to consider to what extent human rights issues may challenge us to re-imagine our theological vision for the future.

The history of human rights abuse since the UDHR was created in 1945 does not suggest that the problems are diminishing. There are numerous issues which will call for a Christian response in the long-term future. Amnesty International offers the following list of human-rights-related websites, all of which deal with serious issues and which require attention to the particular as well as the general: anti-slavery, anti-war/weapons, awareness groups, children and youth, civil liberties, corporate concerns, cultural, death penalty, environmental protection, gay and lesbian civil rights, genital mutilation, government and intergovernmental, specific regions and groups, indigenous peoples, political and legal reform, prisoner support, refugees, relief efforts, religion, social justice, torture, umbrella organizations, victim support and women's rights.

It is out of the particular that improvement to the general comes, provided that the particular is also viewed within an overall strategy. Each of the issues briefly listed above conceals a huge raft of important human rights concerns, any of which may be an important area of Christian engagement. However necessary it may be for us to engage in internal Christian discussion about church structures and doctrinal formulation, there is a large element of self-indulgence about such preoccupation unless it is explicitly related at some point to people at the point of greatest need, for whom Christ was, and is especially, concerned.

It may appear from the preceding paragraphs that the seminal issues of human rights culture must ultimately be left to the arbitration of the technical discussions of philosophers. The reality, however, is that many disciplines can, and do, contribute to the break-up of technical log-jams in unexpected ways. This brings us back to the core task of this study – the specific role of Christology in contributing to the process of creating a broad human rights culture. It would appear that Christology can contribute at various levels.

As Dag Hammarskjold has famously remarked, Freedom from fear could be said to sum up the whole philosophy of human rights. Immediately we encounter yet another paradox of rights talk. In most circumstances torturers will continue to torture and exploiters will continue to exploit until they fear the consequences and are forced to desist. We have also emphasized the role of the kenotic Christ, identifying with the marginalized and the vulnerable. But the non-marginalized majority may continue to discriminate and exclude. Unconditional love, it seems, is not nearly enough to secure the enforcement of rights.

It is true that advocacy may in time generate a new human rights culture which may achieve mass appeal. This remains an important task. Advocacy may generate a sense of obligation and duty which will create an active implementation of rights. But enforcement may sometimes require coercion. Are we now to follow the fateful path of the Augustinian *cogite intrare*? To this question there is no simple answer. Clearly, actions which themselves breach human rights are wrong. But on rare occasions it may be necessary to embrace the lesser evil in order to benefit those who are most seriously wronged.

Declarations of human rights by the United Nations and other bodies remain theoretical ideas until they are recognized and encoded in treaties with legal sanction. Many of these treaties are couched in imprecise language, and their provisions can be evaded. The United Nations has itself produced guidelines for the enforcement of human rights. Nations, organizations or individuals may make complaints to the UN Human Rights Committee. The Committee will produce rulings on the issue and make recommendations for resolving the problem. But the worst violators regularly ignore these procedures, and little can be done. There may be geopolitical reasons why pressure can be exerted on one country and not on another. Large states may literally get away with murder because pressure on them would produce geopolitical instability, while small states may be pressured into some degree of conformity. Here, human rights considerations may inevitably not always be the ultimate concern. To protect some rights while jeopardizing many others would clearly not be in the interest of human flourishing. In every case a judgement has to be made, taking into account the likely outcomes.

We saw the real value of Christian concepts of forgiveness and reconciliation. These may produce a real hope of change and movement, and it would be irresponsible to dismiss their potential on the basis of past failures. The future value of a Christian contribution to rights may quite easily be much greater than its past value, especially in the creation of a culture in which there is openness to movement and transformation. This Christian perspective, based on an understanding of Christ as the centre of faith, may take many different forms, from a conservative doctrinal stance to a form of Christian humanism. Its cumulative effect may be to move societies and communities in the direction of gradual recognition of the need for human rights enforcement at all levels. The enormity of this task only underlines the need for beginning to act as soon as possible, and to act through an intercultural and interdisciplinary conversation.

The way ahead will quite naturally be envisaged differently by people with different Christological perspectives. I have suggested an open, porous Christology which is hospitable to a framework of Christian humanism. This project is intended to be open equally to conversations with more conservative and more liberal conversation partners.[8]

How can Christian perspectives contribute to influencing the violators of human rights at national and at more local levels? It should be remembered that there are millions of Christian communities around the world, large and small. Many of these are already engaged in programmes which support human rights in different areas, an excellent example being the current work of the Church of Scotland in Myanmar (cf. www.fishwrapper.org). Links between churches, national, ecumenical and sometimes mission-oriented, already help to link these concerns. The advent of the

---

8   O'Grady (1979, 72) suggests that Jesus stands on the side of the human. One might say equally the humane. Charles Villa-Vicencio (1992, 184) emphasizes the importance of the simple recognition of human dignity.

Internet has provided a powerful vehicle for advocacy and action – so powerful that governments which violate rights are likely to close down dissenting websites. The obverse of Christian failure is the surprising number of minority rights groups which have first been granted sanctuary and support on church premises. There is huge potential here for the wider recognition of the potential Christian advocacy of rights in a great range of cultures and subcultures.

Beyond such advocacy there is the role of denominational church committees in promoting a higher level of conscience about rights issues and in representation to governments and international bodies. There are obviously cases of mass violation of rights where only international political action can make a difference. There is also the important, but sometimes overlooked, opportunity for individuals to act through their own professional bodies and in supporting advocacy groups outside the churches. A culture supportive of human rights is not created overnight: it develops through a web of numerous connections.

We have seen the nexus between rights, needs and duties, justice and forgiveness, appeals to moral sentiment and appeals to essential human dignity on the basis of secular or religious affirmations, and the significant tensions between these values. It is only when there is a concerted effort to make concrete connections here and address the various dimensions of this nexus that significant progress on the ground becomes likely. The alternative is to remain marooned at the level of theoretical debate, where the different approaches will inevitably, and often quite legitimately, remain.

Compliance with human rights directives requires the recognition of legitimate authority and the willingness to comply. Willingness to comply may stem from a variety of reasons, from the moral to the purely pragmatic. Non-compliance is the Achilles heel of a huge percentage of current human rights activity, and it raises questions of legitimate force – pressure, judicial, economic, political and perhaps military.[9]

---

9   Marc Weller, (in Lyons and Mayall, 2003, 146–68) discusses 'Human Rights in Weak, Divided, and Threatened States' with reference to Somalia:

> The operation was the source of several lessons concerning the management of UN operations – for example, the need for decisiveness and steadiness in response to challenges to UN mandates and for long-term staying power and commitment to operations once they have been established.

In the same volume Nicholas Wheeler writes on 'Enforcing Human Rights':

> Securing compliance requires a solidarist theory of Human Rights enforcement, which goes beyond a pragmatic realism. For solidarism – humanitarian intervention is a moral duty...

> The fact is that no Western government has intervened to defend human rights in the 1990s unless it has been confident that there was little risk of casualties. (Ibid., 179)

> Sanctions often fail. Force may be necessary where there is 'a supreme humanitarian emergency....The future of HR depends on persuading state leaders to change this mind-set and embrace a solidarist ethic of humanitarian responsibility. (Ibid., 196)

In the current climate of global realities human rights action has had more success at some levels than others. To review areas already noted, we have seen that the greatest human rights issue of the current era is world poverty, with all the suffering and multiple deprivation that it brings. *International* agreements on the alleviation of poverty have produced a number of successful initiatives, but on nothing like the scale required. Human rights language has contributed to a greater awareness of the issue, and declarations have been made, recognizing the interconnection between economic and political rights. But national interest, lack of national political will, geopolitical factors and sometimes lack of economic forces have prevented a concerted attack on poverty. Here, human rights action has been most effective at more local levels. With poverty comes disease, and, again, the AIDS crisis and other disease pandemics remain undefeated, although the WHO and other bodies that are not focused on rights issues as such have taken some effective action.

At a *global* level the impact of TNCs is significant. For them, as we have seen, the feelings of their shareholders are inevitably the paramount consideration. If human rights issues are to be effectively addressed at global level, it seems clear that nation-states and corporations have to be persuaded that it is in their own best long-term interests to address rights violations. At a *regional* level such bodies as the European Court of Human Rights and developing parallel bodies elsewhere are beginning to influence national legislatures on rights matters. But, as we have seen, there is wide scope at national level for slippage and non-compliance within the separate legal jurisdictions of individual nations.

At the *national* level there are still frequent conflicts between state law and the rights of individuals. The remnants of Westphalian theory protect traditional national law against both regional courts and individual and group interests. National law may itself embody traditions that are not sympathetic to human rights – for example, the stress on the sovereignty of property in the common law of England. At the group level individual rights may be used to deny the legitimate group rights of such diverse bodies as language minorities and trade unions. In turn, group rights may illegitimately curtail individual rights – the micro-tyranny of the local culture.

And in this spectrum we should never lose sight of the contribution of individuals to rights issues. The twentieth century was notable for remarkable instances of individual struggles, often against society, on behalf of human rights.[10]

It is fair to require now from theology, and especially from Christology, a distinctive response to these issues, if its claim to be able to facilitate rights culture is not to be rendered vacuous. We have seen that, despite a poor record on human rights in a major key, as it were, there are numerous strands of human rights activity in minor keys that permeate the Christian tradition. A humane response to the incarnation of Christ has been active throughout history, sometimes almost underground but never

---

10 Cf. Peter Paris's discussion of King, Tutu, Mandela and Aung San Suu Kyi in his chapter 'Moral Exemplars in Global Community' in Stackhouse and Browning 2001, 191f)

We may also think of individual courage in the 20 July conspirators against Hitler, in courageous action in Rwanda, in the thoughtful and effective action of Peter Dennison in Founding Amnesty International and numerous other instances.

quite extinct. The challenge for the next two millennia will be to turn the minor key rights culture into the major key rights culture – to bring human rights from the margins into the centre of Christian action. There is no reason why this should not take place. Grounds for hope that it can happen lie in the persistence, throughout inhospitable intellectual and political climates, of a Christian awareness of Christ as a vulnerable, self-giving, loving presence. It would be unwise to repeat the Victorian optimism that the climate for a humane applied Christology is becoming more favourable everywhere. In large areas of the world it is not. But the tradition suggests that even small clusters of human rights culture can have a discernible effect on society in the long term, if not immediately. That I take to be a significant outcome of this study.

A humane Christology should be anything but a dilution of the heart of the Christian gospel. Diluted Christology is always open to revision and abuse in support of entrenched political and social power. A humane Christology could be a more progressive or a more traditional Christology (Wildman/Alison). A humane Christology sees Jesus Christ as the decisive instantiation of the vulnerable, self-giving, self-dispossessing divine love. Marion saw that God is love before God is anything else, and that this characterization of God in the Christian tradition is the clear consequence of the events concerning Jesus. A commitment to Jesus Christ as the icon of unconditional love is not in itself sufficient. Millions of unquestionably committed Christians have acted in ways quite contrary to the basic nature of Christ. But it is necessary. If people are to make any kind of worthwhile Christian contribution to rights issues, then they have to face the challenge of discipleship squarely, although they may interpret the task differently through different sorts of Christian culture, evangelical, liberal and whatever. Much of the time they will fail. But they simply have to pick up the task again and keep chipping away at it. There is nothing glamorous or intoxicating about this approach: it has its own justification.[11]

There are different ways of making a difference. As already indicated, I find personal support for attention to rights issues through a progressive Christological tradition of the sort represented today by John Cobb and others. This tradition is open to other Christological streams, catholic and evangelical, to secular reflection on democracy and humanism, to interfaith dialogue. These are all important dimensions of a search for an overlapping, but non-coercive, consensus as part of a continuing research tradition in applied theology. It is perhaps less easy for a reflective, fallibilist Christian tradition to have confidence in the effectiveness of a Christomorphic trace in history over the long-term future than for a triumphalist tradition. Yet I see in the history of this tradition grounds for a responsible confidence in a decisive continuing Christian contribution to human rights and to human flourishing.

---

11 Block and Drucker (1992) illustrate how people helped holocaust victims often as a matter of course, and at great cost to themselves, out of sympathy. This gives some empirical support to Adam Smith's theory of moral sentiments – empathy as prior to reasons. Charles Taylor (in Nussbaum and Sen, 1993, 227f) calls for a 'practical rationality' Cf. also Grant (2001); and Post *et al.*, (2002), especially Post's chapter 'The Tradition of Agape' (ibid., 51ff)

The Current Reality of Human Rights Violations

In its list of human rights issues in October 2004 Amnesty International highlighted the following abuses, among others:

- *Armed conflicts*: sexual violence against women in Columbia, impunity for rape in Bosnia, mass murder in Sudan, unbridled violence in Haiti, Austrian rifle production in Malaysia and French helicopter sales for use in Nepal.
- *Children and juveniles*: murder and recruitment of child soldiers in Sri Lanka and in the Congo, the Beslan school tragedy, huge problems in Liberia.
- *Commonwealth*: violations of the right to food in Zimbabwe, involvement of the military in killings in Jamaica, discrimination against indigenous women in Canada, an imminent execution in Barbados.
- *Conscientious objectors*: imprisonment of COs in Greece, USA, South Korea, Cyprus and Turkmenistan.
- *Crimes against humanity*: military atrocities in Laos, rape used as a weapon in Darfur; suicide attacks on civilians in Israel/Occupied Territories.
- *Death in Custody*: deaths in Lebanon, Kenya, Brazil, Central Asia, China and Syria.
- *Death penalty*: USA, Iran, Jordan, Egypt, Uzbekistan, Belarus, Indonesia, China, Barbados.
- *Detention arrest*: Mauritania, Sudan, Syria, Indonesia, Lebanon, Nepal and Bangladesh. The details are seriously disturbing. Yemen – death by stoning and flogging.
- *Disappearances*: Ecuador, Nepal, Ethiopia, Philippines, Peru, Pakistan, Central Asia and Sudan.
- *Discrimination*: violations in Zimbabwe, Colombia, Bosnia-Herzegovina, Afghanistan, Sudan, Honduras, China, Ethiopia, Laos and Cambodia.

This is only the beginning of the alphabetical list. There are meticulous details of further violations – connected with economic globalization, excessive force, extrajudicial executions, freedom of expression, human rights defenders, impunity, indiscriminate killings, international justice, medical actions, military, police and security transfers, prison conditions, prisoners of conscience, racism, refugees, sexual orientation, torture, trade union matters, trials and the treatment of women.

This book has tried to take due account of the valuable critiques of human rights that have appeared and that underline the need for a constantly critical approach to human rights. The other side of this equation is the huge volume of rights violations which continue to take place with impunity on a daily basis, usually affecting the least articulate of human beings and causing untold suffering. It is particularly on behalf of the voiceless victims that any effort which may contribute to the alleviation of human rights violations becomes hugely worthwhile. It is simply not possible to do too much thinking, advocating and acting for human rights in the twenty-first century.

We have noted that the Christian churches have often themselves been the victims of human rights violations and also that they have themselves been guilty of committing human rights violations, and sometimes continue to do so. This clearly weakens their effectiveness in encouraging a human rights culture. However, there is no time to wait until the churches' internal record is perfect before taking action wherever possible.

At the same time, the churches clearly have an obligation to address human rights violations within their own structures. These may relate to issues of employment, racism, equality, gender and sexual orientation, minority cultures and many other pressing concerns. To what degree are the poor welcomed to the centre of teaching and leadership where that is possible? How central is the role permitted to people with disabilities, when they have the capacity to contribute? To what extent are church structures themselves hegemonic and coercive? Who wields legitimate power?

It is important that conservatives and liberals, as well as people of all perspectives, should be free to live according to their convictions in Christian community. This clearly does not mean, however, that anything goes. For the Christian gospel, there is a decisive criterion in the person of Jesus Christ, the icon of the unconditional love of God. Whatever is contrary to this self-dispossessing love is contrary to the expressed will of God and will not contribute to the divine purpose. It is not always easy to discern the significance of this criterion in controversial times. Yet the icon of unconditional generosity and compassion has led to the abandonment of the persecution of heretics, the abolition of slavery and the empowerment of women in the church, all of which will undoubtedly lead to other steps towards a more compassionate church. There are very serious challenges to be faced. But there are grounds for hope.

Christology and Human Rights in a Science-based Environment

The relationship of Christology to human rights can, and in principle needs to be, developed in many different fields, and I want to say something about science, which shapes so many of the conditions of possibility in our times.

Much traditional discussion on theology and science has concentrated on the physical cosmos – still overshadowed perhaps by debates about creationism. I am going to concentrate on the human dimension. Christian theology argues that the fact of God has consequences for all human life. Christian theology is centred on Jesus Christ, as decisive for the welfare of humanity at every level, in both individual and social contexts. A Christomorphic vision of science and human rights is, then, more or less bound to argue and affirm the values of science in many forms – science as *Geisteswissenschaft* as much as *Naturwissenschaft*.

A Christomorphic vision of human rights and science will embrace human rights in combination with all of the following: physical sciences; economics; life sciences; law; business studies; politics; culture; literature; music; medicine; life sciences; humanities; history; architecture, town planning and engineering; and religion.

It may not be desirable to build all houses in a cruciform shape, as a sub-Barthian view of Christ and culture might suggest. But it is possible to build communities in ways which enhance or diminish humanity and the possibility of exercising human capacities, or in ways which are either consonant or inconsistent with the promise of Jesus Christ to bring life that is more abundant, fair and just into the world. And if the planning is not scientifically accurate, and the houses not soundly built, then none of this can happen and the divine purpose is hindered, simply by ignorance, neglect or greed. To fail to utilize the constructive dimension of science at every level is to neglect the fruits of creation.

If we do not have a scientific approach to the events concerning Jesus – not necessarily at the beginning but somewhere along the line – then all our speculation about the relation of indirect divine action to the motion of red-green anti-quarks will be seriously compromised. This happens, even in the most exalted circles.

If we are looking for a critically rational approach to Christian faith using experience in its various dimensions as an important factor, then the tradition of experience of Jesus, in his life, death and after his death, will be scientifically unavoidable. Here we have a figure who appears, in terms of reasonable probabilities rather than established empirical data, to have been committed to proclaiming and acting out a life of unconditional love, coming from and privileging the marginalized areas of society. A perspective on science and religion that does not highlight this solidarity with the marginalized can scarcely claim to be scientific.

It may be said that this is an unscientific romantic holistic fallacy. You need to generate the resources in the first place in order to be able to spend millions on NMR scanners and so on to improve the health of the poor. But unless there is some effective payback directly to the marginalized, then perhaps you can forget talk of a scientific *Christian* approach to theology and science. We can speak most tellingly of science and kenosis when there is a real outcome for those in whom involuntary kenosis is most starkly apparent.

Beyond the master paradigm of a life of unconditional love there is death and resurrection. We are not God and we cannot pretend to be God. In human terms the kenosis of kenosis tends to lead to complete powerlessness. Faith believes that God brings into being new, authentic existence out of non-being through self-dispossession. This is incarnation inspiration, the instantiation of the divine within the human. In different ways all our language is metaphorical, and incarnational language is no exception. However, I am myself inclined to the view that this incarnation is transformational, not just in terms of our contemporary perception but in terms of the development of some mysterious transcendental reality. I don't want to contrast the imaginative and the spiritual with the physical or even ontological, because this tends to suggest a mechanistic approach to incarnation which is, of course, equally metaphor-laden. But it seems to me that faith reckons to experience through the events concerning Jesus more than just a change of interpretative stance. The 'what' of this remains necessarily unresolved; it remains in provisional categories, traces if you will. Otherwise it falls over into fideism.

History as part of the human sciences is also decisive for the tradition of common Christian experience. Of course, all history is selective and reflects the times in which it is written. But if we do not strive for the best available historical perspectives, we necessarily delude ourselves about the nature of that common experience, in both its good and bad expressions. This is especially relevant to Christianity and human rights. Part of the tradition of the gospel, reflecting early Christian experience, is the Bible. When we cease to reflect critically on this experience the text becomes ossified, and we have incarnation into a text rather than a person.

This experience is fallible, reflecting what God said to people in the past and what people heard God to be saying. It may be revelatory and counter-revelatory by turns.

The tradition of the gospel goes beyond the interpretation of the biblical texts. It includes a history of prayer, worship and Christian social action. It includes the sacraments of baptism and eucharist, through which faith has understood God to be inviting human beings to participate in a mysterious relationship, in a generous communion of hospitality. This, too, is part of the tradition of experience which is part of the warrant for the construction of the critical rationality of faith.

The tradition of the gospel is not simply a tradition of relationality. It is a tradition of relationality transformed. It points to reconciliation, justice and liberation. As such it suggests a critical rationality of human rights, in which the rational is not simply the intelligible, but the just and fair. To be unjust and unfair is ultimately to be unscientific, if unconditional love is the ultimate ground and goal of the way things are. All else is a distortion in the sight of God.

What, then, is justice? What is fairness? Why are rights often contested, and human rights criticized, not least by theologians and lawyers? Everything is capable of distortion: there is no triumphalist solution. Fallibilism is, again, the only scientific attitude. But the necessity of recognizing fallibility is not a ground for inaction. Without tangible and effective outcomes, without enforcement in human rights issues, the gospel of incarnation is not served, and the call to discipleship is masked and immunized by theory.

I return to the multifaceted dimensions of a theological perspective on the human rights implications of science.

- *The physical sciences*: the use of the physical sciences for the enhancement of human society rather than its destruction – the peaceful, rather than the military, use of nuclear power, the use of geology and seismology to warn of approaching tsunamis as well as to conduct blue skies research.
- *The life sciences*: the production and use of drugs in ethically responsible ways rather than simply to make gigantic profits.
- *Economics and business studies*: the deployment of the resources of global market capitalism to begin to meet the needs of the billions who are locked into poverty, with all its concomitant issues of healthcare, education and plain starvation.
- *Law*: the focused deployment of legal resources at every level to support justice, and combat the denial of justice.

- *Politics*: the study of politics as a science which enables democratic participation, which does not muddy the waters of humanitarian efforts by hi-jacking these for political purposes, which promotes reconciliation and conflict resolution.
- *Culture*: scientific approaches which recognizes the need for appropriate balances in different situations between pluralism, multiculturalism, identity politics and integration.

One common characteristic of unscientific thinking is its freezing of temporality. Historical perspectives are viewed ahistorically, provisionality is ruled out, and the present status quo is absolutized. Here, a research tradition of imagination may allow dialogue a wider range of participants, from the voices of past civilizations to the voices – of course, still contemporary but suggestive – of science fiction. But neither past nor present nor putative future is regarded as normative. We cannot be bound by the past or the present, nor can we hi-jack the future.

What is humane? Human communication only became possible through the physical development of the faces of our simian ancestors. Let me go to the other end of imagination and consider the world of space fiction:

> Even as Fassin watched, another infant was thrown from one end of the giant blades, voice a high and anguished shriek. This latest unfortunate missed the prop guards but hit a high-tension stay cable and was almost cut in half. A Dweller in a skiff dipped back into the slipstream, to draw level with the tiny, broken body. He stripped it of its welding kit and let the body go. It disappeared into the mist, falling like a torn leaf.
>
> Dwellers cheerfully admitted that they didn't care for their children. They didn't care for becoming female and getting pregnant, frankly, doing this only because it was expected, drew kudos and means one had in one sense fulfilled a duty. The idea of having to do more, of having to look after the brats afterwards *as well* was just laughable. (Banks, 2004, 246)

The Christian understanding of the human is a fragile, potentially transient and clearly precious contribution. If we are to defend human rights in a swiftly changing environment we shall have to take account of theology and science, not only at the level of cosmological speculation but also at the level of human rights.

Faith beyond Fundamentalism

Not every expression of Christian faith will be helpful in achieving human rights goals. In the twenty-first century we are often reminded of the Crusades and the destructive ideology and action which they embodied. This does not mean that only one perspective will do, namely the progressive viewpoint argued for here. The strength of a viable Christian faith lies in moving forward through reasoned argument and discussion of alternatives – not in endless talk, but in action based on an honest discussion of all the issues. Christian thinking and action, in my view, may derive from catholic, evangelical or more liberal-progressive traditions. It may need the flexibility to derive strength from each of these in different areas, but if it is to contribute to human rights it will have to be a faith which moves decisively beyond fundamentalism in any shape or form.[12]

A spirituality of human rights action

We have already suggested, and it is worth underlining, that an open vision of Christian faith will respect the mystery of God. It will perhaps encompass a touch of mysticism, in so far as it will have reservations about doctrinal absolutes and infallible authorities, whether of sacred texts or sacred communities. It will continue to respect those who differ on these issues, while seeking to advocate alternative perspectives. As a Christian vision it will continue to be centred on Jesus Christ as the way, the truth and the life, but in an inclusive manner. It will be open to dialogue both with other Christian cultures and with non-Christian and non-religious visions. It will be democratic without being either majoritarian or exclusively defined in terms of Western culture, Protestant, Catholic or secular. As a Christian vision it will understand rights and privileges and national interests as servants of the gospel's concern for all humanity rather than an alternative gospel. It will hope to work with all who seek to promote human welfare through justice and reconciliation. And it will continue, despite everything, to trust in the unconditional love of God.

Paradoxically, a call to address the specificity of human rights violation may include a call to a new seriousness about spirituality. Spirituality can mean many different things to many people. I suppose spirituality has an inside and an outside, and these are connected in different ways. You can see the effects of spirituality in the presence of a worshipping congregation in a huge cathedral, in a little country chapel and in a great spiritual gathering on the banks of the Ganges. You can think of spirituality in the work of an artist and in the humanitarian work of caring agencies throughout the world. You can think of true spirituality and you can think of false spirituality. There certainly appears to be something there – something which we can, and do, assess.

---

12 A good example of such a flexible approach to tradition and postmodernity – good from my perspective because it approaches issues from a rather different standpoint to mine – is David Jasper's *The Sacred Desert* (2004). This book moves beyond the postmodern condition, combining deeply traditional Christian icons with the fragmentary art and literature of contemporary culture, creating a space in an age in which theology is all but impossible, yet where we can still be Christian and human. In both image and word, it is profoundly Christocentric, suggesting (rather than arguing) that human and divine creativity intermesh in a *creatio ex nihilo*, in new life in the deadness of the desert sand – a hope that springs up where hope has been extinguished.

This is a book about real deserts, entered into both physically, spiritually and in our imaginations. It thus challenges our bodies, minds and spirits. It is both a critical, academic book and a work of spirituality, of mysticism *contra* mysticism. Saints, travellers, theologians, artists and poets here rub shoulders, all challenging our contemporary consciousness, each participating in their desert wanderings in the silent kenotic self-giving of God. In Mark Rothko's abstract paintings are found icons of that self-dispossession – so very hard, it costs not less than everything – which may finally lead to the knowledge of ourselves and of God. We are directed towards transcendence as the trace that alone gives an ultimate meaning to our lives.

Spirituality seems to have something to do with an attitude, a way of acting and thinking which puts our thoughts and actions in the perspective of relation to God, or to transcendence, whatever that may mean, to a more ultimate ground of meaningfulness. People sometimes do this consciously or unconsciously.

In the Christian tradition, spirituality is often understood as listening for the voice of God in our world and in our lives. There have, of course, been great spiritual giants in the Christian past. But for us it means perhaps just stopping to think occasionally and trying to imagine the reality of God in relation to our world and the way in which we live our lives. Creating this space for reflection affects us all differently at different times. We may respond by paying more attention to private prayer and meditation. We may respond by becoming more involved in public worship and in the work of the churches. We may simply come to see our daily lives as being themselves an expression of spirituality, of lives lived and relationships developed with an integrity which seeks to reflect the decency and justice which the prophet Amos long ago identified as God's will for his creation.

And that is good. Of course, we struggle sometimes, when we look at the decidedly ambiguous state of the world and the churches, to ask ourselves what sort of prayer and meditation, what sort of worship, what sort of church work, what sort of daily lives is best. And here Christian faith offers us a kind of icon – a pattern, a shape for a spirituality in the events concerning Jesus.

The Christian response to this pattern has been very mixed through the ages, and has sometimes been very extreme. Jesus Christ is the way, the truth and the life. Here is the most precious thing, the divine love incarnate. People who do not see this are the enemies of God and of life. Let's kill them all. A spiritual vision, you might begin to think, is like a loaded gun, and it is irresponsible for people like us even to touch it.

It has often been as bad as that. But fortunately it has not always been as bad as that. Despite what sometimes seem to have been our best collective efforts, something has shone through the icon of the Christ event that has also inspired countless, often unremembered, acts of compassion and generosity, and these have transformed human lives in great ways and small. When we read the kind of reports about the churches that hit the newspapers we may often have the impression of bodies which are eternally consuming their own smoke and being pathetically self-absorbed. This study suggests that the Christ of the New Testament is not like that and that is why he is worth our lifelong attention. Like all of us, Jesus of Nazareth depended heavily on his family and friends. But his words and his actions were surprisingly and strikingly outward-looking rather than inward-looking. The parable of the Good Samaritan is typical in the way in which it breaks most of these rules of tribal behaviour by which we all still tend to live. It is all about inclusion rather than exclusion.

Religion is so often about exclusion. In Scotland those of us with Presbyterian links are familiar with a form of Calvinism which has as one of its main planks the doctrine of election. When we wake up in the morning and say to ourselves, 'We are God's elect', it's almost better for our endorphins than going to the gym – and a lot less trouble! The problem is that, when some are elect, the others tend to become unelect.

This is where I begin to think of human rights. Spirituality can be an important vehicle for concentrating our attention – for good or for bad. Jesus comes through the New Testament as always being there for those who no one else within the tribe will speak up for – as the voice of the voiceless in all circumstances. I want to suggest that a Christian spirituality which is centred on Jesus has a great deal to do with support for human rights. Jesus comes across as someone whose whole existence is moulded and illuminated by his compassionate relation to others, not only in giving but in receiving, teaching and learning, in amazing mutuality and reciprocity. Jesus is totally devoted to God. But God relates to him through this self-giving which is, at the same time, the self-dispossession of God. Jesus reluctantly, but deliberately, puts himself at risk. Unsurprisingly, he is tortured and killed. Utterly surprisingly, that does not seem to be the end of the matter. The women – minor characters to this day in the Christian narrative – come to understand that the world has been turned upside down.

Do we need to know this? Give us Barabbas. The last 2,000 years have produced plenty of victims. But the spirituality of Jesus suggests that victimhood is not the last word. There is always hope of transformation, because the world has once been turned upside down and nothing is ever again quite as static as it looks. The love of God is not quite dead and may do awesome things in unexpected places. It is not owned by any tribe – by the Christian tribe, the white tribe, the male tribe. It is for all humanity, whoever is in need, because through the marginalized the marginalized God is still in Christ, reconciling the world to himself.

Ever since we members of Homo sapiens began to knock the Neanderthals on their heads back in our caves – very successfully it has to be said – people have struggled to cope with violence, its limits and its justification. We have learned to be sceptical of the doctrine of the just war. This was a major step forward. On the other hand, we may think that, as Robert Runcie once put it, no wars are just but some wars can be justified. The Jesus of the gospel story (for example, Matthew 24) begins from where people are: the love of many will grow cold. Jesus, however, suggests an alternative sequel. The man who holds out to the end will be saved and the gospel of this kingdom will be proclaimed throughout the earth as a testimony to all nations; then the end will come.

Blessed are the poor in spirit: should we ever just sit on our hands and watch the vulnerable being destroyed? And how should we feel about those soldiers who die bravely for their country and for their families? Well, of course, the horrors of war in the past were perpetrated by other countries. Yet war makes us all desperate because, in conflict, we are usually terrified out of our minds.

What can be said as we contemplate the long lists on memorial tablets, and the tablets everywhere from here to that other black tablet, the Vietnam Veterans Memorial Wall and beyond? In 1918 people looked to a bright future created out of all that sacrifice and were often cruelly disappointed. But they had a point. If there is to be any scrap of meaning out of holocaust, then men's love should not grow even colder. Can we say that in our society in Britain in 2006 our solidarity with the marginalized and the oppressed is more clearly demonstrated in action than it was in Central Europe half a century ago?

War is a blunt instrument at the best of times. And yet tyrants may have to be resisted, if not for our own sakes, then to preserve the most vulnerable. Human rights are not an invitation to acquiescence. Otherwise all is lost.[13]

The gospel texts point us firmly to the goal of all this talk. Man's love should not grow cold. The Bible speaks of the fruits of the spirit – love, peace, justice, patience, kindness, active compassion. The gospel does not settle all arguments and close down conversation. But it is a word of encouragement. It suggests that the nature of all reality has a bias towards constructive, rather than destructive, activity; that we are encouraged to see a little way beyond ourselves. The promise of the gospel is that there is a loving God, often almost despite all appearances; that there is compassion even beyond the shock and awe and the beheadings and genocides of our time. There is aspiration beyond expectation, hope after hope. Where is God ever to be found in the complexity of modern conflict? Here is part of a poem by Godfrey Rust, 'September 11th, 2001':

…Where was God
on September the Eleventh? He was begging
in old clothes in the subway
beneath the World Trade Centre.
He was homeless in Gaza,
imprisoned in Afghanistan,
running the gauntlet to her school in the Ardoyne,
starving in Somalia,
dying of Aids in an Angolan slum,
suffering everywhere in this fast-shrinking world;
and boarding a plane unwittingly in Boston,
heading for an appointment on the 110th floor.
When the time came he stretched out his arms once again to take
the dreadful impact that would pierce his side.
His last message on his fading cell phone
once more to ask forgiveness for them all, before
his body fell under the weight of so much evil.

(© Godfrey Rust. Reproduced with kind permission)

---

13 Biology student Sophie Scholl lay anxiously in her condemned cell in Munich in 1943, a day or two before she was beheaded for resistance to the Nazis, and had a dream about a child:

> One sunny day I was bringing a child in a long white dress for baptism. The path to the church led over a steep hill. But I held the child firmly and safely in my arms. Then suddenly there was before me a crevasse. I had just enough time to lay the child down safely on the other side – and then I fell into the depths.

The child is our ideal; it will prevail despite every obstacle. We may be pathfinders, but we must die before our goal is reached. (Quoted from Aicher-Scholl, 1993; my translation)

Reflection on contemporary events suggests the continuing interlinking of human rights concerns. In 2005 the world was shocked by the consequences of the Asian tsunami. In many areas, notably Sri Lanka and Indonesia, internal conflicts made the provision of aid much more difficult. In Burma the denial of freedom of information meant that the scale of the problem simply could not be assessed. Central to the whole region was the problem of the positive right to an economic standard sufficient for the maintenance of human dignity and the unlikely chance of that becoming a possibility. The presence of a totalitarian regime in Myanmar raises again the issue of connections between democracy and human rights, but concern for democracy/ humanitarian relief should not be a front for Western imperial expansion. The same period put the spotlight on the problems of defending democracy by undemocratic means – detention without trial in the United States and Britain, the appalling civilian death toll in Iraq. Yet the problems of the ancient democracies were certainly no worse than those in other areas – the poisoning of the opposition leader in Ukraine underlined the viciousness of some alternative strategies.[14]

Perhaps the most difficult problem to address is the huge, but inevitably unrecorded, number of human rights abuses that occur in places where access is difficult, because of totalitarian regimes, lack of infrastructure and information technology, and the absence of significant numbers of educated and articulate people who are able to report abuses effectively. It is this silent wall of abuse, as much as its reported enormity of scale, that is the greatest challenge to action. This is where informal consensus on practical action is most urgently needed. This is where Christian faith has a clear task of assisting on every possible front. Anything less is unacceptable.[15]

The promise of the gospel and the art of the possible

Christian faith believes that human rights abuse is not the last word in God's purposes for humanity. The divine love which is at the centre of the universe is actualized in the mystery of incarnation, and reconciliation has been achieved in the events concerning Jesus Christ. This is an inclusive process which promises the fulfilment of love to all humanity regardless of other considerations. The hope of

---

14 Dealing with this daunting scenario requires determination and persistence. As Charles McCoy has put it:

> Dealing with Human Rights requires the continuing interaction and integration of persons from multiple disciplines, persons engaged in ethical reflection and action, and persons active in the policy arenas where human rights are being shaped and continuously reshaped. (McCoy, 2002, 174)

15 For attention to the causes and effects of underreporting in many areas of the world I am particularly indebted to a lecture by Professor James Ron in Princeton University in April 2005. On this scale of problems, consensus becomes the only reasonable strategy – a strategy to which religion has to be unequivocally committed. As David Hollenbach has said, 'The consensus could be the result of the common exercise of a shared practical reason' (Hollenbach, 2003, 242).

love is the motor and basis of perseverance in Christian charitable actions in all circumstances:

> Resistance to genocide is not just an affirmation of universalism in which every human being is entitled to rights and equal treatment by virtue of being born. It is more than seeing humanity in the Jews, more than seeing the bonds that connect us. It is also a cherishing, a celebration of all the differences – individual and group – that allow for human flourishing, set firmly within the context of universal worth. (Monroe, 2004, 266)

But this vision has an important eschatological dimension. Clearly, the triumph of love is very far from complete. The evils of the twentieth century, though different in kind, have been arguably as great as those of previous centuries. How might Christian faith, centred as it is in Christology, work most effectively in the human rights arena in the future?

We have seen that human rights engagement takes place at different levels, intellectual and practical. Often its effectiveness is related to going global by going local. In local action Christologies of different sorts have been instrumental in encouraging action on many specific issues. Christians of diverse persuasions have been effective in discouraging contemporary slavery, in fighting poverty and disease, in acting for justice, peace and reconciliation, in the emancipation of women in society and in the churches, and in civil rights struggles for cultural minorities of all sorts, black, gay, linguistic and other. They campaign for negative rights, such as freedom from torture and oppression, and for positive rights, such as sufficient nourishment, clean water and available medicine. All of this is worthwhile and will doubtless continue to be effective.

It is important to focus on carefully targeted projects that correspond to available enthusiasms and resources. Projects which lack adequate planning, resources and willpower almost inevitably fail and may in fact exacerbate the problem. This applies to large-scale political interventions and small-scale projects alike. A carefully focused strategy may be described as the art of the possible and is the way of practical reason.

Beyond this, however, lies the eschatological vision. This calls for a theological version of 'rooted cosmopolitanism' which encourages a continuing effort of Christian solidarity in tackling human rights enforcement. This means solidarity both among the churches and with all kinds of religious and secular organizations in achieving agreed human rights outcomes. This will not take place until churches and theology learn to distinguish clearly between unity and uniformity. What matters is not the metaphysical underpinning of human rights effort, but a concerted effort to work together towards relieving the oppressed and feeding the hungry throughout the world.[16] The extent to which this happens will no doubt be a measure of the credibility of Christian witness in the society of the future. But what ultimately matters is how

---

16 Jeffrey Sachs (2005) suggests that an investment of approximately US$150 billion over the next decade could lead to the elimination of poverty by 2025 – a calculation dependent on the responsible distribution of this sum by the aid-receiving governments.

effectively action in solidarity contributes to the creation of the justice, peace and human rights which are the promise and the goal of the divine love.

We have juxtaposed the art of the possible with the promise of the gospel. This is, of course, all too apposite to the difficult choices facing human rights enforcement. It is pointless to attempt actions without the resources to complete the job effectively. To that extent all initiatives need to be carefully tailored to the logistics. On the other hand, the greatest single current abuse of human rights – which may not be a specific abuse but results in endless suffering – lies in the fact of global poverty. Totally eliminating poverty would probably be impossible, even with the best political will in the world – and this is clearly lacking. Yet even though a contribution modest enough to be resourced would make a huge difference, there is little prospect of this happening in the immediate future. In this respect, we just have to acknowledge failure, with all its unpleasant consequences. Nevertheless, this should not inhibit governmental and other organizations from seriously pursuing achievable goals. A balance between realism and idealism, and the discernment to know the difference, is part of the art of the possible in the framework of the promise of the gospel.

When we penetrate more deeply into the matter of realism, formidable problems emerge. The UNHRC in its 61st session in 2005 had a very modest agenda, and even this may well be ignored by those who have the power to act. Christology involves churches. The WCC has had human-rights-related committees of various kinds for many years, from the World Missionary Council of 1910 to the CCIA and affiliated groups. However, the power of CCIA has waned sharply in recent decades, as churches have failed to produce the intellectual enthusiasm and financial resources necessary to make a significant impact. The picture at denominational level is similar. The WARC has long urged human rights engagement, but it, too, has been hampered in many fields – notably on contraception, women's rights and gay rights – by sharp doctrinal disagreements. Anglicans, Lutherans, Methodists and others have encountered similar barriers. The Roman Catholic Church has spoken and acted impressively on behalf of justice and poverty issues, but has faced even sharper divisions in areas of personal lifestyle choice, contraception and AIDS, abortion and the concept of liberation or emancipatory theology itself. General Councils produce resounding declarations, but the net effect is often ludicrously short of the aspiration.

It may be appropriate to end with one of the sharpest challenges to the theme of Christ and human rights yet seen: the churches' response to AIDS. Donald Messer, in his *Breaking the Conspiracy of AIDS* (2004) makes a passionate plea for the Christian church to taken a much more proactive and compassionate approach to AIDS sufferers and AIDS prevention. He chronicles the historic aversion of churches to AIDS patients because of the putative connection with inappropriate sexual relationships, and stresses the continuing catastrophic consequences of this neglect. He pleads eloquently for the confession that we are all HIV-positive, that the church has AIDS and that Christ has AIDS:

> I did not take God to the AIDS hospital in Tambaram. God was already there seeking to offer comfort, care and compassion. I felt Jesus' presence there, wiping the brows of so many who sweated profusely. Jesus was already there, comforting those whose bodies were shivering from pain-induced cold...Every new HIV infection is like another nail pounded into the body of our Lord. (Messer, 2004, xiv)

The figures are staggering. Forty million people are living with the disease, and 22 million have died. We are forced to reflect that, compared even with serious issues like torture, the sheer scale of this disaster as a human rights issue is gigantic. Yet the churches are still largely in denial. Messer pleads for 'a new holy boldness' in the church in the age of AIDS:

> The cross wrapped in the red ribbon of AIDS reminds the church of God's saving mission in Christ and our ecclesial calling to join in God's liberating and loving ministry in the world. (Ibid., 21)

He calls for a radical shift in Christian attitudes, for a more realistic engagement with the reality of human sexual behaviour. He notes the disproportionate effect of AIDS on poor, marginalized women throughout the world. He underlines the dependence of AIDS issues on economics, debt relief, healthcare provision, good sex education and proper counselling. In particular, he calls for a change in attitudes towards homosexuality where homophobic violence is often still endemic. While conceding that global evidence of such a positive change is very scarce, Messer commends the gospel of hope as a transformative force. Against inertia he places faith, hope and courage.

But what has this complex topic to do with human rights? Messer himself rightly stresses the need to protect the human rights of all people. As for Christology, Jesus was always there for the unclean and the leper:

> The church's profession of human rights, however, will ring hollow if stigmatization and discrimination against people with HIV/AIDS are allowed to continue within the church. If laypeople and clergy diagnosed with HIV lose their positions of leadership within the church, then the church loses any authority it may have to speak for human rights within the broader society. (Ibid., 74)

The issue could hardly be put more plainly and the challenge made more sharply than this.[17] As Christians we believe that God is love. We believe that God was in

---

17   A good practical example of targeted theological engagement with AIDS is the work of Professor Julian Müller and his team of graduate students, who have used Wentzel van Huyssteen's work on postfoundationalism to articulate a theology of solidarity:

> It is practical theology that is 'HIV positive.' In other words, it is a practical theology that is local and contextual, but in such a way that it identifies with the people in the context. It is not a system of theories, which is formulated and then imposed on a certain situation, but a story of understanding, which grows from a real situation. It is a story developing out of an interaction between researcher(s) and a context. It is postfoundationalist theology. In other words it finds its identity in a balance and dialogue between theological tradition and the context. (Muller, 2004)

Christ reconciling the world to himself. Jesus Christ is the form of Christ in the world, the form of unconditional love. What exactly does this imply? In *Unlimited Love: Altruism, Compassion and Service* (2003) Stephen Post reports on the work of his Institute for Research on Unlimited Love, showing the positive benefits of altruism and compassion, despite the difficulties encountered. Compassion goes beyond empathy to sympathy. It is worth recording the Institute's definition of unlimited love:

> The essence of love is to affectively affirm as well as to unselfishly delight in the well-being of others, and to engage in acts of care and service on their behalf; unlimited love extends this love to all others without exception, in an enduring and constant way. Widely considered the highest form of virtue, unlimited love is often deemed a Creative Presence underlying and integral to all reality: participation in unlimited love constitutes the fullest experience of spirituality. Unlimited love may result in new relationships and deep community may emerge around helping behaviour, but this is secondary. Even if connections and relations do not emerge, love endures. (Post, 2003, preface.)

Faced with this reality how is Christian faith to honour its duty to 'get real'? It may be that Ignatieff's maxim, discussed in Chapter 3, that human rights goes global by going local, becomes the cutting edge of enforcement. While striving for international cosmopolitan action remains important, the best way to achieve this may be through the successful implementation of local strategies.[18] These may be, and probably ought to be, coordinated to point the way to a joined-up worldwide programme. But the best momentum will be generated through the vision and courage of those who press for concentrated attention on localized human rights issues, whether these involve single individuals or groups, large or small. 'Where two or three are gathered together, there am I in the midst of them.' That is the promise of the gospel.

One final comment. We may sometimes wonder what connection there could possibly be between the world of the academy and the particular and practical realities of human rights enforcement. Here is a quote from Ignacio Ellacuria:

> Finally, we may ask what these aspirations can possibly have to do with the world of academic monographs and university communities. Here is one response.
> We, as an intellectual community, must analyse causes; use imagination and creativity together to discover remedies; communicate to our public a consciousness that inspires the freedom of self-determination; educate professionals with a conscience, who will be the immediate instruments of transformation; and continually hone an educational institution that is academically excellent and ethically orientated. (Ignacio Ellacuria, SJ, Rector, University of Central America Santa Clara Commencement Address, 1983)

---

18 One local movement which makes a significant impact is Jim Wallis's Sojourners organization., which reconceives the polarization between the religious right and secularism in North America, and seeks to build bridges to justice action through an evangelical social movement. The abuse of religion does not take away the proper use. The movement is open also to more agnostic people who are concerned about justice. This perspective, characterized in Brian Maclaren's phrase as 'a generous orthodoxy' corresponds in many ways to the viewpoint of this study (cf. Newlands, 1997).

Bibliography

Aicher-Scholl (1993), *Die Weisse Rose*, Frankfurt am Main: S. Fischer.

Alison, J. (1993), *Knowing Jesus*, London: SPCK.

Alison, J. (2001), *Faith Beyond Resentment*, London: Darton, Longman and Todd.

Alison, J. (2003), *On Being Liked*, New York: Crossroad Publishing.

Althaus-Reid, M. (2004), *From Feminist Theology to Indecent Theology*, London: SCM.

Amesbury, R. (2005), *Morality and Social Criticism*, London: Palgrave Macmillan.

Amnesty International (1975), *Report on Torture*, London: Duckworth.

An-Na'im, A. (1993), *Human Rights in Cross-Cultural Perspective,* Philadelphia, PA: University of Pennsylvania Press.

An-Na'im, A., Gort, J., Jansen, H. and Vroom, H. (1995), *Human Rights and Religious Values. An Uneasy Relationship*, Grand Rapids, MI: Eerdmans.

Appiah, K. (2005), *The Ethics of Identity*, Princeton, NJ: Princeton University Press.

Appleby, R. (2003), *Religion, Human Rights and Social Change*, London: Routledge.

Aslan, R. (2005), *No God but God*, New York: Random House.

Baier, A. (1991), *A Progress of Sentiments: Reflections on Hume's Treatise*, Cambridge, MA: Harvard University Press.

Baier, A. (1994), *Moral Prejudices*, Cambridge, MA: Harvard University Press.

Baillie, D. (1948), *God was in Christ*, London: Faber.

Bainton, R. (1953), *The Reformation of the Sixteenth Century*, London: Hodder & Stoughton.

Bainton, R. (1963), *Studies on the Reformation*, London: Hodder & Stoughton.

Banks, I. (2002), *Dead Air*, New York: Little, Brown.

Banks, I.M. (2004), *The Algabraist*, London: Orbit.

Barnhizer, D. (ed.) (2001), *Effective Strategies for Protecting Human Rights*, Aldershot: Ashgate.

Bauer, J. and Bell, D.A. (eds) (2001), *The East Asian Challenge to Human Rights*, Cambridge: Cambridge University Press.

Bauman, R. (2000), *Human Rights in Ancient Rome*, London: Routledge.

Baur, J. (ed.) (1977), *Zum Thema Menschenrechte*, Stuttgart: Calwer.

Beckford, R. (1998), *Jesus is Dread: Black Theology and Black Culture in Britain*, London: Darton, Longman & Todd.

Bell, D.A. (2000), *East Meets West. Human Rights and Democracy in East Asia*, Princeton: Princeton University Press.

Bell, D.A. (2001), *Liberation Theology after the End of History*, London: Routledge.

Bernhardt, R. (1994), *Christianity without Absolutes*, London: SCM.

Bernstein, R. (2002), *Radical Evil*, Oxford: Blackwell.

Biggar, N. (ed.) (2003), *Burying the Past. Making Peace and Doing Justice after Civil Conflict*, Washington, DC: Georgetown University Press.

Biggar, N. *et al.* (1986), *Cities of Gods*, New York: Greenwood Press.

Block, G. and Drucker, M. (1992), *Rescuers*, New York: Holmes and Meier.

Bloom, I., Martin, J. and Proudfoot, W. (eds) (1996), *Religious Diversity and Human Rights*, New York Columbia University Press

Blount, B. (2001), *Then the Whisper put on Flesh – New Testament Ethics in an African-American Context*, Nashville, TN: Abingdon Press.

Boswell, J., McHugh, F. and Verstraeten, J. (eds) (2000), *Catholic Social Thought: Twilight or Renaissance?*, Leuven: Leuven University Press.

Boyd, A. (1998), Baroness Cox – A Voice for the Voiceless, Oxford: Lion Press.

Brown, M. Anne (2002), *Human Rights and the Borders of Suffering: The Promotion of Human Rights in International Politics*. Manchester: Manchester University Press.

Cahill, L. (1980), *Towards a Christian Theology of Human Rights, Journal of Religious Ethics*, 8(8), 277ff.

Cairns, D. (1973), *The Image of God in Man*, London: Collins.

Cameron, J.K. (1981), 'Scottish Calvinism and the Principle of Intolerance' in B.A. Gerrish (ed.), *Reformatio Perennis*, Pittsburgh, PA: Pickwick Press.

Campbell, T., Ewing, K.D. and Tomkins, A. (2001), *Sceptical Essays on Human Rights*, Oxford: Oxford University Press.

Campbell, T. *et al.* (1986), *Human Rights: From Rhetoric to Reality*, Oxford: Blackwell.

Card, C. (2002), *The Atrocity Paradigm*, Oxford: Oxford University Press.

Cavanaugh, W. (1998), *Torture and Eucharist*, Oxford: Blackwell.

Chan, M. (2000), *Christology from Within and Ahead*, Leiden: Brill.

Clayton, R. and Tomlinson, H. (2000), *The Law of Human Rights*, Oxford: Oxford University Press.

Cobb, J. (2002), *Postmodernism and Public Policy*, New York: SUNY.

Comstock, G. (1993), *Gay Theology without Apology*, New York: Pilgrim Press.

Cooper, K. and Gregory, J. (eds) (2004), *Retribution, Repentance and Reconciliation*, Woodbridge: Boydell & Brewer.

Cowan, J. *et al.* (2001). *Culture and Rights: Anthropological Perspectives*, Cambridge: Cambridge University Press.

Critchley, J. (1999), *The Ethics of Deconstruction: Derrida and Levinas*, West Lafayette, IN: Purdue University Press.

Crompton, L. (2003), *Homosexuality and Civilization*, Cambridge, MA: Harvard University Press.

Cronin, K. (1992), *Rights and Christian Ethics*, Cambridge: Cambridge University Press.

Daniels, N. (1982), 'Grounding Rights and a Method of Wide Reflective Equilibrium', *Inquiry*, XXV, 227–306.

Derrida, J. (1992), 'Force of Law: The Mystical Foundation of Authority', in D. Cornell *et al.* (eds), *Deconstruction and the Priority of Justice*, New York: Routledge.

Dershowitz, A. (2004), *Rights from Wrongs: A Secular Theory of the Origin of Rights*, New York: Basic Books.

DeVries, D. (1996), *Jesus Christ in the Preaching of Calvin and Schleiermacher*, Louisville: Westminster John Knox Press.

Dillistone, F. (1968), *The Christian Understanding of Atonement*, London: Nisbet.

Donnelly, J. (1985), *The Concept of Human Rights*, London: Croom Helm.

Donnelly, J. (1989), *Universal Human Rights in Theory and Practice*, Ithaca, NY: Cornell University Press.

Donnelly, J. (1993), *International Human Rights*, Boulder, CO: Westview Press.

Douglass, R.B. and Hollenbach, D. (1994), *Catholicism and Liberalism*, Cambridge: Cambridge University Press.

Douzinas, C. (2000), *The End of Human Rights: Critical Legal Thought At the Turn of the Century*, Oxford: Hart.

Drinan, R.F. (2001), *The Mobilization of Shame*, New Haven, CT: Yale University Press.

Drombrowski, D. (2001), *Rawls and Religion: The Case for Political Liberalism*, Albany, NY: SUNY.

Dworkin, R. (1977), *Taking Rights Seriously*, Cambridge, MA: Harvard University Press.

Ebeling, E. (1991), *Evangelische Evangelienauslegung*, Tuebingen: Mohr.

Edmonton,S. (2004), *Calvin's Christology*, Cambridge: Cambridge University Press.

Eide, A. *et al.* (1992), *The UDHR: A Commentary*, Oslo: Scandinavian University Press.

Elwood, D. (1990), *Human Rights: A Christian Perspective*, Quezon City: New Day.

Ericson, Maria (2001), *Reconciliation and the Search for a Shared Moral Landscape: An Exploration Based upon a Study of Northern Ireland and South Africa*, New York: Peter Lang.

Evans, R.A. and Evans, A.F. (eds) (1983), *Human Rights: A Dialogue Between the First and Third Worlds*, New York.

Evans, T. (1998), *Human Rights Fifty Years On: A Reappraisal*, Manchester: Manchester University Press.

Ewing K.D. (1999), 'Just Words and Social Justice', *Review of Constitutional Studies*, 15, 53–75..

Ewing, K.D. (2000), 'A Theory of Democratic Adjudication', *Alberta Law Review*, 38(3).

Ewing, K.D. (2001a), 'Constitutional Reform and Human Rights', *Edinburgh Law Review*, 5(3).

Ewing, K.D. (2001b), 'The Unbalanced Constitution', in T. Campbell, K.D. Ewing and A. Tomkins (eds), *Sceptical Essays on Human Rights*, Oxford: Oxford: University Press, 103ff.

Ewing, K.D. (2003a), 'The Case for Social Rights', in T. Campbell, J. Goldsworthy and Adrienne Stone (eds), *Protecting Human Rights: Instruments and Institutions*, Oxford: Oxford University Press, 323ff.

Ewing K.D. (2003b), 'Human Rights', in *The Oxford Handbook of Legal Studies*, ed. P. Cane and M. Tushnet, Oxford: Oxford University Press, 298ff.

Falk, R. (2000), *Human Rights Horizons*, London: Routledge.

Felice, W. (1996), *Taking Suffering Seriously. The Importance of Collective Human Rights*, New York: SUNY.

Fenn, R. (2001), *Beyond Idols: The Shape of a Secular Society*, New York: Oxford University Press.

Fergusson, D. (2004), *Church, State and Civil Society*, Cambridge: Cambridge University Press.

Fiorenza, E.S. and Haering, H. (1999), 'The Non-ordination of Women and the Politics of Power', *Concilium*, 3.

Forsythe, D. (1999), *Human Rights and Peace*, Lincoln: University of Nebraska Press.

Forsythe, D. (2000), *Human Rights in International Relations*, Cambridge: Cambridge University Press.

Forsythe, D. (2005), *The Humanitarians: The International Committee of the Red Cross*, Cambridge: Cambridge University Press.

Francis, D. (2002), *People, Peace and Power: Conflict Transformation in Action*, London: Pluto Press.

Freeman, S. (ed.) (2003), *The Cambridge Companion to Rawls*, Cambridge: Cambridge University Press

Frend, W. (1969), 'Liberal Christianity in the Early Church', in A. Stephenson (ed.), *Liberal Christianity in History*, London: Modern Churchmen's Union.

Garland, D. (1991), *Punishment and Modern Society*, Oxford: Oxford University Press.

Garnsey, P. (1996), *Ideas of Slavery from Aristotle to Augustine*, Cambridge: Cambridge University Press.

Gearon, L. (ed.) (2002), *Human Rights and Religion*, Brighton: Sussex Academic Press.

Gearty, C. (2003), 'Reclaiming our Tradition: Rights, Diversity and Catholic Social Teaching', The Alan Bray Lecture.

Gearty, C. and Tomkins, A. (eds) (1996), *Understanding Human Rights*, London: Mansell.

Genovese, E. (1998), *A Consuming Fire: The Fall of the Confederacy in the Mind of the White Christian South*, Athens and London: University of Georgia Press.

Geras, N. (1995), *Solidarity in the Conversation of Humankind*, London: Verso.

Gewirth, A. (1982), *Human Rights*, Chicago: University of Chicago Press.

Gewirth, A. (1996), *The Community of Rights*, Chicago: Chicago University Press.

Ginsburg, C. (1995), 'Killing a Chinese Mandarin: The Moral Implications of Distance', in O. Hufton (ed.), *Historical Change and Human Rights*, New York: Basic Books.

Glendon, M. (1991), *Rights Talk: The Impoverishment of Political Discourse*, London and New York: Macmillan/The Free Press.

Goldenberg, D. (2003), *The Curse of Ham. Race and Slavery in Early Judaism, Christianity and Islam*, Princeton, NJ: Princeton University Press.

Goldewijk, B. and Fortman, B. (1999), *Where Needs Meet Rights*, Geneva: WCC.

Gorringe, T. (1996), *God's Just Vengeance – Crime, Violence and the Rhetoric of Salvation*, Cambridge: Cambridge University Press.

Grant, C. (2001), *Altruism and Christian Ethics*, Cambridge: Cambridge University Press.

Greenberg, K.J. (ed.) (2005), *The Torture Papers*, Cambridge: Cambridge University Press.

Grell, O. and Scribner, R. (1996), *Tolerance and Intolerance in the European Reformation*, Cambridge: Cambridge University Press.

Griffith, J. (1967), *The Politics of the Judiciary*, London: Fontana.

Guroian, V. (1999), 'Human Rights and Christian Ethics – An Orthodox Critique', *Journal of the Society of Christian Ethics*, 17, 301ff.

Haffner, S. (2002), *Defying Hitler*, London: Weidenfield and Nicolson.

Haight, R. (1985), *An Alternative Vision*, New York: Paulist Press.

Haight, R. (2001), *Jesus, Symbol of God*, Maryknoll: Orbis.

Halama, J. (ed.) (2003), *The Idea of Human Rights*, Prague: Charles University.

Halliday, F. (2002), *Two Hours that Shook the World*, London: Saqi Books.

Harnack, A. von (1986), *What is Christianity?*, Philadelphia, PA: Fortress Press. First published 1900.

Harnack, A. von and Hermann, W. (1907), *Essays on the Social Gospel*, New York: Oxford University Press.

Hart, D.B. (2001), 'The Whole Humanity: Gregory of Nyssa's Critique of Slavery', *Scottish Journal of Theology*, 54, 51ff.

Hastrup, K. (ed.) (2001), *Human Rights on Common Ground — The Quest for Universality*, The Hague: Kluwer Law International.

Hauerwas, S. (1983), *The Peaceable Kingdom*, Notre Dame, IN: University of Notre Dame Press.

Hayden, P. (2001), *The Philosophy of Human Rights*, St Paul, MN: Paragon.

Haynes, D. (1989), 'Israel in Barth's Church Dogmatics', PhD dissertation, Emory.

Haynes, S. (1991), *Prospects for Holocaust Theology*, Atlanta, GA: Scholar's Press.

Haynes, S. (2002), *Noah's Curse – The Biblical Justification of American Slavery*, New York: Oxford University Press.

Heffling, C. (ed.) (1996), *Our Selves, Our Souls and Bodies*, Oxford: Cowley Publications.

Hegarty, A. and Leonard, S. (1999), *Human Rights: An Agenda for the 21st Century*, London: Cavendish Publishing.

Helmick, R.G. and Petersen, R.L. (2001), *Forgiveness and Reconciliation*, Radnor, PA: Templeton Foundation Press.

Hengel, M. (1977), *Crucifixion*, London: SCM Press.

Herdt, J. (1997), *Religion and Faction in Hume's Moral Philosophy*, Cambridge: Cambridge University Press.

Herman, D. (1997), *The Antigay Agenda*, Chicago: Chicago University Press.

Heyd, D. (ed.) (1996), *Toleration – An Elusive Virtue*, Princeton, NJ: Princeton University Press.

Hick, S., Halpin, E and Hoskins, E. (eds) (2000), *Human Rights and the Internet*, London: Macmillan.

Hill, G. (1999), *The Triumph of Love*, London: Penguin Books.

Hill, M. (ed.) (2002), *Religious Liberty and Human Rights*, Cardiff: University of Wales Press.

Hilton, B. (1988), *The Age of Atonement*, Oxford: Oxford University Press.

Hogan, L. (2000), *Human Rights*, Dublin: Trocaire.

Hollenbach, D. (2003), *The Global Face of Public Faith*, Georgetown: Georgetown University Press.

Horton, K. and Patapan, H. (2004), *Globalisation and Equality*, London: Routledge.

Hufton, O. (ed.) (1995), *Historical Change and Human Rights*, Oxford Amnesty Lectures 1994, New York: Basic Books.

Hurlbut, E. (1847), *Essays on Human Rights and their Political Guaranties*, Edinburgh: Maclachlan Stewart.

Ignatieff, M. (1979), *A Just Measure of Pain: The Penitentiary in the Industrial Revolution, 1750–1850*, London: Macmillan.

Ignatieff, M. (2000), *The Rights Revolution*, Toronto: Anansi Press.

Ignatieff, M. (2001), *Human Rights as Politics and Idolatry*, Princeton, NJ: Princeton University Press.

Ignatieff, M. (2004), *The Lesser Evil. Political Ethics in an Age of Terror*, Princeton, NJ: Princeton University Press.

Insole, C. (2004), *The Politics of Human Frailty*, London: SCM Press.

Ishay, M. (1997), *The Human Rights Reader*, New York: Routledge.

Isherwood, L. (1999), *Liberating Christologies*, New York: Pilgrim Press.

Isherwood, L. (2001), *Introducing Feminist Christologies*, Sheffield: Sheffield Academic Press.

Jasper, D. (2004), *The Sacred Desert*, Oxford: Blackwell.

Jenkins, P, (2002), *The Next Christendom*, New York: Oxford University Press.

Jones, P. (1994), *Rights*, New York: St Martin's Press.

Jones, T. (2003), *The Dark Heart of Italy*, London: Faber and Faber.

Jordan, M. (1997), *The Invention of Sodomy*, Chicago: Chicago University Press.

Jordan, M. (2001), *The Ethics of Sex*, Oxford: Blackwell.

Juviler, P. *et al.* (1993), *Human Rights for the 21st Century – A US–Soviet Dialogue*, New York: ME Sharpe.

Karatnycky, A. (ed.) (2001), *Freedom in the World*, The Annual Survey of Political Rights and Civil Liberties, 2000–2001, New York: Freedom House.

Katz, S. (1994), *The Holocaust in Historical Context*, I, Oxford: Oxford University Press.

Kearney, R. (2001), *The God Who May Be*, Bloomington: Indiana University Press.

Keenan, J. (2004), *Moral Wisdom*, Lanham, MD: Rowman and Littlefield.

Kelsay, J. and. Twiss, S. (1994), *Religion and HR*, New York: The Project on Religion and Human Rights.

Kennedy, D. (2002), 'The International HR Movement: Part of the Problem?', *Harvard Human Rights Journal*, 101, 101–25.

Kennedy, H. (2004), *Just Law*, London: Chatto and Windus.

Kirkpatrick, D.D. (2004), 'The Return of the Warrior Jesus: "Glorious Appearing", *New York Times*, 4 April.

Kissinger, W. (1975), *The Sermon on the Mount – A History of Interpretation and Bibliography*, Metuchen, NJ: Scarecrow Press.

Knight, D. and Paris, P. (eds) (1989), *Justice and the Holy*, Atlanta: Scholars Press.

Knox, J. (1949), *History of the Reformation in Scotland*, Edinburgh: Nelson & Sons.

Kolakowksi, L. (1990), *Modernity on Endless Trial*, Chicago: University of Chicago Press.

Kristoff, N.D. (2004), 'Jesus and Jihad', *New York Times*, 16 July.

Kuipers, R. (1997), *Solidarity and the Stranger: Themes in the Social Philosophy of Richard Rorty*, Lanham, MD: University Press of America.

Kymlicka, W. (1989), *Liberalism, Community and Culture*, Oxford: Clarendon Press.

Lane, A.N.S. (1997), 'Interpreting the Bible', *Apollos*, 275ff.

Laursen, J. and Nederman, C. (1998), *Beyond the Persecuting Society*, Philadelphia, PA: University of Pennsylvania Press.

Lee, J.Y. (1995), *Marginality: The Key to Multicultural Theology*, Minneapolis: Fortress Press.

Leighton, R. (1875), *Work*, London: Longmans Green.

Levinson, S. (ed.) (2004), *Torture*, Oxford: Oxford University Press.

Lewis, B. (2004), *The Crisis of Islam*, New York: Random House.

Lincoln, B. (2003), *Holy Terrors – Thinking about Religion after September 11*, Chicago: University of Chicago Press.

Little, D. (1993), 'The Nature and Basis of Human Rights', in G. Outka and J. Reeder (eds), *Prospects for a Common Morality*, Princeton, NJ: Princeton University Press, 73ff.

Little, D. (1999), 'Rethinking Human Rights: A Review Essay on Religion, Relativism and Other Matters', *Journal of Religious Ethics*, 271), 151f.

Little, D., Kelsay, J. and Sachedina, A. (1988), *Human Rights and the Conflict of Cultures*, Columbia, SC: University of South Carolina Press.

Loffreda, B. (2000). *Losing Matthew Shepard*, London: Macmillan Press.

Loughlin, G. (2004) 'Gathered at the Altar: Homosexuals and Human Rights', *Theology and Sexuality*, 10(2), 73–82.

Lubac, Henri de (1998), *Medieval Exegesis, I, II*, Grand Rapids: Eerdmans.

Lyons, G. and Mayall, J. (eds) (2003), *International Human Rights in the 21st Century: Protecting the Rights of Groups*, Lanham, MD: Rowman and Littlefield.

McCoy, C.S. (ed.) (2002), *Promises to Keep: Prospects for Human Rights*, Berkeley, CA: GTU Center for Ethics and Social Policy.

MacDonogh, G. (1989), *A Good German: Adam von Trott zu Solz*, London: Quartet Books.

MacLaren, D. (2003), 'Reconciliation: Linking Spirituality with Development', *Studies in World Christianity*, 9(2), 223ff.

Marion, J-L. (1995), *God Without Being*, Chicago: Chicago University Press.

Maritain, Jacques (1943), *The Rights of Man and Natural Law*, trans. Doris C. Anson, New York: Charles Scribner's Sons.

Markham, I. (2003), *A Theology of Engagement*, Oxford: Blackwell.

Markham, I. and Abu-Rabi I. (eds) (2002), *11 September: Religious Perspectives on the Causes and Consequences*, Oxford: Oneworld.

Marquand, D. and Nettler, R. (2000), *Religion and Democracy*, Oxford: Blackwell.

Matheson, P. (1995), *Argula von Grumbach*, Edinburgh: T & T Clark.

Matscher, F. and Petzold, H. (eds) (1988), *Protecting Human Rights: The European Dimension – Studies in Honour of Gerard Wiarda*, Cologne: Karl Heymanns Verlag KG.

Messer, D. (2004), *Breaking the Conspiracy of AIDS*, Minneapolis: Fortress Press.

Miller, A.O. (1977), *A Christian Declaration on Human Rights*, Grand Rapids, MI: Eerdmans.

Minow, M. (1990), *Making All the Difference: Inclusion, Exclusion, and American Law*, Ithaca, NY: Cornell University Press.

Minow, M. (1999), *Between Vengeance and Forgiveness: Facing History after Genocide*, Boston, MA: Beacon Press.

Mobilization for the Human Family (2000), *Religion and Politics*, Claremont, CA: Pinch Publications.

Mohr, R. (1988), *Gays/Justice*, New York: Columbia University Press.

Moltmann, J. (1974), *The Crucified God*, New York: Harper & Row.

Monroe, K.R. (2004), *The Hand of Compassion*, Princeton, NJ: Princeton University Press.

Morgan, E. (2002), *Cathures*, Glasgow/Manchester: Carcanet Press.

Muehling-Schlapkohl, M. (2000), *Gott ist Liebe*, Marburg: Elwert Verlag.

Müller, J. (2004), 'HIV/AIDS: Narrative, Practical Theology, and Postfoundationalism. The Emergence of a New Story' at: www.julianmuller.co.za/emergence_story.pdf.

Murphy, A. (2001), *Conscience and Community*, University Park, PA: State University of Pennsylvania Press.

Muzaffar, C. (2002), *Rights, Religion and Reform*, London: Routledge Curzon.

Nederman, C. (2000), *Worlds of Difference*, University Park, PA: Pennsylvania State University Press.

Nederman, C. and Laursen, J. (1996), *Difference and Dissent*, New York: Rowan and Littlefield.

Newlands, G. (1997), *Generosity and the Christian Future*, London: SPCK.

Newlands, G. (2002), *John and Donald Baillie: Transatlantic Theology*, New York: Peter Lang.

Newlands, G. (2004), *The Transformative Imagination*, Aldershot: Ashgate.

Newlands, G. (2006), *Traces of Liberality*, Oxford: Peter Lang.

Nickson, A. (2002), *Bonhoeffer on Freedom*, Aldershot: Ashgate.

Niebuhr, R.R. (1963), *The Responsible Self: An Essay in Christian Moral Philosophy*, New York: Harper & Row.

Niebuhr, R.R. (1964), *Schleiermacher on Christ and Religion*, New York: Scribners.

Nino, C. (1991), *The Ethics of Human Rights*, Oxford: Clarendon Press.

Nouwen, H. (1972), *The Wounded Healer*, New York: Doubleday.

Nurser, J. (2003), 'The "Ecumenical Movement", Churches, "Global Order" and Human Rights: 1938–1948, *Human Rights Quarterly*, 25(4), 841–81.

Nurser, J. (2005), *For All Peoples and All Nations – The Ecumenical Church and Human Rights*, Washington, DC: Georgetown University Press.

Nussbaum, M. (2000), *Women and Human Development: The Capabilities Approach*, Cambridge: Cambridge University Press.

Nussbaum, M. and Olyan, S. (1998), *Sexual Orientation and Human Rights*, Oxford: Oxford University Press.

Nussbaum, M. and Sen, A. (eds) (1993), *The Quality of Life*, Oxford: Clarendon Press.

O'Donovan, O. and O'Donovan, J. (1999), *From Irenaeus to Grotius*, Grand Rapids, MI: Eerdmans.

O'Grady, R. (1979), *Bread and Freedom*, Geneva: WCC.

Olivetti, M.M. (ed.) (1999), *Incarnation*, Milan: CEDAM.

O'Neill, O. (2000), *Bounds of Justice*, Cambridge: Cambridge University Press.

O'Neill, O. (2002), *A Question of Trust*, Cambridge: Cambridge University Press.

Outka, G. and Reader, J. (1993), *Prospects for a Common Humanity*, Princeton, NJ: Princeton University Press.

Patterson, O. (1995), 'Freedom, Slavery and the Modern Construction of Human Rights', in O. Hufton (ed.), *Historical Change and Human Rights*, New York: Basic Books.

Patterson, O. (1998), *Rituals of Blood*, New York: Basic Books.

Pelikan, J. (1985), *Jesus Through the Centuries*, Cambridge, MA:Yale University Press.

Perry, M. (1998), *The Idea of Human Rights*, New York: Oxford University Press.

Placher, W. (1994), *Narratives of a Vulnerable God*, Louisville: Westminster John Knox Press.

Placher, W. (2001a), *Jesus The Savior – The Meaning of Jesus Christ for Christian Faith*, Louisville:Westminster John Knox Press.

Placher, W. (2001b), 'Visiting Prisoners' in *The Blackwell Companion to Postmodern Theology*, Oxford; Blackwell.

Poling, J.N. (1991), *The Abuse of Power: A Theological Problem*, Nashville, TN: Abingdon Press

Poling, J.N. (2002), *Render Unto God: Vulnerability, Family Violence, and Pastoral Change*, St Louis, MO: Chalice Press.

Polkinghorne, J. (ed.) (2001), *The Work of Love: Creation as Kenosis*, Grand Rapids, MI: Eerdmans.

Post, S. (2003), *Unlimited Love: Altruism, Compassion and Service*, Philadelphia, PA: Templeton Foundation.

Post, S., Underwood, L., Schloss, J. and Hurlbut, W. (2002), *Altruism and Altruistic Love*, Oxford: Oxford University Press.

Potter, H. (1993), *Hanging in Judgement*, London: SCM.

Prejean, H. (1993), *Dead Man Walking: An Eyewitness Account of the Death Penalty in the USA*, New York: Vintage Books.

Prejean, H. (2004), *The Death of Innocents: An Eyewitness Account of Wrongful Executions*, New York: Random House.

Putnam, H. (2004), *Ethics without Ontology*, Cambridge, MA: Harvard University Press.

Rabben, L. (2002), *Fierce Legion of Friends*, Brentwood, MD: The Quixote Center.

Rawls, J. (1971), *A Theory of Justice*, Boston, MA: Harvard University Press.

Rawls, J. (2001) *Justice as Fairness*, Cambridge MA: Belknap Press.

Ray, B. (ed.) (2000), *John Rawls and the Agenda of Social Justice*, New Delhi: Anamika.

Reid, E. (2001), 'Human Rights, the Churches and the Common Good', *Political Theology*, 3(1), 19ff.

Rendel, M. (1997), *Whose Human Rights?*, Stoke on Trent: Trentham Books.

Rice, C. (1981), *The Scots Abolitionists 1833–1861*, Baton Rouge: Louisiana State University Press.

Richards, D. (1986), *Toleration and the Constitution*, New York: Oxford University Press.

Richards, D. (1998), *Women, Gays and the Constitution*, Chicago: Chicago University Press.

Richards, D. (1999), *Identity and the Case for Gay Rights*, Chicago: Chicago University Press.

Richardson, R. (ed.) (1998), *Understanding Schleiermacher*, Lewiston: Mellen.

Rieff, D. (2002), *A Bed for the Night: Humanitarianism in Crisis*, New York: Simon and Schuster.

Rivera-Pagán, L (2002), *Essays from the Diaspora*, Chicago: Chicago Lutheran School of Theology at Chicago.

Rivera-Pagán, L. (2003), 'A Prophetic Challenge to the Church: The Last Word of Bartolomé de las Casas', *PTS Bulletin*, XXIV(2), 216ff.

Rorty, R. (1998), 'Human Rights, Rationality and Sentimentality', *Philosophical Papers. Volume 3*, Cambridge: Cambridge University Press.

Ruether, R. (1983), *Sexism and God Talk: Toward a Feminist Theology*, Boston, MA: Beacon Press.

Runzo, J., Martin, M. and Sharma, S. (2003), *Human Rights and Responsibilities in the World Religions*, Oxford: Oneworld.

Ruston, R. (2004), *Human Rights and the Image of God*, London: SCM Press.

Ruthven, M. (1978), *Torture: The Grand Conspiracy*, London: Weidenfield & Nicolson.

Sachs, J. (2005), *The End of Poverty*, New York: Penguin Press.

Scarry, E. (1985), *The Body in Pain*, Oxford: Oxford University Press.

Schleiermacher, F. (1928), *The Christian Faith*, ed. H.R. Mackintosh and J.S. Stewart, Edinburgh: T & T Clark.

Schleiermacher, F. (2002), *Lectures on Philosophical Ethics*, ed. R. Louden, trans L.A. Huish, Cambridge: Cambridge University Press.

Schmidinger, H. (ed.) (2002), *Wege zur Toleranz: Geschichte einer europäischen Idee in Quellen*, Darmstadt: Wissenschaftliche Buchgesellschaft.

Schmidt-Leukel, P. (2004), 'Buddhism and the Idea of Human Rights', *Studies in Interreligious Dialogue*, 14(2), 2126–34.

Schmidt-Leukel, P., Köberlin, G.K. and Götz, J.T. (2001), *Buddhist Perceptions of Jesus*, St Ottilien: EOS Verlag.

Schussler Fiorenza, E. (1983), *In Memory of Her: A Feminist Reconstruction of Christian Origins*, New York: Crossroads.

Schussler Fiorenza, E. (1993), *Discipleship of Equals: A Christian and Feminist Ekklesialogy*, London: SCM Press.

Schussler Fiorenza, E. and Haering, H. (eds) (1999), *The Non-ordination of Women and the Politics of Power*, New York: Concilium.

Shue, H. (1980), *Basic Rights: Subsistence, Affluence and US Foreign Policy*, Princeton, NJ: Princeton University Press.

Shue, H. (1998), 'Negative Duties Towards All, Positive Duties Towards Some', *Journal of Religious Ethics*, 26(2), Fall.

Shukpak, M. (1993), 'The Churches and HR: Catholic and Protestant Views as reflected in Church Statements', *Harvard Human Rights Journal*, 6, 127ff.

Shute, S. and Rorty, R. (eds) (1993), *On Human Rights. The Oxford Amnesty Lectures 1993*, New York: Harper Collins.

Skinner, Q. (1998), *Liberty before Liberalism*, Cambridge: Cambridge University Press.

Spong, J. (1999), *Here I Stand: My Struggle for a Christianity of Integrity*, San Francisco: Harper Collins.

Stackhouse, M. (1984), *Creeds, Society and Human Rights: A Study in Three Cultures*. Grand Rapids, MI: Eerdmans.

Stackhouse, M.L. and Browning, D.S. (2001), *God and Globalization. Vol. 2: The Spirit and the Modern Authorities*, Harrisburg, PA: Trinity Press International.

Stackhouse, M. and Obenchain, D. (2002), *God and Globalization. Vol. 3: Christ and the Dominions of Civilization*, Harrisburg, PA: Trinity Press International.

Stackhouse, M. and Paris, P. (eds) (2000), *God and Globalization. Vol 1: Religion and the Powers of Common Life*, Harrisburg, PA: Trinity Press International.

Storrar, W and Morton, A. (eds) (2004), *Public Theology for the 21st Century*, Edinburgh: T & T Clark.

Stout, J. (2003), *Democracy and Tradition*, Princeton, NJ: Princeton University Press.

Stuart, E. (1995), *Just Good Friends*, Oxford: Mowbray.

Stuart, E. (2003), *Gay and Lesbian Theologies*, Aldershot: Ashgate.

Sullivan, A. (1999), *Love Undetectable*, New York: Vintage.

Sundman, P. (1996), *Human Rights, Justification and Christian Ethics*, Stockholm, Uppsala University Press.

Swanton, C. (1992), *Freedom: A Coherence Theory*, Indianapolis: Hackett.

Swartley, W.M. (2003), *Homosexuality: Biblical Interpretation and Moral Discernment*, Scottdale, PA: Herald Press.

Swidler, A. (ed.) (1982), *Human Rights in Religious Traditions*, New York: Pilgrim Press.

Swidler, L. (ed.) (1991), *Human Rights: Christians, Marxists and others in Dialogue*, New York: Paragon House.

Talbott, W. (2005), *Which Rights Should Be Universal?*, Oxford: Oxford University Press.

Taylor, C. (1999), *A Catholic Modernity?*, ed. J.L. Heft, New York: Oxford University Press.

Taylor, M.L. (1990), *Remembering Esperanza*, Minneapolis: Fortress Press.

Taylor, M.L. (2001), *The Executed God: The Way of the Cross in Lockdown America*, Minneapolis: Fortress Press.

Taylor, M.L. (2005), *Politics, Religion and the Christian Right*, Minneapolis: Fortress Press.

Ter, H. and Busutil, J. (eds) (2003), *Freedom to do God's Will: Religion, Fundamentalism and Social Change*, London: Routledge.

Terrell, J.M. (1998), *Power in the Blood? The Cross in the African American Experience*, New York: Orbis.

Tice, T. (ed.) (1993), *Schleiermacher Seminar Papers*, Washington: American Academy of Religion.

Tice, T. (ed.) (1994), *Schleiermacher Seminar Papers*, Chicago: American Academy of Religion.

Tierney, B. (1997a), *Rights, Law and Infallibility in Medieval Thought*, Aldershot: Variorum.

Tierney, B.(1997b), *The Idea of Natural Rights*, Chico: Scholars Press.

Traer, R. (1991), *Faith in Human Rights: Support in Religious Traditions for a Global Struggle*, Washington, DC: Georgetown University Press.

Trible, P. (1984), *Texts of Terror*, Philadelphia, PA: Fortress Press.

Troeltsch, E. (1931), *The Social Teaching of the Christian Churches*, trans. O. Wyon, London: George Allen & Unwin.

Tutu, D. (1999), *No Future without Forgiveness*, New York: Doubleday.

Vanhoozer, K.J. (ed.) (2003), *Cambridge Companion to Postmodern Theology*, Cambridge Companions to Religion, Cambridge: Cambridge Unviersity Press.

Van Huyssteen, J.W. (1999), *The Shaping of Rationality: Toward Interdisciplinarity in Theology and Science*, Grand Rapids, MI: William B. Eerdmans.

Verheyden, J. (ed.) (1975), *Schleiermacher's Life of Jesus*, Philadelphia, PA: Fortress Press.

Villa-Vicencio, C. (1992), *A Theology of Reconstruction*, Cambridge: Cambridge University Press.

Vorster, J. (1999), 'Calvin and Human Rights', *Ecumenical Review*, 1, 205ff.

Wallis, J. (2005), *God's Politics*, San Francisco: Harper Collins.

Walzer, M. (1983), *Spheres of Justice: A Defense of Pluralism and Equality*, New York: Basic Books.

Wardle, L.D. *et al.* (eds) *Marriage and Same-Sex Unions: A Debate*, Westport, CT: Praeger.

Wasserstein, B. (1994), *Britain and the Jews of Europe*, New York: Oxford University Press.

Wattles, J. (1996), *The Golden Rule*, Oxford: Oxford University Press.

Weingartner, E. (1999), *Protecting Human Rights*, Geneva: CEC/United Church of Canada.

Weingartner, E. (1994), *Protecting Human Rights: A Manual for Practitioners*, Switzerland: Council of European Churches.

Weithman, P. (ed.) (1997), *Religion and Contemporary Liberalism*, Notre Dame, IN: University of Notre Dame Press

Wengst, K. (1988), *Humility*, Philadelphia, PA: Fortress Press.

West, R. (ed.) (2001), *Rights*, Aldershot: Ashgate.

Weston, B. and Marks, S. (eds) (1999), *The Future of International Human Rights*, New York: Transnational Publishers.

Wildman, W. (1998), *Fidelity with Plausibility – Modest Christologies in the Twentieth Century*, New York: SUNY.

Wilkinson, L.P. (1979), *Classical Attitudes to Modern Problems*, London: Kimber.

Williams, R. (2001), 'Beyond Liberalism', *Political Theology*, 3(1), 64ff.

Wilson, R. (ed.) (1997), *Human Rights, Culture and Context*, London and Chicago: Pluto Press.

Wintermute, R. (1995), *Sexual Orientation and Human Rights*, Oxford: Clarendon Press.

Witte, J. (1996), 'Moderate Religious Liberty in the Theology of John Calvin', *Calvin Theological Journal*, 31, 359ff.

Witte, J. (2001), 'The Spirit of the Laws, the Laws of the Spirit', in BM.L. Stackhouse and D.S. Browning (eds), *God and Globalization. Vol. 2: The Spirit and the Modern Authorities*, Harrisburg, PA: Trinity Press International, 76–106.

Witte, J. (2005), *The Reformation of Rights*, Cambridge: Cambridge University Press.

Witte, J. and Van der Vyver, J. (1996), *Religious Human Rights in Global Perspective. Vol. I: Religious Perspectives; Vol. II: Legal Perspectives*, The Hague: Martinus Nijhoff.

Wolterstorff, N. (1983), *Until Justice and Peace Embrace*, Grand Rapids, MI: Eerdmans.

Zagorin, P. (1991), *Ways of Lying*, Cambridge, MA: Harvard University Press.
Zagorin, P. (2003), *How the Idea of Religious Toleration Came to the West*, Princeton: Princeton University Press.

Websites

www.coe.int/T/E/Human rights
www.globetrotter.berkeley.edu/humanrights/bibliographies
www.iabolish.com (American Anti-Slavery Group)
www.georgenewlands.com
www.oneworld.net
www1.umn.edu/humanrts
www.warc.ch/dcw/rw982/02

Index